Company Acquisition of Own Shares

Sixth Edition

Company Acquisition of Own Shares

Sixth Edition

Nigel Dougherty
Barrister, Erskine Chambers

Anne Fairpo
Barrister, Thirteen Old Square Chambers

JORDANS

Published by
Jordan Publishing Limited
21 St Thomas Street
Bristol BS1 6JS

British Library Cataloguing-in-Publication Data

A catalogue record for this book is available from the British Library.

ISBN 978 1 84661 245 9

Typeset by Letterpart Ltd, Reigate, Surrey

Printed in Great Britain by CPI Antony Rowe, Chippenham and Eastbourne

PREFACE

This book aims to provide for the practitioner a comprehensive analysis of the law relating to own share acquisitions, from the perspective of both company law and tax law. Significant changes to this area of English company law were made by the Companies Act 2006, making it easier for a limited company to purchase its own shares. Much interest has been focused on this power, and its increasing use by the business community highlights its practical importance. However, the own share purchase provisions cannot properly be understood outside the legal context to which those provisions belong – an own share purchase is but one species of own share acquisition, although perhaps the most important species. This book examines the whole area, including a number of difficult points. Also included are the provisions regulating the giving by a company of financial assistance for the purpose of an acquisition of relevant shares.

The precedents included in the book aim to cover the main types of transaction in this area which the practitioner may be required to implement.

The law is stated as at 1 February 2013, including the expected effect of the Finance Act 2013. However, other changes lie on the horizon. In April 2013, the Financial Conduct Authority will replace the Financial Services Authority, although it may be expected that the immediate impact of the introduction of an alternative regulator will be modest, at least so far as company share acquisitions are concerned. Perhaps of rather more significant consequence, the government's proposed implementation of the Nuttall Review on employee share ownership is likely to make own share acquisitions even easier and more attractive to companies and their shareholders.

Finally, we should record our considerable debt to Michael Wyatt who oversaw this work for each of its previous five editions. He has provided both of us with a firm foundation upon which to build. Any errors are, of course, our own.

Nigel Dougherty and Anne Fairpo
February 2013

CONTENTS

TABLE OF CASES

References are to paragraph numbers.

TABLE OF STATUTES

References are to paragraph numbers.

TABLE OF STATUTORY INSTRUMENTS

References are to paragraph numbers.

TABLE OF EC MATERIALS

References are to paragraph numbers.

TABLE OF OTHER MATERIALS

References are to paragraph numbers.

TABLE OF ABBREVIATIONS

ACT	Advance Corporation Tax
CA	Companies Act
CA 2006	Companies Act 2006
CGT	Capital Gains Tax
CTA 2010	Corporation Tax Act 2010
DTI	Department of Trade and Industry
EEA	European Economic Area
EMI	Enterprise Management Incentives
FA	Finance Act
FID	Foreign income dividend
FSA 1986	Financial Services Act 1986
FSMA 2000	Financial Services and Markets Act 2000
ICTA 1988	Income and Corporation Taxes Act 1988
IFRSs	International Financial Reporting Standards
IHT	Inheritance tax
IHTA 1984	Inheritance Tax Act 1984
ITA 2007	Income Tax Act 2007
ITEPA 2003	Income Tax (Earnings and Pensions) Act 2003
ITTOIA 2005	Income Tax (Trading and Other Income) Act 2005
OECD	Organisation for European Co-operation and Development
plc	Public limited company
SDRT	Stamp Duty Reserve Tax
TCGA 1992	Taxation of Chargeable Gains Act 1992
TMA 1970	Taxes Management Act 1970
UITF	Urgent Issues Task Force

Case reports

AC	Appeal Cases
All ER	All England Law Reports
App Cas	Appeal Cases
BCC	British Company Cases
BCLC	Butterworths Company Law Cases
Ch *or* Ch D	Chancery Reports
CLR	Commonwealth Law Reports
EWCA Civ	England and Wales Court of Appeal Division

EWHC	England and Wales High Court
KB	King's Bench Division Reports
M & W	Meeson and Welsby
PCC	Palmer's Company Cases
QB *or* QBD	Queen's Bench Division Reports
SJ	Solicitor's Journal
STC	Simon's Tax Cases
TC	Tax Cases Reports
WLR	Weekly Law Reports

Chapter 1

INTRODUCTION

THE SCOPE OF THIS BOOK

1.1   This book seeks to cover the company law and fiscal consequences attaching to acquisitions and redemptions of their own shares by companies incorporated in Great Britain. The three main ways in which a company today may acquire its own shares are by way of gift, purchase and forfeiture (for non-payment of calls in respect of shares which are not fully paid up); all three are considered in detail. Also considered is the law relating to shares being held by a nominee for the company, and to a public company providing financial assistance for an acquisition of shares in itself or a subsidiary of a public company providing financial assistance for an acquisition of shares in that public company.

OWN SHARE PURCHASES: THE POSITION BEFORE 1982

1.2   It was established in *Trevor v Whitworth*[1] that a company limited by shares or a company limited by guarantee and having a share capital was not able to purchase its own shares. Any such purported purchase amounted to a return or reduction of share capital, and was illegal and void unless sanctioned by the court. This rule did not apply to an unlimited company (*Re Borough Commercial and Building Society*[2]) which, if duly authorised by its articles of association, may reduce its share capital in any way. The rule came to be reinforced by what is now s 136 of the Companies Act (CA) 2006, which, in general, prevents a body corporate from becoming a member of a company which is its holding company (see **2.31**); and also by CA 2006, ss 677–683 which, within limits, restrict a public company from giving financial assistance for an acquisition of shares in itself or a company from giving financial assistance for the acquisition of shares in a public company that is its holding company (see Chapter 11).

THE CHANGE OF DIRECTION

1.3   The Jenkins Committee report in 1962 (Cmnd 1749) did not consider that any real need existed to allow companies to purchase their own shares, and therefore it did not recommend any change in the law. However, the ensuing

---

[1]   (1887) 12 App Cas 409.
[2]   [1893] 2 Ch 242.

years saw the UK's accession to the EU and a growing awareness of the possibilities which a change in the law might open up. The Second EU Directive on company law of 13 December 1976[3] set out, in Arts 19–22, the parameters within which the legislation of any Member State was to allow (if at all) public companies to purchase their own shares. A Green Paper was published in 1980 by the Government entitled *The purchase by a company of its own shares* (Cmnd 7944), and this led to the enactment, as ss 45–62 of the CA 1981, of provisions conferring power on a company to purchase its own shares and to issue and redeem redeemable shares of any class. Upon consolidation, these provisions became CA 1985, ss 159–181. Meanwhile, CA 1980, s 35 had re-cast the rule in *Trevor v Whitworth*, allowing, for the first time, a company to hold fully paid shares in itself where it has acquired them otherwise than for valuable consideration. In 2003, a refinement of the legislation allowed, for the first time, quoted public companies to hold shares in themselves which they have purchased as 'treasury' shares (a term borrowed from across the Atlantic). This trend of making it easier for a company to acquire its own shares was continued by the CA 2006, which removed the requirements for express authority to make a share repurchase to be contained in a company's articles and for a special resolution to be necessarily obtained before a company can enter into a contract for an off-market purchase of own shares.

REDEEMABLE SHARES

1.4   The power for a company to issue redeemable preference shares was first introduced by CA 1928, s 18. Before then, shares could only be redeemed pursuant to a duly sanctioned reduction of capital, as occurred in *Re Dicido Pier Company*.[4] Although that section, which ultimately became CA 1948, s 58, permitted a company to issue redeemable preference shares, it did not empower the issue of redeemable ordinary shares (or, for that matter, redeemable shares of any other class not being preference shares). Although one could usually recognise a preference share as such, as being a share that would be expected to confer on its holder the right to some element of preferential treatment as compared to the holders of some other class of share, the expression 'preference share' is not defined by statute. With effect from 15 June 1982, it has been permissible for a company to issue redeemable shares of any class. Thus a company may nowadays issue ordinary shares, with some of them being expressed to be redeemable and others not. CA 2006, s 685 further simplifies the use of redeemable shares by allowing the shareholders to delegate power to the directors to set the terms of any redeemable shares upon the issue of those shares.

---

[3]   Directive 77/91/EEC [1977] OJ L26/1.
[4]   [1891] 2 Ch 354.

THE POSSIBLE ADVANTAGES

1.5 The possible advantages which arise from allowing companies to purchase their own shares, and to issue redeemable ordinary shares, include the following.

(a) The problems associated with the unmarketability of the shares in an unquoted company may be alleviated. If an investor knows that, notwithstanding the absence of a market in the shares of an unquoted company, he may in the future be able to liquidate his investment by allowing the company itself to buy him out, he may be more prepared to invest. Similarly, if an entrepreneur knows that he may be able to rid the company of an outside investor as a shareholder by causing the company to purchase the investor's shares, the entrepreneur may be more prepared to look for an outside equity investor. In cases where weight is attached to these factors, the appropriate course may be to issue the investor with redeemable shares.

(b) It may contribute to the efficient management of a company's business if dissident or apathetic shareholders can be bought out by the company. In some cases, there may be no ready market for the shares in question and the other shareholder or shareholders may not have sufficient free capital to buy out the dissenting interest.

(c) When a family shareholder with a significant number of shares retires or dies (and there are no children to succeed him), the other members of the family may not be able to afford to buy his shares. There may be cases where the only option (apart from liquidating the company) is to sell shares to a third party and, where this results in loss of family control, it could have harmful effects on the company's trade.

(d) A very similar situation can arise when a shareholder dies, and there is no alternative to the estate selling shares, if a liability to inheritance tax is to be met.

(e) The efficacy of an employees' share scheme may be increased if the company can purchase its own shares, particularly in the case of an employee who is leaving the employment of the company.

(f) Where a particular shareholder is required, under the company's articles, to sell his shares, the relative balance of power between the other shareholders can be preserved if the company itself buys the shares.

(g) A public company may be able to increase its earnings per share; if earnings stay constant while the number of issued shares goes down, the earnings per share figure must go up.

FEASIBILITY: THE TAX CONSEQUENCES

1.6   The tax consequences of a commercial transaction play a large part in arriving at the decision whether the transaction is feasible or not. This is due partly to the substantial rates at which income tax is levied in the UK, and partly to the widely held belief that taxation represents an undesirable overhead expense which should be avoided if at all possible. As will be shown, the TCGA 1992 contains complex provisions designed to cause the proceeds of sale of some own share purchases to be taxable in their entirety as capital and not as income. The lower rates of capital gains tax, compared with income tax, has tended to push the balance of advantage towards capital treatment.

FINANCIAL ASSISTANCE

1.7   CA 2006, ss 677–683 abolished the prohibition on a private company giving financial assistance for the acquisition of its own shares or the shares in another private company. In the light of the changes in the CA 2006, the 'whitewash procedure', previously contained in ss 155-158 of the CA 1985 has been removed. Financial assistance is no longer a specific concern for private companies, unless the shares that would be acquired, or have been acquired, are shares in a public company which is a holding company of the private company providing, or proposing to provide, 'financial assistance'.

1.8   Subject to defined exceptions, a public company is prohibited from providing financial assistance for the acquisition of shares in itself. Companies (including private companies) that are subsidiaries of public companies are similarly prohibited from giving financial assistance for the acquisition of shares in a public company.

1.9   Irrespective of the nature of the company, it remains important for directors to bear in mind that the fact that a transaction does not involve the provision of unlawful financial assistance does not necessarily mean that it is in accordance with their duties as directors.

PROPOSED REFORMS

1.10   In July 2012, the Nuttall Review recommended various changes to the law governing company own share purchases in order to promote employee share ownership. Following consultation, the Government has proposed amendments to the Companies Act 2006 which (if approved) will significantly affect aspects of the own share purchase regime, in particular:

(a)   allowing private companies to pay for their own shares in instalments, particularly where the buy-back is for the purposes of an employee share scheme;

(b) allowing private companies to hold their own shares in treasury and to deal with such shares as treasury shares; and

(c) allowing shareholder authorisation for a contract for an off-market purchase of a company's own shares, the variation of such a contract and the release of the company's rights under such a contract, to be given by way of simply an ordinary resolution (not a special resolution, as at present).

It is anticipated that such changes will take effect, if approved, from 6 April 2013.

THE REST OF THE BOOK

1.11 The next nine chapters analyse the company law relating to the various types of own share acquisition. Chapter 11 explains the law relating to the provision by a company of financial assistance for an acquisition of its own shares or its holding company. The ensuing chapters deal with the tax consequences of the various types of own share acquisition; and the concluding chapter considers some tax and commercial planning ideas.

Chapter 2

THE RULE AGAINST OWN SHARE ACQUISITIONS

THE GENERAL RULE

2.1   The rule in *Trevor v Whitworth*[1] prohibiting own share acquisitions (see **1.2**) was, subject to certain exceptions, enacted with effect from 22 December 1980, when the predecessor (CA 1980, s 35(1)) of what later became s 143(1) CA 1985 and is now CA 2006, s 658(1) was brought into force. Section 658(1) lays down the general principle that no limited company may acquire its own shares, whether by purchase, by subscription or otherwise, except as permitted by Part 18 of the CA 2006. The ensuing provisions of s 658 and of s 659 identify the exceptions to this general rule, and describe the consequences of an infringement.

EXCEPTIONS TO THE GENERAL RULE

2.2   Section 658(1) excludes from the application of this general principle acquisitions which are expressly contemplated by Part 18 of the CA 2006. By these means, the permitted acquisitions that might be made by a limited company include the redemption of redeemable shares, the purchase of own shares (whether out of capital or otherwise) and the acquisition of treasury shares.

2.3   Section 659 makes it clear that the following transactions comprise further exceptions to the general principle that a limited company may not acquire its own shares:

(a)   a limited company may acquire any of its own fully paid shares otherwise than for valuable consideration (s 659(1));

(b)   a limited company may acquire any of its own shares by means of:

    (i)   the acquisition of shares in a reduction of capital duly made (s 659(2)(a));

    (ii)   the purchase of shares in pursuance of an order of the court under CA 2006, s 98 (litigated objection to resolution for a public company to be re-registered as private), s 721(6) (litigated objection to

---

[1]   (1887) 12 App Cas 409.

redemption or purchase of shares out of capital), s 759 (in the event of a breach of the prohibition of public offers by a private company) or Part 30 (protection of members against unfair prejudice) (s 659(2)(b)); and

(iii) the forfeiture of shares, or the acceptance of shares surrendered in lieu, in pursuance of the articles for failure to pay any sum payable in respect of the shares (s 659(2)(c)).

NON-COMPLIANCE

2.4　Probably the most significant consequence for a company purporting to act in contravention of s 658 is that the purported acquisition is expressly made void (CA 2006, s 658(2)(b)).

2.5　Section 658(2)(a) also makes contravention of s 658 a criminal offence. A purported act in contravention of s 658 renders the company itself and every officer of the company who is in default liable to a fine and, in the case of an officer, imprisonment for up to two years if he is tried on indictment or up to twelve months in England (in Scotland and Northern Ireland, six months) if he is tried summarily (CA 2006, s 658(3)).

THE OPERATION AND EFFECT OF THE EXCEPTIONS

2.6　The exceptions to the general rule in s 658(1) are now considered below.

(1)　Gratuitous transfers to the company

2.7　CA 2006, s 659(1) recognises that a company limited by shares may acquire any of its own fully paid shares otherwise than for valuable consideration. This provision represents a departure from the pre-1980 law, as it allows a company to be a member of itself. The acquisition can be made either in a situation where the company is acting as a trustee and receives shares in itself to hold on trust, or where the company becomes the owner of the shares, receiving them by means of an *inter vivos* or testamentary gift. Thus where, as in *Re Castiglione's Will Trusts*,[2] a testator bequeaths shares in a company to the company itself, directing that the shares be transferred to the company, it is today possible for the testator's wishes to be carried out to the letter, there being no necessity (as there was in that case) for the company to arrange for the shares to be transferred to its nominees.

2.8　In a change to the position under the CA 1985, s 143(3), CA 2006, s 659(1) would permit a company limited by guarantee and having a share capital to acquire its own shares. However, in practice, this change is unlikely to be significant. There would seem to be little perceived need for such a company

---

[2]　[1958] Ch 549.

to do so. Moreover, as from 22 December 1980, it has not been possible for a company to be formed as, or become, such a company (see CA 2006, s 5(1) and (2)).

2.9   The requirement that the shares be fully paid up before they can be acquired by the company is an obstacle in the path of the perpetration of fraud against the company's creditors. A purported gift of partly paid shares to the company itself would be void (CA 2006, s 658(2)).

Procedure

2.10   All that is required to enable a company to acquire its own shares otherwise than for valuable consideration is for the donor or settlor to make out a stock transfer form in favour of the company and present it, together with his share certificate and a copy of the settlement or deed of gift, to the board of directors. The transfer will be subject to any restrictions in the company's articles of association applying to the transfer of shares. In the case of a bequest of shares to the company, the procedure will be determined by those provisions of the company's articles that deal with the transmission of shares. Thus, if reg 30 of the 1985 Table A (Companies (Tables A–F) Regulations 1985, SI 1985/805) or arts 28 and 29 of the Model Articles for Private Companies Limited by Shares (Sch 1 to the Companies (Model Articles) Regulations 2008, SI 2008/3229) apply, the directors could pass a resolution providing that the company should be registered as the holder of the shares, and the passing of that resolution (or, at any rate, a minute thereof) should constitute the giving of a 'notice' to the company, which notice would then be deemed to be an instrument of transfer executed by the deceased member, thereby bringing into operation any restrictions in the articles applying to transfers of shares.

2.11   Assuming that the company's articles do not frustrate the intention of the donor or settlor, the registration process involves the company's name and particulars being entered in the register of members, so as to result in the company becoming a member of itself and the holder of the shares in question. Any voting rights attaching to the shares would normally be exercisable by the directors in a manner which they considered to be *bona fide* in the interests of the company as a whole (*Re Smith & Fawcett Ltd*[3]). However, where the company is a public company, the exercise of the voting rights may be prohibited altogether (see **3.10**).

Directors' report

2.12   Whenever a company acquires any of its own fully paid shares otherwise than for valuable consideration, the directors' report with respect to any relevant financial year must state:

---

[3]   [1942] Ch 304.

(a)   the number and nominal value of the shares acquired by the company during that year; and

(b)   the maximum number and nominal value of shares which, having been acquired by the company (whether or not during that year), are held at any time during that year by the company or which are disposed of by it (in which case, if the company disposed of them for money or money's worth, the amount or value of the consideration in each case must be stated).

Where the number and nominal value of the shares of any particular description are to be stated as having been acquired or as being held, there must also be stated the percentage of the called-up share capital which shares of that description represent (Small Companies and Groups (Accounts and Directors' Report) Regulations 2008, SI 2008/409, Sch 5, para 6; Large and Medium-Sized Companies and Groups (Accounts and Reports) Regulations 2008, SI 2008/410, Sch 7, paras 8 and 9).

2.13   The following is an illustration of wording which could be used in the directors' report:

> During the year, the Company was appointed a trustee of the _____ Settlement and received, in its capacity as such trustee and without giving any valuable consideration therefor, a total of ____ fully paid Ordinary shares of £1 each in the capital of the Company, representing ____ per cent of the called-up share capital, upon trust to hold the same in accordance with the trusts of the aforementioned settlement. That number of shares represents the maximum number of such shares held by the Company during the year.

(2)   An authorised redemption or purchase of shares

2.14   A redemption or purchase of shares in accordance with Chapters 3 to 5 of Part 18 of the CA 2006 is a permitted exception to the general rule preventing a company from acquiring its own shares. The redemption of shares is discussed in Chapters 4 and 7, and own share purchases are dealt with in Chapters 5, 6, 7 and 8.

(3)   A reduction of capital duly made

2.15   A reduction of capital in accordance with CA 2006, ss 641–649 will often not involve any acquisition by the company of its own shares. Instead, the company will often be repaying share capital which is in excess of the company's wants or extinguishing or reducing the liability in respect of share capital which has not been fully paid up. Although in *British and American Trustee and Finance Corporation v Couper*[4] it was held that there was nothing to prevent the reduction of capital procedure from being used to validate an

---

[4]   [1894] AC 399.

acquisition by a company of its own shares by means of a purchase of them, that decision appears to have been overridden by the provisions first introduced by the CA 1981 which apply specifically to own share purchases. Just as redeemable preference shares were removed from the scope of a reduction of capital in 1928 (see **1.4**), so too were own share purchases and redeemable ordinary shares in 1982.

2.16 An example of a reduction of capital involving an acquisition by the company of its own shares is where a company agrees with a particular shareholder to acquire his shares in consideration for the transfer to him of some asset owned by the company. Such an exchange contract does not constitute a purchase and sale of either the shares or the other asset, since the ordinary meaning of a 'sale' of shares is a transfer of the shares for cash (*Re Westminster Property Group plc*[5]). That ordinary meaning almost certainly applies to the word 'purchase' in CA 2006, ss 690–723. As the transaction is not, therefore, capable of being treated as an own share purchase, it can only be implemented lawfully by means of a reduction of capital.

(4)   A purchase of shares pursuant to a court order

2.17   There are four separate situations to which this exception applies:

A.   *Public company re-registering as private*

2.18   Where a special resolution has been passed by a public company to be re-registered as a private company, CA 2006, s 98 enables the making of an application to the court for the resolution to be cancelled. In the case of a company limited by shares, the application may be made by either:

(a)   not less than 50 of the company's members, or

(b)   the collective holders of not less than 5% in nominal value of the company's issued share capital or any class of it (*Eckerle v Wickeder Westfalenstahl GmbH*[6]),

being, in either case, persons who did not consent to or vote in favour of the resolution (CA 2006, s 98(1)). If the company has issued treasury shares, those treasury shares are to be disregarded in calculating the 5% figure (CA 2006, s 98(1)(a)). The application must be made within 28 days after the passing of the resolution, and may be made on behalf of the persons entitled to make the application by such one or more of their number as they may appoint in writing for the purpose (CA 2006, s 98(2)). Notice of the application should be given immediately to the Registrar of Companies in accordance with CA 2006, s 99, both by the applicant(s) and by the company once served with notice of such an application. The making of the application prevents the resolution

---

[5]   [1985] 2 All ER 426 at 433g.
[6]   [2013] EWHC 68 (Ch).

from having effect except where it is withdrawn or where it is confirmed by an order of the court and a copy of that order has been delivered to the Registrar of Companies (CA 2006, s 97(2)). The court is given an unfettered discretion as to what order to make, and it is expressly provided that the court's order may provide for the purchase by the company of the shares of any of its members and for the reduction accordingly of its capital (CA 2006, s 98(5)). The statutory predecessor of CA 2006, s 98 was CA 1980, s 11, which was enacted at a time when an own share purchase could lawfully be achieved only by means of a reduction of capital confirmed by the court.

B.   *Objection to redemption or purchase of shares out of capital*

2.19   Where a private company passes a special resolution to approve a payment out of capital for the redemption or purchase of its shares an application can be made for the cancellation of the resolution. The application can be made by either:

(a)   any member of the company who did not consent to or vote in favour of the resolution, or

(b)   any creditor of the company.

The application must be made within 5 weeks after the passing of the resolution, and may be made on behalf of the persons entitled to make the application by such one or more of their number as they may appoint in writing for the purpose (CA 2006, s 721(2)). Notice of the application should be given immediately to the Registrar of Companies in accordance with CA 2006, s 722, both by the applicant(s) and by the company once served with notice of such an application. While the making of an application does not operate to prevent a company from acting on the basis of the original resolution authorising the payment, it is likely that a company will be slow to do so in circumstances where the court might cancel the resolution. Again, the court is given an unfettered discretion as to the order that it might make, although the court is given express power to provide for the purchase by the company of the shares of any of its members and for the reduction of the company's capital and make any alteration in the company's articles that might be required by this provision (CA 2006, s 721(6)).

C.   *Breach of prohibition of public offers by a private company*

2.20   Section 755, CA 2006 prohibits a private limited company from offering to the public any securities of the company or allotting or agreeing to allot any shares or debentures of the company with a view to their being offered to the public. The question of what is an 'offer to the public' is given a specific meaning by s 756. An offer to persons already connected with the company such as existing shareholders or employees, or certain members of their close family will not involve an 'offer to the public'. Similarly, offers to others that are non-renounceable or which are only renounceable in favour of such 'connected' persons will also fall outside the prohibition. If a private company makes an offer to the public, but does so on terms that it undertakes to re-register as a private company (either before the shares are allotted or within 6 months of the offer being made), it will not be in breach of the prohibition (s 755(3), CA 2006). If, notwithstanding this prohibition, a company allots shares in breach of s 755, CA 2006, the allotment itself remains valid, as does any agreement to allot or sell shares (s 760, CA 2006). Where it has breached the prohibition, a member of the company at the time the offer was made (or who became a member as a result of the offer) or a creditor of the company who was a creditor at the time during which the offer was made or the Secretary State may apply to the court under s 758, CA 2006. If the court is satisfied that the company has acted in contravention of s 755, the court may require the company to re-register as a public company or make an order for the compulsory winding-up of the company or make some other order to remedy the breach in some other way. By s 759, the scope of such a 'remedial order' confers upon the court a wide discretion, although it is specifically provided that such an order may require a person 'knowingly concerned in the contravention' to purchase any shares allotted, or agreed to be allotted, pursuant to an offer to the public at such price and on such terms as the court thinks fit (s 759(3), CA 2006). As such, a director of the company might be required to purchase the shares concerned. However, in the event such a remedial order is made against the company itself, the court may provide for the reduction of the company's capital accordingly (s 759(5), CA 2006).

D. Unfairly prejudicial conduct

2.21 A member of a company has the right under CA 2006, s 994 to apply to the court complaining that, inter alia, the company's affairs are being or have been conducted in a manner which is unfairly prejudicial to the interests of its members generally or those of some part of its members including himself, or that any actual or proposed act or omission of the company is or would be so prejudicial. CA 2006, s 996 gives the court a wide power to make an order giving relief in respect of the matters complained of, and it is expressly provided that the court's order may provide for the purchase by the company of the shares of any of its members and for the reduction accordingly of its capital (CA 2006, s 996(2)(e)). Before the changes brought in by the CA 1985, the statutory predecessor of CA 2006, s 996(2) was CA 1980, s 75(4), which was enacted at a time when an own share purchase could lawfully be achieved only by means of a reduction of capital confirmed by the court.

(5) The forfeiture or surrender of shares

2.22 In times when it was common for shares to be issued partly paid up, the right for a company to forfeit shares for non-payment of calls was seen as necessary to prevent co-adventurers from defaulting on their obligation to pay up their shares when duly called upon to do so, and was accordingly recognised as valid. Today, CA 2006, s 659(2)(c) is the main statutory authority for the proposition that a forfeiture or surrender of shares is, within stated limits, a valid and lawful means whereby a company may acquire its own shares without buying them and without being given them. Section 659(2)(c) permits the forfeiture of shares, or the acceptance of shares surrendered in lieu, in pursuance of the articles for failure to pay any sum payable in respect of the shares. This restates the general principle laid down by the case-law, and accords with the terms of every version of Table A from that of the Companies Act 1862 onwards.

2.23 Other statutory authority governing the forfeiture of shares lies in the terms of Table A (regs 18–22 in the 1985 Table A and arts 56–61 of the Model Articles for Public Companies, although it is not a matter addressed in the Model Articles for Private Companies Limited by Shares, which make no provision for nil or partly paid shares). Because a forfeiture of shares deprives the shareholder of his property, a company must comply strictly with the procedure on forfeiture laid down in its articles of association; any inaccuracy or irregularity renders the forfeiture invalid (*Johnson v Lyttle's Iron Agency*[7]). There must be properly appointed directors to make a call or declare a forfeiture of shares (*The Garden Gully United Quartz Mining Company v McLister*[8]). A power purporting to enable a company to forfeit shares for non-payment of a member's debts generally is invalid (CA 2006, s 659(2)(c); *Hopkinson v Mortimer Harley & Co Ltd*[9]). To be valid, a forfeiture must be for failure to pay 'any sum payable in respect of' the shares to be forfeited.

Effect of a valid forfeiture

2.24 Where a person has had any of his shares forfeited, he must cease to be a member in respect of them but remains liable to the company for the unpaid calls, plus interest thereon (reg 21 of the 1985 Table A; art 60(3)(d) of the Model Articles for Public Companies). The requirement that he should cease to be a member in respect of them must be fulfilled by the removal from the register of members of his name as their holder and its replacement by the name of the company itself as being the holder of the shares (CA 2006, s 112). The forfeiture includes all dividends or other moneys payable in respect of the forfeited shares but not paid before the date of forfeiture. The company may sell or re-allot the forfeited shares, and if it does so the new member is entitled to be credited with all sums which had been paid in respect of the shares prior to the forfeiture (*Re Randt Gold Mining Company*[10]). As the former member may not wish to co-operate, a purchaser of the shares from the company may derive a good title to the shares through a statutory declaration made by a director or the secretary of the company and a transfer of the shares executed by some person duly authorised for the purpose by the directors (as described in regs 20 and 22 of the 1985 Table A; art 61 of the Model Articles for Public Companies). Pending the sale of forfeited shares, the company remains their holder. If the company is a public company, it must comply with CA 2006,

---

[7]   (1877) 5 Ch D 687.
[8]   (1875) 1 App Cas 39.
[9]   [1917] 1 Ch 646.
[10] [1904] 2 Ch 468.

s 662 (see **3.10**). It is clear that a cancellation of forfeited shares by a *public* company in accordance with s 662 is valid and is not a reduction of capital requiring the court's consent under CA 2006, s 641. However, there is nothing in the Act or in the 1985 Table A or in the Model Articles for Private Companies Limited by Shares to allow a *private* company to cancel forfeited shares; such a company, having acquired the shares, should either remain their holder or sell them.

Contrast with the company's exercise of a lien

2.25 A forfeiture of shares differs in two key respects from the mere exercise by a company of a lien which it has over a member's shares (in accordance with the company's articles, such as those in regs 8–11 of the 1985 Table A or arts 52 and 53 of the Model Articles for Public Companies):

(i) the exercise of the lien empowers the company to sell the shares to a third party, but does not authorise the company to acquire the shares itself;

(ii) a lien may (if the articles so provide) arise in respect of any indebtedness by the member to the company, and not just (as in the case of a forfeiture) for failure to pay 'any sum payable in respect of' the shares.

Directors' report

2.26 Where shares in a company are acquired by it by forfeiture or surrender in lieu of forfeiture, the directors' report with respect to any relevant financial year must state:

(i) the number and nominal value of the shares acquired in that way by the company during that year; and

(ii) the maximum number and nominal value of shares which, having been acquired in that way by the company (whether or not during that year), are held at any time during that year by the company or which are disposed of by it (in which case, if the company disposed of them for money or money's worth, the amount or value of the consideration in each case must be stated) or cancelled.

Where the number and nominal value of the shares of any particular description are to be stated as having been acquired or cancelled, or as being held, there must also be stated the percentage of the called-up share capital which shares of that description represent (Small Companies and Groups (Accounts and Directors' Report) Regulations 2008, SI 2008/409, Sch 5, para 6; Large and Medium-Sized Companies and Groups (Accounts and Reports) Regulations 2008, SI 2008/410, Sch 7, paras 8 and 9).

2.27 The following is an illustration of wording which could be used in the directors' report:

During the year, the Company acquired by forfeiture for non-payment of calls a total of ____ Ordinary shares of £1 each in the capital of the Company, representing ____ per cent. of the called-up share capital. That number of shares represents the maximum number of such shares held by the Company during the year. Later in the year the Company sold ____ of these shares, realising a total of £____.

THE SCOPE OF THE GENERAL RULE

2.28 In *Acatos & Hutcheson plc v Watson*[11] it was held that where company A has a (non-controlling) shareholding in company B, neither CA 1985, s 143 (the predecessor to CA 2006, s 658) nor the rule in *Trevor v Whitworth*[12] prevents company B from acquiring a controlling interest in company A. It makes no difference to this conclusion what size the shareholding is, or whether it is company A's only asset, or what company B's motive is for acquiring company A. The only possible exception would be where company A acquired the minority shareholding in company B as part of a single scheme pursuant to which company B would then acquire the issued share capital in company A; the objective of such a scheme being to enable company B to achieve the same substantive commercial result as an own share purchase without it actually being an own share purchase. Only in the latter, fairly extreme, situation was there any chance of the court being persuaded to lift the veil of incorporation and treat the acquisition of shares in company A by company B as a breach of what is now s 658. Otherwise, the validity of such a transaction could not be attacked under s 658. In the *Acatos & Hutcheson* case itself, company A had been set up as a vehicle through which to make an offer for the entire issued share capital of company B, the shares in which were listed on the Stock Exchange. Various shareholders connected with the same family exchanged their shares in company B for shares in company A, thereby resulting in company A coming to hold about 29.4% of the issued share capital in company B. Subsequently, the intention to make an offer for company B was abandoned. The shareholders in company A then wanted to be restored to their original position as shareholders in company B and to dispose of company A. As a liquidation of company A would have created unacceptable tax liabilities, it was proposed that company B should now acquire the whole of the issued share capital in company A. The court granted a declaration confirming the validity of that proposed transaction. It was noted that if the law were to the opposite effect, a perfect defence to any contested corporate take-over would be for the target company to acquire some shares in the proposed bidder company.

UNLIMITED COMPANIES

2.29 Unlimited companies are not restricted by legislation as to whether and how they may acquire their own shares or reduce their capital. The members of

---

[11] [1995] 1 BCLC 218.
[12] (1887) 12 App Cas 409.

an unlimited company are, in the winding up of the company, liable to discharge its debts in so far as they cannot be discharged out of the company's property. The absence of legislation restricting own share acquisitions or reductions of capital can therefore be justified on the basis that its existence would not give any significant additional protection to creditors of the company. Conversely, in the case of limited companies, the protection of creditors is the main rationale of such legislation.

TRANSACTIONS WHICH ARE NOT 'ACQUISITIONS'

2.30 The scope of CA 2008, s 658 must, it is considered, be limited to transactions in which the company acquires, or would be acquiring, the legal title to shares in itself. Thus, where a nominee or bare trustee of the company acquires shares in the company, that cannot be an acquisition by the company itself, otherwise CA 2006, ss 660–669 (discussed in the following chapter) would be founded on a misconceived premise. When one takes into account also the changes to the law on financial assistance effected by the CA 2006 (see Chapter 11), it follows that there is nothing in s 658 that would, for example, prevent a private company from assisting to purchase fully paid shares in the company from Y, on terms that X shall hold them on trust for the company. In commercial terms, that transaction might be regarded as an 'acquisition' by the company of its own shares, but it would not be an 'acquisition' for the purposes of s 658.

MEMBERSHIP OF HOLDING COMPANY; CA 2006, S 136

2.31 CA 2006, ss 658–659 are supplemented by CA 2006, s 136, subs (1) of which lays down the general rule that, save as permitted by Chapter 4 of Part 8 of the CA 2006:

> '(a) a body corporate cannot be a member of a company that is its holding company and (b) any allotment or transfer of shares in a company to its subsidiary is void.'

These prohibitions apply as much to a nominee acting on behalf of a subsidiary as to the subsidiary itself (s 144). And, in relation to a company other than a company limited by shares (eg an unlimited company or a company limited by guarantee), the references to 'shares' are to be construed as references to the interest of its members as such, whatever the form of that interest (s 143).

Exceptions

2.32 The prohibitions do not apply where the subsidiary is concerned only as personal representative or trustee unless, in the latter case, the holding company or a subsidiary of it is beneficially interested under the trust (s 138(1)). For the purpose of ascertaining whether the holding company or a subsidiary is so interested, there is to be disregarded:

(a) any interest held only by way of security for the purposes of a transaction entered into by the holding company or subsidiary in the ordinary course of a business which includes the lending of money (CA 2006, s 138(2)(a));

(b) any residual interest or right of recovery under a pension scheme or an employees' share scheme (CA 2006, ss 138(2)(b), 139 and 140); and

(c) any rights that the holding company or subsidiary has in its capacity as trustee, including any right to receive expenses, or remuneration or an indemnity out of the trust property (CA 2006, s 138(2)(c)).

The interests set out in (b) and (c) above are addressed further at **3.23** et seq.

2.33 Further, the prohibitions do not apply where the subsidiary holds shares in its holding company in the ordinary course of its business as an 'intermediary', ie a person who:

(a) carries on a *bona fide* business of dealing in securities;

(b) is a member or has access to a regulated market as defined in Art 4.1(14) of Directive 2004/39/EC of the European Parliament and of the Council on markets in financial instruments or, in the case of an European Economic Area State that has not implemented that Directive, as defined in Council Directive 93/22/EEC on investment services in the securities field; and

(c) does not carry on any of the following businesses:

   (i) any business which consists wholly or mainly in the making or managing of investments;

   (ii) any business which consists wholly or mainly in, or is carried on wholly or mainly for the purpose of, providing services to persons who are 'connected' with the subsidiary (within the meaning of the Corporation Tax Act 2010 (CTA 2010), s 1122);

   (iii) the business of effecting or carrying out of contracts of insurance;

   (iv) any business which consists in managing or acting as trustee in relation to a pension scheme or which is carried on by the manager or trustee of such a scheme in connection with or for the purposes of that scheme;

   (v) any business which consists in operating or acting as trustee in relation to a 'collective investment scheme' (Financial Services and Markets Act 2000 (FSMA 2000), s 235) or is carried on by the operator or trustee of such a scheme in connection with or for the purposes of the scheme (CA 2006, s 141(3)).

2.34 For these purposes:

(a) 'securities' includes options, futures and contracts for differences, and rights or interests in those investments;

(b) 'trustee' and 'the operator' are, in relation to a collective investment scheme, to be construed in accordance with FSMA 2000, s 237(2) (CA 2006, s 141(4)).

All expressions defined in s 141 must be read with FSMA 2000, s 22 (including any relevant order under that section) and FSMA 2000, Sch 2 (CA 2006, s 141(5)).

2.35 Where a body corporate becomes a holder of shares in a company without infringing s 136(1), but subsequently the relevant prohibition in s 136(1) is infringed in respect of those shares (either as a result of the body corporate becoming a subsidiary of that company, or as a result of a change in circumstances), it may continue to be a member of that company; but for so long as that prohibition would otherwise apply:

(a) it is denied any right to vote in respect of those shares on written resolutions or at meetings of the company or at meetings of any class of its members (s 137(4)); and

(b) it may validly receive an allotment of fully paid shares in the company made by way of capitalisation of reserves of the company; but those bonus shares are likewise denied any voting rights (s 137(3), (4)). As no other issue or transfer of shares in its holding company may be made to the subsidiary, it can have no entitlement under any pre-emption provisions relating to issues or transfers of shares in its holding company.

2.36 In other circumstances, the exact consequences of an infringement of s 136 remain unclear; but it is considered that, in order to give effect to the words of s 136(1), the infringing share allotment should be regarded as a nullity. For example, if a parent company beneficially owns 75% of the issued share capital (consisting of a single class of ordinary shares) of a subsidiary and then purports to allot some shares in itself to that subsidiary, it is considered that this breach of s 136(1) must result in that share allotment being a nullity for all company law purposes – the shares would have no voting rights or entitlement to participate in any dividend or in any surplus arising upon a liquidation of the parent company.

Chapter 3

SHARES HELD BY A COMPANY'S NOMINEES

THE POSITION BEFORE THE COMPANIES ACT 1980

3.1   It was held in *Kirby v Wilkins*[1] and confirmed in *Re Castiglione's Will Trusts*[2] that there is nothing to prevent fully paid shares in a limited company from being transferred to a person to hold as nominee for the company, as long as the company itself does not provide any consideration for the transfer. Nor was such a transaction rendered invalid by the nominee being obliged to exercise the voting rights attached to the shares in accordance with the directions of the company. Where the shares transferred to the nominee were only partly paid, the nominee was personally liable to answer calls (*Cree v Somervail*[3]).

THE CURRENT LAW

3.2   With effect from 22 December 1980, express provision has been made for the case where any shares in a limited company are *issued* to a nominee for the company, or where partly paid shares are *transferred* to the company's nominee and rules have been provided to cover the case where *any* shares, whether fully paid or partly paid, in a *public* company are held by a nominee for the company. These provisions implemented Art 18 of the Second Company Law Directive (77/91/EEC). The relevant provisions governing shares held by a company's nominee are now collected together in CA 2006, ss 660–676.

Sections 660–661 of the Companies Act 2006

3.3   Section 660 of the CA 2006 applies to companies (whether public or private) limited by shares or limited by guarantee and having a share capital. Where shares in the company are taken by a subscriber to the memorandum as nominee for the company, or are *issued* to a nominee of the company, or where the nominee acquires them from a third person only partly paid up, s 660(2) requires, as a general principle and subject to certain exceptions, the shares to be treated for all purposes as being held by the nominee on his own account, and any beneficial interest of the company in the shares to be ignored.

---

[1]   [1929] 2 Ch 444.
[2]   [1958] 1 Ch 549.
[3]   (1879) 4 App Cas 648.

3.4   If the company calls on the nominee to pay any amount for the purpose of paying up, or paying any premium on, the shares, and the nominee fails to pay the amount called within 21 days, s 661(2) renders jointly and severally liable with him to pay the amount called:

(a)   the other subscribers to the memorandum; or

(b)   the directors of the company at the time of the issue or acquisition of the shares.

3.5   If proceedings are brought against such a subscriber or director for recovery of the call, s 661(3) gives the court power to relieve that defendant, either wholly or partly, from any actual or apparent liability of his on such terms as it thinks fit, where it appears to the court that he has acted honestly and reasonably and that, having regard to all the circumstances of the case, he ought fairly to be excused from liability. Moreover, the subscriber or director need not wait until proceedings are actually commenced against him. If he has reason to apprehend that a claim will or might be made against him for the recovery of the call, he may apply to the court for the relief, and the court has power to grant it (CA 2006, s 661(4)).

3.6   This power to grant relief is similarly worded to that conferred by s 1157 of the CA 2006; the power to grant relief is discretionary and the burden of proof is on the defendant (*Re J Franklin & Son Ltd*[4]). It seems likely that the power would be exercised mainly where the defendant was unaware of the existence of the nomineeship; co-subscribers of the memorandum or non-executive directors might not be aware of such a nomineeship, and s 126 of the CA 2006 provides that no notice of any trust, express, implied or constructive, is to be entered on the register of members of an English company. Section 234(2) of the CA 2006 expressly allows a company (usually by its articles) to indemnify any director against any liability incurred by him in connection with any application under s 661 of the CA 2006 in which relief is granted to him by the court. Thus the legal costs incurred by the director could be payable by the company if its articles (or any contract with the director) contain such a provision. The fact that nowadays shares are seldom issued less than fully paid suggests that proceedings under s 661 are likely to be rare events.

3.7   The following are the exceptions to the general principles laid down by s 660 as previously stated:

(a)   Where the company is a public company and the nominee for the company acquires the shares otherwise than by subscription and with financial assistance given to him directly or indirectly by the company for the purpose of or in connection with the acquisition, and the company has a 'beneficial interest' in the shares, the nominee is not treated as

---

holding the shares for his own account and the company's beneficial interest in them is recognised (CA 2006, 660(3)(a)). However, in these circumstances the provisions of s 662 of the CA 2006 come into play (see **3.16** et seq). Also, if the nominee fails to pay the amount of a call on the shares within 21 days, the directors of the company at the time when he acquired the shares still become jointly and severally liable with him to pay that amount (CA 2006, s 661(2)). The meaning to be given to the expression 'financial assistance' in s 660(3)(a) is not made clear by the CA 2006 (not least because the partial definition of that term contained in s 677 is only for the purposes of ss 677–682 of the CA 2006). It should also be noted that the reference to 'financial assistance' here is, in any event, wider in its effect than in ss 677–682, since it may have been given 'in connection with the acquisition' and not just for the purpose of it.

(b) Where the company, because it is acting in the capacity of nominee or trustee, itself has no 'beneficial interest' in the shares which are acquired for it by the nominee, the provisions of s 660(1) and (2) do not apply (CA 2006, s 660(3)(a)). It is thought that the word 'acquired' here means acquired by way of issue or by way of transfer, as opposed to meaning merely acquired by way of transfer. In these circumstances the nomineeship is fully recognised, and if the nominee fails to pay calls made in respect of the shares, the directors or other subscribers are not liable. The nominee would remain liable, but would normally have a right of indemnity against the company, which in turn would normally have a right of indemnity against the beneficial owner or trust fund. In determining for this purpose whether or not the company has any 'beneficial interest' in the shares, various residuary rights which the company may have are to be disregarded, such rights being mainly related to trusts, pension schemes and employees' share schemes. These residuary rights, and the way in which they are to be disregarded, are described in detail at **3.27** et seq.

3.8 In view of the deletion of what was CA 1985, s 145(2)(b), the provisions of CA 2006, s 660(1) and (2) will now apply in relation to shares issued in consequence of an application made before 22 December 1980 or transferred in pursuance of an agreement to acquire them made before that date. However, this is likely to be of little practical relevance; there is no reason to suppose that such an application or agreement would still be unperformed.

Sections 662–669 of the Companies Act 2006

3.9 Prior to the Companies Act 1980, there were no restrictions as to the length of time for which a nominee might continue to hold shares for the company. Nor were there any restrictions as to the exercise of the voting rights attached to the shares, beyond the restriction to be deduced from the law relating to the role and duties of directors, that the voting rights would normally be exercisable by the directors in a manner which they considered to be *bona fide* in the interests of the company as a whole (*Re Smith & Fawcett*

Ltd[5]). That position continues to apply in the case of private companies. However, Arts 20–22 of the Second Company Law Directive imposed special requirements in respect of public companies. Now s 662 of the CA 2006 sets out five separate situations in which a *public* company must cancel shares held by itself or by another and in which the exercise of the voting rights is denied. A 'public' company is defined by s 4(2) of the CA 2006.

(a)   Forfeiture or surrender

3.10   The first situation is where shares in the public company are forfeited, or surrendered to the company in lieu, in pursuance of the articles for failure to pay any sum payable in respect of those shares, whether as part of the subscription price or by virtue of a call having been made on partly paid shares. The company must, within three years from the forfeiture or surrender, cancel the shares and diminish the amount of its share capital by the nominal value of those shares, unless the shares or any interest of the company in them are previously disposed of (CA 2006, s 662(1)(a), (2), (3)(a)). The company may not, pending the cancellation, exercise any voting rights in respect of the shares, and any purported exercise of those rights is void (CA 2006, s 662(5) and (6)).

(b)   Surrender of shares pursuant to the Building Societies Act 1986

3.11   The second situation is where shares are surrendered to a company that is a building society under s 102C(1)(b) of the Building Societies Act 1986, where a claimed trustee account holder has made a false declaration as to his status and right to receive shares as the holder of such an account.

(c)   Shares otherwise acquired by the company

3.12   The third situation is where the public company acquires any of its fully paid shares otherwise than for valuable consideration and has a 'beneficial interest' in those shares (CA 2006, s 662(1)(c)), eg if the company were to receive a bequest of the shares. The various residuary rights which are to be disregarded in determining for this purpose whether or not the company has any 'beneficial interest' in the shares are described in detail at **3.27** et seq.

3.13   It is not readily apparent from the terms of s 662(1)(c) of the CA 2006 that this factual situation is the only one to which the paragraph applies, as the paragraph states that it applies 'where shares in the company are acquired by it (otherwise than in accordance with [Part 18] or Part 30' of the CA 2006 (these are set out at **2.2**) and the company has a beneficial interest in the shares. However, an acquisition of shares purporting and failing to fall within Part 18 of the CA 2006 is void (CA 2006, s 658(2)), so the company could not have any beneficial interest in any such shares. Accordingly, the only factual situation which remains is the one specified in the introductory wording of s 659(1),

---

[5]   [1942] Ch 304.

ie where the company acquires any of its fully paid shares otherwise than for valuable consideration (CA 2006, s 659(1)).

3.14   The public company must, within three years from the time it receives the shares, cancel them and diminish the amount of its share capital by their nominal value, unless the shares or any interest of the company in them are previously disposed of (CA 2006, s 662(1)(c), (2), (3)(b)). The company may not exercise any voting rights in respect of the shares pending the cancellation, and any purported exercise of those rights is void (CA 2006, ss 662(5) and (6)).

(d)   Fully paid shares transferred to a nominee

3.15   The fourth situation is where a nominee of the public company acquires shares in the company from a third person without financial assistance being given directly or indirectly by the company and the company has a 'beneficial interest' in those shares (CA 2006, s 662(1)(d)). Here, the shares must be fully paid, as otherwise the company would be debarred from having a beneficial interest in them (CA 2006, s 660; see **3.3**). The various residuary rights which are to be disregarded in determining for this purpose whether or not the company has any 'beneficial interest' in the shares are described in detail at **3.27** et seq. The company must, within three years from the acquisition, cancel the shares and diminish the amount of its share capital by the nominal value of the shares, unless it disposes of its interest in the shares beforehand (CA 2006, s 662(3)(b)). The nominee may not, pending the cancellation, exercise any voting rights in respect of the shares, and any purported exercise of those rights is void (CA 2006, s 662(5) and (6)).

(e)   Financial assistance plus beneficial interest

3.16   The fifth situation is where a person acquires shares in the public company with financial assistance given to him directly or indirectly by the company for the purpose of or in connection with the acquisition and the company has a 'beneficial interest' (CA 2006, s 662(1)(e)). Here, the shares may be either fully paid or partly paid but must be acquired from a third party by way of transfer and not from the company itself by way of subscription (CA 2006, s 660(3)). The company must within one year from the acquisition cancel the shares and diminish the amount of its share capital by the nominal value of the shares, unless it disposes of its interest in the shares beforehand (CA 2006, s 662(3)(c)). The person who acquires the shares may not exercise any voting rights in respect of them pending the cancellation, and any purported exercise of those rights is void (CA 2006, s 662(5) and (6)). Whether or not the company committed an illegal act in providing the financial assistance is a matter to be determined by reference to ss 677–683 of the CA 2006 (see Chapter 11).

3.17   In the case of all five situations ((a)–(e), above), where the cancellation results in the nominal value of the company's issued share capital becoming less than £50,000 (or the prescribed euro equivalent, currently €57,100), the company must apply for re-registration as a private company (CA 2006, s 664).

Failure to cancel the shares or to re-register before the end of the one- or three-year period renders the company and every officer in default liable to a fine and, for continued contravention, to a daily default fine (CA 2006, s 667(2)). Failure to re-register also has the effect of prohibiting the company (as a 'deemed' private company) from offering any of its shares or debentures to the public or from allotting or agreeing to allot any of its shares or debentures with a view to their being offered for sale to the public (CA 2006, ss 661(1) and 755); in other respects, however, the company retains its status as a public company until it is eventually re-registered (CA 2006, s 666(2)).

3.18   The directors 'may take any steps necessary to enable the company to carry out its obligations' to cancel shares (s 664). The effect of s 662(4) is that the public company is not obliged, when cancelling any shares by virtue of s 662, to comply with the formal procedure for a reduction of capital under Chapter 10 of Part 17 of the CA 2006 (which requires, in the case of a public company, the passing of a special resolution and an application to the court for a confirmatory order). Where a company cancels shares in order to comply with s 662, it must within one month after the shares are cancelled give notice to the Registrar of Companies specifying the shares cancelled and such notice must be accompanied by a statement of capital (s 663(1)–(3)).

3.19   If the cancellation of shares under s 662 requires the company to re-register as a private company, the directors 'may resolve that the company should be so re-registered' (s 664(1)). Such a resolution may involve the passing of a resolution altering the company's memorandum so that it no longer states that the company is to be a public company and make such other alterations to the company's name and articles as are necessary in connection with it becoming a private company (CA 2006, ss 662(4), 664(1), (2)). A printed copy of any such resolution passed by the directors must be sent to the Registrar of Companies within 15 days of its passing (CA 2006, s 30(1)). The application for re-registration must be made on prescribed form RR02 and be signed by a director or secretary of the company or an authorised person, and must contain a statement of the company's proposed name on re-registration. It must be delivered to the Registrar of Companies together with a printed copy of the articles of association of the company as altered by the resolution (CA 2006, s 664(4)). If the Registrar is satisfied that the company may be re-registered under s 664, the company is re-registered accordingly and the Registrar must issue the company with a new certificate of incorporation, by virtue of which the company becomes a private company and the alterations in the company's name and articles set out in the resolution take effect (s 665(4)). This certificate is conclusive evidence that the requirements of the CA 2006 in respect of re-registration have been complied with, and that the company is a private company (CA 2006, s 665(5); on the effect of certificates issued by the Registrar see *Re CL Nye Ltd*[6]).

---

[6]   [1971] Ch 442.

Private company re-registering as a public company

3.20 Where, after shares in a *private* company:

(a) are forfeited in pursuance of the company's articles, or are surrendered to the company in lieu of forfeiture, or

(b) are acquired by the company otherwise than for valuable consideration and the company has a 'beneficial interest' in the shares, or

(c) are acquired by a nominee of the company from a third person without financial assistance being given directly or indirectly by the company and the company has a 'beneficial interest' in those shares, or

(d) are acquired by any person with financial assistance given to him directly or indirectly by the company for the purpose of or in connection with the acquisition and the company has a 'beneficial interest' in those shares,

the company is re-registered as a public company, the obligations to cancel the shares, the ban on exercising the voting rights attaching to them, and the potential obligation to re-register as a private company, described at **3.10** and **3.17–3.19** above, apply as if the company had been a public company at the time when the relevant acquisition occurred, except that the three-year or one-year period (as appropriate) starts to run from the date when the company is re-registered as a public company (CA 2006, s 668(1), (2) and (3)). The various residuary rights which are to be disregarded in determining for these purposes whether or not the company has any 'beneficial interest' in the shares are described in detail at **3.27**.

Reserve fund

3.21 Where shares or an interest in shares in a public company are acquired by itself or by its nominee and are shown as an asset in the company's balance sheet, an amount equal to the value of the shares or interest must be transferred out of profits available for dividend to a reserve fund. This amount is then not available for distribution (CA 2006, s 669(1) and (2)).

Directors' report

3.22 Whenever:

(a) a nominee of a company acquires shares in the company from a third person without financial assistance being given directly or indirectly by the company and the company has a 'beneficial interest' in those shares, or

(b)   any person acquires shares in a company with financial assistance given to him, directly or indirectly, by the company for the purpose of or in connection with the acquisition and the company has a 'beneficial interest' in the shares,

the directors' report with respect to any relevant financial year must state:

(i)   the number and nominal value of the shares acquired by the nominee or other person during that year; and

(ii) the maximum number and nominal value of shares which, having been acquired as described at (a) or (b) above (whether or not during that year), are held at any time during that year by the nominee or other person or which are disposed of by him (in which case, if he disposed of them for money or money's worth, the amount or value of the consideration in each case must be stated).

Where the number and nominal value of the shares of any particular description are to be stated as having been acquired or as being held, there must also be stated the percentage of the called-up share capital which shares of that description represent (Small Companies and Groups (Accounts and Directors' Reports) Regulations 2008, SI 2008/409, Sch 5, paras 6 and 7; Large and Medium-Sized Companies and Groups (Accounts and Reports) Regulations 2008, SI 2008/410, Sch 7, paras 8 and 9).

A 'beneficial interest'

3.23   The following paragraphs describe the matters which are to be disregarded in determining whether a company has a 'beneficial interest' in its own shares.

3.24   Where shares in a company are held on trust for the purposes of a 'pension scheme' or an 'employees' share scheme', there is to be disregarded any 'residual interest' of the company, being an interest which has not 'vested in possession' (CA 2006, s 672(1)). A 'residual interest' is a right (including a right dependent on the exercise of a discretion vested by the scheme in the trustee or any other person) of the company to receive any of the trust property if:

(a)   all the liabilities (including ones which may result from the exercise of such a discretion) arising under the scheme become satisfied or provided for; here, the interest is treated as vesting in possession at that time, whether or not the amount of property receivable pursuant to that interest is then ascertained (CA 2006, s 672(2), (3) and (4)(b)); or

(b)   the company ceases to participate in the scheme; or

(c) the trust property at any time exceeds what is necessary for satisfying the liabilities (including ones which may result from the exercise of such a discretion) arising or expected to arise under the scheme.

In a case falling within (b) or (c), the residual interest vests in possession when the company becomes entitled to require the trustee to hand over any of the property receivable pursuant to that right (CA 2006, s 672(4)).

3.25 Where by virtue of **3.24** a residual interest is to be disregarded in determining whether s 660 or s 661 of the CA 2006 (acquisition of shares by a nominee for the company) applies at the time when shares are issued or acquired, but the residual interest vests in possession before the shares are disposed of or fully paid up, those sections apply as if the shares had been issued or acquired on the date on which the interest vests (CA 2006, s 672(5)). The same applies for the purposes of ss 662–668 of the CA 2006 in relation to an acquisition of shares by a public company (CA 2006, s 672(6)).

3.26 Where shares in a company are held in trust for the purposes of an 'employees' share scheme', there is to be disregarded any charge or lien on, or right of set-off against, any benefit or other right or interest under the scheme for the purpose of enabling the employer or former employer of a member of the scheme to obtain the discharge of a monetary obligation due to him from the member (CA 2006, s 673(2)); and for this purpose a director of a company is deemed to be employed by it (CA 2006, s 676). Where the trust is for the purposes of a 'pension scheme', there is in addition to be disregarded any right to receive from the trustee of the scheme, or as trustee of the scheme to retain, any amount that can be recovered or retained under s 61 of the Pension Schemes Act 1993 (deduction of contributions equivalent premium from refund of scheme contributions) or otherwise as reimbursement or partial reimbursement for any state scheme premium paid in connection with the scheme under Part 3 of that Act (CA 2006, s 673(1)).

3.27 Where a company is a personal representative or trustee, there are to be disregarded any rights which the company has in that capacity including, in particular, any right to recover its expenses or be remunerated out of the trust property and any right to be indemnified out of that property for any liability incurred by reason of any act or omission of the company in the performance of its duties as personal representative or trustee (CA 2006, s 674).

3.28 At **3.24** and **3.26** above, the expression 'employees' share scheme' has its ordinary meaning given by s 1166 of the CA 2006, ie:

'a scheme for encouraging or facilitating the holding of shares in or debentures of a company by or for the benefit of –

(a) the bona fide employees or former employees of –
   (i) the company,
   (ii) any subsidiary of the company, or

(iii)   the company's holding company or any subsidiary of the company's
holding company, or
(b)   the spouses, civil partners, surviving spouses, surviving civil partners, or
minor children or step-children of such employees or former employees.'

A 'scheme' is, according to the *Oxford English Dictionary*, simply a plan or
design. An employees' share scheme is to be distinguished from each
acquisition of shares which may occur under it. A contract for the acquisition
of shares, being a contract entered into between an employee and his
employer-company, is not itself a 'scheme'; rather, it is simply one of the many
share acquisition contracts which a scheme is likely to result in.

Chapter 4

THE ISSUE OF REDEEMABLE SHARES

THE COMPANIES ACT 1981

4.1   With effect from 15 June 1982, s 58 of the CA 1948 (which gave power to companies to issue redeemable preference shares) was repealed (CA 1981, s 62(2)) and replaced by provisions empowering the issue of redeemable shares of any class. These provisions are now contained in Chapter 3 of Part 18 of the CA 2006, the relevant sections being ss 684–689.

THE COMPANIES ACT 2006

4.2   With effect from 1 October 2009, the CA 2006 significantly altered the regime governing the issue of redeemable shares. Among the more significant changes private companies are now able to issue redeemable shares without the need for a specific authority in their articles, provided, of course, that the articles do not exclude or restrict the issue of such redeemable shares. Further, whether by way of a provision in the articles or by way of ordinary resolution, shareholders in either a public or a private limited company may delegate to the directors the responsibility of determining the terms, conditions and manner of redemption of such redeemable shares. Alongside modified filing procedures concerned with the allotment or redemption of redeemable shares, the CA 2006 also makes provision for a company and a shareholder to reach agreement for the payment due on redemption of the redeemable shares to be deferred.

THE POWER TO ISSUE

4.3   Section 684(1) of the CA 2006 confers, subject to the ensuing provisions of Chapter 3 of Part 18 of the CA 2006, power on a limited company having a share capital to issue shares which are to be redeemed or are liable to be redeemed at the option of the company or the shareholder.

4.4   In the case of private limited companies, there is no longer any need (as there had been under CA 1985, s 159(1)) for the issue of redeemable shares to be specifically authorised by the company's articles. With effect from 1 October 2009 s 684(1), CA 2006 provides a statutory authority for the issue of redeemable shares, which applies to all private limited companies having a share capital whenever they were formed. However, that authority is not absolute. In particular, by s 684(2), the articles of such a private limited company may have the effect of excluding or restricting the issue of redeemable shares.

4.5   An example of such a restriction may arise from the authorised share capital of a company incorporated before 1 October 2009 and contained in its memorandum of association immediately before that date. As a result of para 42(2) of Sch 2 to the Companies Act 2006 (Commencement No 8, Transitional Provisions and Savings) Order 2008 (SI 2008/2860), any such provision is automatically to be treated, on and after 1 October 2009, as being a provision of the company's articles setting out the maximum amount of shares that may be allotted by the company. A company seeking to issue shares (including redeemable shares) beyond that maximum will need first to remove or increase that limit. By paras 42(2) and (5) of that 2008 Order, such a limit may be amended or revoked by an ordinary resolution, by a special resolution amending the articles removing or altering such a limit or by the adoption of new articles that make no provision as to the maximum number of shares that might be allotted.

4.6   Other prohibitions or restrictions may arise in the articles. Often these will be capable of being amended by special resolution to remove or modify the scope of the prohibition or restriction. However, it is possible that such a provision might be entrenched (and hence impose additional restrictions on amending or repealing such a provision) in accordance with s 22(2), CA 2006. Moreover, while an issue of redeemable shares would not at common law involve a variation of the rights of the holders of an existing class of shares, it is possible that the articles of a company will provide that an issue of redeemable shares shall be deemed to involve a variation of the rights of some other existing class or classes of shares. If so, the process of varying such class rights or obtaining class consents will need to be followed.

4.7   In contrast to the position with private companies, a public company limited by shares (whenever formed) requires specific authority in its articles to issue redeemable shares (s 684(3)). A public company incorporated on or after 1 July 1985 but before 30 September 2009 will have the necessary authority to issue redeemable shares of any class if its articles adopt reg 3 of Table A (in the Companies (Tables A to F) Regulations 1985, SI 1985/805). For public companies incorporated after 1 October 2009, it too will have the necessary power, if its articles adopt art 43 of Sch 3 to the Companies (Model Articles) Regulations 2008 (see further **4.9** below). Relevant to companies incorporated before 1 July 1985 but on or after 15 June 1982, reg 3 of (Part I of) Table A in the First Schedule to the CA 1948, as amended by CA 1981, Sch 3, para 20 also contained that full authority. However, any public company incorporated before 15 June 1982 whose articles of association adopt reg 3 of (Part I of) the 1948 Table A or any of the earlier Table As will *not* have the necessary authority – any such power that it might have would relate merely to redeemable *preference* shares under s 58 of the CA 1948.

4.8 Accordingly, a public company having a share capital that was incorporated prior to 15 June 1982 but which has not updated its articles must, if it is to have power to issue redeemable shares pursuant to the 1985 Act (and not just redeemable *preference* shares), pass a special resolution to amend its articles. Where such a special resolution is passed to amend the articles so that they include an article which merely sets out the terms and manner of redemption of the redeemable shares, that resolution cannot be construed as also amending the articles to give the required authority also to issue the redeemable shares; see *Re Patent Invert Sugar Company*,[1] where a similar point arose in the context of a company needing authority in its articles before being able to pass a special resolution to reduce its share capital. A precedent for an article to be inserted into pre-15 June 1982 articles of a public company is the following:

POWERS RELATING TO REDEEMABLE SHARES

#. Subject to the provisions of the Companies Act 2006, the Company may issue shares which are to be redeemed or are to be liable to redeemed at the option of the Company or the holder on such terms, conditions and manner as the directors may determine.

4.9 This follows the scheme of art 43(2) of the Companies Act 2006, Model Articles for Public Companies (as set out in Sch 3 to the Companies (Model Articles) Regulations 2008) which provides:

'The company may issue shares which are to be redeemed, or are liable to be redeemed at the option of the company or the holder, and the directors may determine the terms, conditions and manner of redemption of any such shares.'

THE EXISTENCE OF IRREDEEMABLE SHARES

4.10 The general power of any company to issue redeemable shares is exercisable subject to the condition that no redeemable shares may be issued at a time when there are no issued shares of the company which are not redeemable (CA 2006, s 684(4)). The object of the legislation is presumably to prevent a company from exacerbating a situation where its only issued shares are redeemable shares, which might then be redeemed, leaving it with no issued shares at all. However, the Act merely places a restriction on the *issue* of redeemable shares – it does not prevent validly issued redeemable shares from being *redeemed* at a time when there are no irredeemable shares in issue. It is considered that the only situations in which s 684(4) could possibly be relevant are the following.

(a) The situation where a company has issued both redeemable and irredeemable shares, and either the irredeemable shares are the subject of a reduction of capital confirmed by the court under s 641 of the CA 2006,

---

[1]   (1885) 31 Ch D 166.

or effected by a private company under s 642 or they are purchased by the company pursuant to a court order (see **2.17** et seq). However, it is doubtful whether the court would ever make such an order if the only shares to be left in issue were redeemable ones.

(b) A public company might have issued partly paid irredeemable shares in addition to fully paid redeemable ones. If the irredeemable shares were all held by one person who subsequently failed to pay calls on the shares, these shares might be forfeited by the company, which might then fail or omit to dispose of them within the ensuing three years, with the result that the shares would then have to be cancelled (see **3.10**).

4.11 A company is prohibited from purchasing its own shares under Chapter 4 of Part 18 of the CA 2006 if as a result of the purchase there would no longer be any member of the company holding shares other than redeemable shares (CA 2006, s 690(2)). Thus, s 684(4) could not be relevant to an own share purchase made in such circumstances. In effect, ss 684(4) and 690(2) complement each other. The existence of s 684(4) also has the effect of preventing the subscribers of the memorandum of a company from being allotted redeemable shares following the incorporation of the company, unless other irredeemable shares were issued previously.

CONDITIONS FOR REDEMPTION

4.12 Once redeemable shares have been validly issued, they may only be redeemed upon fulfilment of the following conditions.

(a) The shares may not be redeemed unless they are fully paid (CA 2006, s 686(1)).

(b) The company must pay over the redemption money on the redemption, unless the terms of redemption of shares provide that the amount payable on redemption may, by agreement between the company and the holder of the shares, be paid on a later date (CA 2006, s 686(2)).

(c) There are restrictions as to the source (within the company's own accounts) of the payment which the company makes for the redemption (CA 2006, s 687(1), (2)). These restrictions are the same as those which apply where a company purchases its own shares under Chapter 4 of Part 18 of the CA 2006, and are considered in Chapter 7.

Subject to the above points, the procedure to be gone through upon redemption will be determined by the terms of redemption.

THE TERMS AND MANNER OF REDEMPTION

4.13 Section 685 of the CA 2006 provides that a redemption of shares may be effected on such terms, conditions and in such manner:

(a) as is determined upon by the directors of the company, where the directors are either authorised to do so by the company's articles or by a resolution of the company (ss 685(1)–(3)).

(b) in the alternative to (a), as is stated in the company's articles (s 685(4)).

4.14 Where it is sought to give directors authority to issue redeemable shares by way of a resolution of the company, such a resolution may be given by way of an ordinary resolution, even though it amends the company's articles (s 658(2)).

4.15 Where the directors are permitted to determine the terms, conditions and manner of redemption, they must do so before the shares are allotted and any obligation of the company to state, in a statement of capital, the rights attached to the shares is extended to the terms, conditions and manner of redemption of any redeemable shares (s 685(3)).

4.16 Taking into account s 658(1) of the CA 2006, in order for a redemption of redeemable shares to be valid, the terms and manner of redemption must comply with the provisions of Chapter 3 of Part 18. The directors' resolution or the article or articles governing redemption must specify the main details of those requirements. Subject to observing the general statutory scheme, there exists considerable freedom as to what, in any given case, those details should be. Where the directors are permitted to determine terms and conditions and manner of redemption, they must do so before the redeemable shares are allotted. However, the terms, conditions and manner of redemption of issued redeemable shares (whether issued pursuant to terms etc determined by the directors before issue or by way of the company's articles) cannot be amended by special resolution, provided always that the company also goes through the appropriate procedure for a variation of the rights attaching to any class of shares (see CA 2006, s 630).

4.17 The most important points to be covered by the terms of redemption will be the timing of the redemption (which can be either fixed to some specific date, or confined to some specified period, or determined by some major event, or left entirely at large); whether the shares are redeemable at the option of the company or of the shareholder, or both; and the amount of the redemption moneys, or a formula by which the redemption moneys are to be computed. Such a formula can either be a fixed one or (applying the word 'formula' more loosely) one which depends wholly or mainly on the judgment or discretion of some identifiable person, who should preferably be both independent and expert in valuing shares (eg the company's auditors). The CA 2006 allows the terms of redemption of shares in a limited company to provide that the amount payable on redemption may, by agreement between the company and the holder of the shares, be paid on a later date than the redemption date (s 686(2)). However, unless the shares are ultimately redeemed in accordance with such a provision, the shares must be paid for on redemption.

4.18 Details of the manner of redemption must also be specified in the resolution of the directors before the allotment of the redeemable shares or in the company's articles. Subject to the possibility of an agreed deferral of payment upon redemption, other details should be specified and not left, in the author's view, to be determined by the company's directors (or any other person) at some future date. The party at whose option the shares are to be redeemed will usually be required to exercise that right by sending a notice of redemption to the other. The share certificate(s) relating to the shares in question will be sent to the company, and the company will pay over the redemption moneys. No stock transfer form should be used, because the existence of the shares is being terminated in accordance with the very terms of that existence – there is no sale, gift or other transfer of shares taking place.

4.19 The following is a precedent for two articles setting out a straightforward set of terms for cumulative redeemable preference shares. Here, the preferential dividends must be actually declared by the company; and it is the company which has the sole option to redeem the preference shares.

#1. The authorised share capital of the Company at the date of the adoption of these Articles is divided into Ordinary Shares of £1 each and 7 per cent Cumulative Redeemable Preference Shares of £1 each (hereinafter called 'Preference Shares').

#2. The Preference Shares shall confer upon the holders thereof the following special rights and privileges and shall subject them to the following restrictions:

(A) As to dividend:

The Preference Shares shall confer on their holders the right to be paid out of the profits of the Company available for dividend and resolved to be distributed in respect of any financial year a fixed cumulative preferential dividend at the rate of 7 per cent per annum on the capital for the time being paid up thereon, such dividend ranking for payment in priority to the payment of any dividend on any other class of Shares. Any Preference Shares issued after the commencement of any financial year shall be entitled to the aforementioned preferential dividend but at a rate equal to such portion of 7 per cent per annum as corresponds to the part of the financial year for which such Shares remain issued.

(B) As to voting:

The holders of the Preference Shares shall have no right as such to receive notice of or to attend or vote at any general meeting of the Company unless either:

(i)   at the date of the notice convening the meeting (or, in the absence of any such notice, on the date of the meeting) the dividend on such Shares or any part thereof is 6 months or more in arrear (for which purpose such dividend shall be deemed to be payable yearly on the 31st day of December); or

(ii) the business of the meeting includes a resolution for winding up the Company, or for reducing the capital of the Company, or for authorising the terms of a contract in pursuance of which the Company may purchase any Shares or dispose of its undertaking, or any resolution varying or abrogating any of the special rights and privileges attaching to the Preference Shares.

(C) As to ranking:

No further Shares ranking either as to dividend or as to capital in priority to or on an equal footing with the Preference Shares shall be created or issued except with the consent or sanction of the holders of such Preference Shares given in the manner provided for by the Act in the case of a variation in the rights attaching to such Shares.

(D) As to redemption:

The Preference Shares shall be redeemable and redeemed in the following manner and upon and subject to the following terms and conditions:

(i) The Company shall have the option at any time to redeem at par all or any of the fully paid up Preference Shares for the time being in issue. Such right shall be exercisable subject to the provisions of the Companies Act 2006. If there is more than one holder of Preference Shares and less than all the Preference Shares then in issue are to be redeemed on this occasion, the same proportion (ignoring any fractional differences) of every holder's Preference Shares must be redeemed, unless different proportions shall have been agreed beforehand between the directors and every holder of Preference Shares.

(ii) Not less than 28 Clear Days' notice in writing of its intention so to redeem shall be given by the Company to the holders of the Preference Shares to be redeemed. The notice shall fix the time, date and place for such redemption. At the time, date and place so fixed the holders of the Preference Shares to be redeemed shall be bound to deliver up to the Company the certificates thereof for cancellation and thereupon the Company shall pay to them in respect of those Shares both the redemption moneys payable and:

(a) any arrears or deficiency of the preferential dividend (whether earned or declared or not) calculated down to the due date of redemption; and

(b) the amount of any preferential dividend which has been declared but not paid.

(iii) If the holder of any Preference Shares to be redeemed fails to comply with his obligation to deliver up the certificates of those Shares at the time, date and place fixed in accordance with sub-paragraph (ii) of this paragraph (D), the Company may elect either:

(a) to waive that obligation and proceed immediately with the redemption of those Shares, upon such (if any) additional terms as to indemnity as the Company may reasonably require, or

(b) to defer the redemption of those Shares until such time as certificates can be produced in respect of them; in which case the holder shall remain bound to deliver them up but shall not be entitled to any payment from the Company until the certificates are delivered to the Company, and, notwithstanding any other provision of this Article, he shall not become entitled to any actual or notional preferential dividend (or any arrears of dividend) on the Shares in respect of any period following the due date of redemption so fixed.

(E)   As to return of capital:

The Preference Shares shall confer on their holders the right in a winding up, or on any reduction of capital involving repayment of capital, in priority to the holders of any other class of Shares, to repayment of the capital paid up on such Preference Shares and to payment of such further sum as is equal to any arrears or deficiency of the said fixed dividend (whether earned or declared or not) calculated down to the date of repayment, but shall confer no further right to participate in the profits or assets of the Company.

4.20   An alternative arrangement is for such an article to provide that the preferential dividend becomes automatically a debt of the company on some fixed date or dates in the year, without the need for the company actually to declare the dividend. The shareholder may well prefer to have the dividends becoming payable automatically; whereas the company may prefer to retain control over the timing of when its dividends become due and payable. The following is a precedent for a cluster of four articles which include such an alternative arrangement. Here, the preference shares also carry a right of conversion into irredeemable ordinary shares and redeemable deferred shares. The rights of redemption and conversion are exercisable by the shareholder only.

SHARE CAPITAL

#1.   The share capital of the Company at the date of the adoption of these Articles is divided into Ordinary Shares of £1 each and Cumulative Convertible Redeemable 8 per cent Preference Shares of £1 each ('Preference Shares').

#2.   The Preference Shares shall be neither issued nor transferred except in multiples of 5 Preference Shares.

#3.   The Preference Shares shall confer on their holders the following special rights and privileges and shall subject them to the following restrictions:

(A)   As to dividend:

(1)   The holders of the Preference Shares shall be entitled in respect of each Financial Year of the Company to a fixed cumulative preferential dividend at the rate of 8 per cent per annum on the capital for the time being paid up on such Shares, such dividend:
   (a)   accruing on a daily basis in respect of any such Share throughout the period during which such Share remains in issue as a Preference Share, and
   (b)   ranking for payment in priority to the payment of any dividend on any other class of Shares.

(2)   The preferential dividend in respect of each Financial Year shall initially be calculated on the assumption that it is payable in two equal instalments on the 31st May and on the 30th November immediately following that Financial Year (such dates being hereinafter called 'Instalment Dates'). If any instalment of preferential dividend is not paid in full on or before its Instalment Date, that instalment shall be increased by an amount equivalent to simple interest calculated on a daily basis at the rate of 8 per cent per annum on the amount of such instalment remaining unpaid.

(3)   If the Company's profits available for distribution on any Instalment Date are sufficient to pay both:
   (a)   the entire instalment of preferential dividend prospectively payable on that date in respect of all the Preference Shares, and
   (b)   all (if any) arrears of preferential dividend,
   that instalment and those arrears (if any) shall automatically, and without any resolution of the Directors or of the Company, become a debt due from, and immediately payable by, the Company to the holders of the Preference Shares.

(4)   If paragraph (3) above does not apply in respect of any Instalment Date, the instalment of preferential dividend prospectively payable on that date, together with all (if any) arrears of preferential dividend, shall not become a debt due from (and immediately payable by) the Company to the holders of the Preference Shares until such date or dates (including that Instalment Date, as to part of the total amount) as the Directors may determine having regard to:
   (a)   the level of the Company's profits available for distribution; and
   (b)   the duty hereby imposed on them to enable the preferential dividend and all (if any) arrears to be paid at the earliest reasonable opportunity without prejudicing the Company's business.

This paragraph (4) remains subject to paragraphs (1) and (2) above.

(5)   For the avoidance of any doubt, it is hereby declared that following a conversion of any Preference Shares in accordance with paragraph (D) of this Article, those converted Shares shall cease to be entitled to any further payment of preferential dividend as such.

(6)   For so long as any Preference Shares remain in existence as such, the Directors shall not recommend or pay any dividend in respect of any Share of any other class unless they resolve that the level of the Company's profits available for distribution, together with the Company's prospects generally, are such that it is highly probable that the Company will, after paying that other dividend, remain able to pay on the two Instalment Dates in the ensuing period of twelve months each instalment of preferential dividend prospectively payable on those dates.

(B)   As to voting:

The holders of the Preference Shares shall have no right as such to receive notice of, or to attend or vote at, any general meeting of the Company unless either:

(i)   at the date of the notice convening the meeting (or, in the absence of any such notice, on the date of the meeting) any instalment of preferential dividend remains unpaid in full for more than 6 months after its Instalment Date; or

(ii)   the business of the meeting includes a resolution for winding up the Company, or for reducing the capital of the Company, or for authorising the terms of a contract in pursuance of which the Company may purchase any Shares or dispose of its undertaking, or any resolution varying or abrogating any of the special rights and privileges attaching to the Preference Shares.

(C)   As to ranking:

No further Shares ranking either as to dividend or as to capital in priority to or on an equal footing with the Preference Shares shall be created except with the consent or sanction of the holders of such Preference Shares given in the manner provided for by the Act in the case of a variation in the rights attaching to such Shares.

(D)   As to conversion and redemption:

The Preference Shares are convertible and redeemable, and may be converted and redeemed in the following manner and upon and subject to the following terms and conditions:

(1)   Any holder of Preference Shares is entitled to give to the Company a notice of conversion and redemption (a 'Conversion Notice') in respect of all (and not just any part of) the Preference Shares registered in his name.

(2)   A Conversion Notice may be given only so as to result in a conversion of the holder's Preference Shares in any year after 2015, and so that such conversion shall occur only on either the 30th June or 31st December or on any other date in the year previously notified by the Directors to the holders of the Preference Shares for this purpose. A Conversion Notice must state the date as at which the Shares are to be converted (the 'Conversion Date') and must be given to the Company not less than 28 Clear Days before that date. A Conversion Notice must be accompanied by any and every share certificate issued in respect of the Preference Shares to which it relates. A Conversion Notice which does not comply with all the requirements of this paragraph shall be entirely null and void.

(3)   The Company may, within 21 days after it receives a duly given Conversion Notice from a holder of Preference Shares, by notice in writing (a 'Deferral Notice') given to that holder, elect that two out of every 5 of his Preference Shares shall be converted into Ordinary Shares of £1 each and that the remaining three Preference Shares shall be converted into Redeemable Deferred Shares of £1 each ('Deferred Shares') carrying the rights and restrictions specified in the next following Article. If the Company does so elect, the Preference Shares in question shall be converted accordingly into Ordinary Shares and Deferred Shares.

(4)   If a Conversion Notice is duly given and no Deferral Notice is duly given in response to it, on the Conversion Date:

(a)   40 per cent of the Preference Shares to which that Conversion Notice relates shall be converted into Ordinary Shares of £1 each, ranking on an equal footing with the other Ordinary Shares in issue on that date (and thereby ceasing to be redeemable), and

(b)   the remaining 60 per cent shall be redeemed; except that if all or any of those Shares cannot then be redeemed without infringing any of the provisions of the Act relating to the redemption of redeemable shares, those Shares which cannot then be redeemed shall be converted into Deferred Shares.

(5)   The redemption price of any Preference Shares which are to be redeemed shall be equal to;

(a)   the nominal value of those Shares, plus

(b)   an amount equal to any arrears of preferential dividend in respect of those Shares, plus

(c)   either:

    (i)   if the Conversion Date is also an Instalment Date, an amount equal to the instalment of preferential dividend prospectively payable on that date, or

    (ii)   otherwise, an amount equivalent to the preferential dividend accrued at a daily rate over the period beginning immediately after the last preceding Instalment Date and ending with the Conversion Date.

(6)   If on the Conversion Date any Preference Shares are to be redeemed, the Company shall on that date cancel the certificates in respect of those Shares, record the redemption and cancellation of the Shares in its register of Members, and pay the entire redemption price of those Shares to their last holder or to such other person as he may direct.

(E)   As to return of capital:

In a winding up of the Company or on any reduction of capital involving repayment of capital, the holders of any Preference Shares then in issue shall have the right, out of (in a winding up) any surplus assets remaining after payment of the liabilities of the Company, and in priority to the holders of any other class of Shares, to repayment of the capital paid up on such Preference Shares and to payment of such further sum as is equal to:

(a)   any arrears of preferential dividend, plus

(b)   an amount equivalent to the preferential dividend accrued at a daily rate over the period beginning immediately after the last preceding Instalment Date and ending with the date of repayment,

but shall confer no further right to participate in the profits or assets of the Company.

#4.   If any Preference Shares are converted into Deferred Shares in accordance with the last preceding Article, each Deferred Share shall confer on its holder:

(A)   no right to any dividend;

(B)   no right to receive any notice of, or to attend or vote at, any general meeting of the Company;

(C)   the right in a winding up of the Company to receive, after payment has been made of the full amount of the capital paid up on every Share of every other class but before any further sum is paid in respect of any Share of any other class, an amount equal to:

(i)   the capital paid up on the Deferred Share, plus

(ii)   an amount equal to any arrears of preferential dividend which had accrued in respect of that Share before the Conversion Date when the Deferred Share came into being as such by way of conversion from a Preference Share, plus

(iii) either:

(a)   if that Conversion Date was also an Instalment Date, an amount equal to the instalment of preferential dividend notionally payable on that date, or

(b)   otherwise, an amount equivalent to the preferential dividend accrued at a daily rate over the period beginning immediately after the last preceding Instalment Date and ending with that Conversion Date,

but shall carry no further right to participate in the winding up; and

(D)   the right to be redeemed on any anniversary of the Conversion Date when the Deferred Share came into being as such by way of conversion from a Preference Share. This right of redemption shall be subject to:

(i)   the provisions of the Companies Act 2006, and

(ii)   the Directors being of the opinion that the Company retains sufficient profits available for distribution to enable it, taking into account the Directors' opinion as to the Company's general prospects, to pay, in respect of any Preference Shares which remain in existence as such, the dividend becoming prospectively payable either on that anniversary date (if it is also an Instalment Date) or on the next following Instalment Date, together with any arrears of such dividend, and also each instalment of preferential dividend prospectively payable on the following two Instalment Dates, and

(iii) the Directors resolving, no later than 28 days before the anniversary date, that the Company can reasonably redeem the Deferred Share without prejudicing the Company's business.

If the Directors do so resolve, they shall immediately give notice in writing to each holder of Deferred Shares of the Company's intention to redeem all or part of those Shares on the forthcoming anniversary date. The notice shall specify the number of Deferred Shares to be redeemed, and shall fix the time, date and place for such redemption. At the time, date and place so fixed the holders of the Deferred Shares to be redeemed shall be bound to deliver up to the Company all or any certificates in respect of those Shares for cancellation, and thereupon the Company shall pay to them in respect of those Shares the same amount that would have been the redemption price of the Preference Shares from which the Deferred Shares in question were converted if those Preference Shares had, on their Conversion Date, been redeemed instead of being converted into Deferred Shares. If the holder of any Deferred Shares to be redeemed fails to comply with his obligation to deliver up any certificates for those Shares at the time, date and place so fixed, the Company may elect either:

(a) to waive that obligation and proceed immediately with the redemption of those Shares, upon such (if any) additional terms as to indemnity as the Company may reasonably require, or

(b) to defer the redemption of those Shares until the following year.

4.21 The following is a precedent for an article where a company is to have two classes of ordinary share, with one class redeemable and the other not. Here, the redeemable shares can be redeemed at the option of either the shareholder or the company after an initial period of time has elapsed. In order for this short form of article to be likely to work, the redeemable shares should represent no more than a smallish proportion of the issued share capital – otherwise there could be a significant risk of the company having insufficient distributable profits to cover the valuation to be placed on the redeemable shares. If the redeemable shares must be a substantial proportion of the issued share capital, it may be desirable to structure the article in such a way that these shares are to be redeemed in instalments over a number of years.

#1. The authorised share capital of the Company at the date of the adoption of these Articles is divided into Ordinary Shares of £1 each and 'A' Ordinary Redeemable Shares of £1 each (hereinafter called 'A Shares'). The 'A' Shares shall rank equally with the Ordinary Shares in all respects except that the 'A' Shares shall be redeemable and redeemed in the following manner and upon and subject to the following terms and conditions:

(A) Subject to the provisions of the Companies Act 2006, at any time after 31st December 2016:

  (i) any holder of 'A' Shares shall be entitled to give to the Company a notice (a 'Redemption Demand') demanding that all or any part of the 'A' Shares registered in his name shall be redeemed in accordance with this Article;

  (ii) the Company shall be entitled to give to every holder of 'A' Shares a notice of redemption (a 'Redemption Notice') in respect of all or any part of the 'A' Shares registered in his name. If there is more than one holder of 'A' Shares and Redemption Notices are given in respect of less than all the 'A' Shares then in issue, the Redemption Notices must be in respect of the same proportion (ignoring any fractional differences) of every holder's 'A' Shares, unless different proportions shall have been agreed beforehand between the directors and every holder of 'A' Shares.

(B) A Redemption Demand shall be treated as requiring the 'A' Shares to which it relates to be redeemed at the Company's registered office at eleven o'clock in the morning 21 days after the date when it is delivered to the Company, unless, within 7 days after receiving the Redemption Demand, the Company gives to the holder of
'A' Shares who gave the Redemption Demand a notice postponing the redemption date by no more than 7 days and/or specifying a different place and/or time for the redemption to occur, in which case the date and/or place and/or time of the redemption shall be varied accordingly.

(C) A Redemption Notice must give not less than 21 Clear Days' notice of the Company's intention to redeem the 'A' Shares to which the notice relates. The notice shall fix the time, date and place for such redemption.

(D)   At the time, date and place of redemption (determined under paragraph (B) or (C) of this Article), every holder of 'A' Shares to be redeemed shall be bound to deliver up to the Company the certificates thereof for cancellation, and thereupon the Company shall pay to such holder the redemption moneys payable, determined under paragraph (E) of this Article. If the holder of any 'A' Shares to be redeemed fails to comply with his obligation to deliver up the certificates of those Shares at the time, date and place of redemption, the Company may elect either:

   (i)   to waive that obligation and proceed immediately with the redemption of those Shares, upon such (if any) additional terms as to indemnity as the Company may reasonably require, or

   (ii)   to defer the redemption of those Shares until such time as certificates can be produced in respect of them.

(E)   The Directors shall compute the redemption price of every 'A' Share which is to be redeemed by reference to the following formula:

> four times 'A' divided by 'C'
>
> Where:
>
> A = the average of the pre-tax profits or losses, as shown in the statutory profit and loss account of the Company and its wholly owned subsidiaries (if any) for the three financial years of the Company immediately preceding the date when the relevant Redemption Notice or Redemption Demand is given, being years for which statutory accounts have been published; and
>
> C = the number of fully paid Shares in issue as at the date when the relevant Redemption Notice or Redemption Demand is given.
>
> The redemption price (being the price of one 'A' Share) shall be subject to a minimum value of zero and shall be rounded down to the nearest whole penny. The Directors may, for the purpose of computing the redemption price, seek such advice as they think fit from the auditors (if any) of the Company or any independent expert, and all costs so incurred shall be borne by the Company.

(F)   If for any reason the redemption price cannot be determined in accordance with paragraph (E) of this Article by the time and date of redemption, the relevant Redemption Notice or Redemption Demand shall be deemed to be entirely void, unless by that time and date a redemption price is agreed between the Directors and the relevant holder of 'A' Shares.

4.22   In the last precedent, an alternative to using a formula to calculate the redemption price would be for para (E) to require the redemption price to be determined by an independent expert as that figure which represents in his opinion the fair value of an 'A' Share. Such a provision would need to specify whether the expert's valuation was to be done by taking into account any discount for the minority status (if applicable) of the holding of 'A' Shares, or by ignoring any such discount. As share valuations by experts often take a significant time to produce, it may also be necessary to structure the whole article in such a way that the redemption date is delayed until the share valuation is available.

THE EFFECT OF A REDEMPTION

4.23 The effect of a redemption by a company of its own shares is that, upon redemption, the shares are treated as cancelled and the amount of the company's issued share capital is diminished by the nominal value of the shares redeemed (CA 2006, s 688).

NO CONVERSION UNDER SECTION 684 FROM IRREDEEMABLE TO REDEEMABLE

4.24 It is noteworthy that s 684 only permits the *issue* of redeemable shares; there is nothing in s 684 to permit a conversion of issued irredeemable shares into redeemable shares (*Re St James' Court Estate Ltd*[2]). In order to achieve such a result, the company must pass appropriate resolutions and effect a reduction of capital. In *Forth Wines Ltd, Petitioner*,[3] the Court of Session confirmed that a resolution converting ordinary (irredeemable) shares into redeemable deferred shares was within the powers of the company under the predecessor to s 641, which empowers a company to 'reduce its share capital in any way' (now, s 645(3)). Although the conversion of the ordinary shares into redeemable deferred shares did not itself constitute a reduction of share capital, it provided a mechanism whereby that share capital could be paid off at a future date.

CONVERSION FROM REDEEMABLE TO IRREDEEMABLE

4.25 There is no reason, however, why shares which were originally issued as redeemable shares should not subsequently become irredeemable. This could happen if the right of redemption is limited to a specific period of time, and that period expires without the right having been exercised. Alternatively, that result could be achieved by means of a resolution altering the articles and varying the rights attaching to the shares (subject to the appropriate procedure for doing so; CA 2006, s 630).

THE LIABILITY OF THE COMPANY

4.26 Where a company issues redeemable shares, it cannot be made liable in damages in respect of any failure on its part to redeem any of the shares (CA 2006, s 735(2)). An aggrieved shareholder may sue the company for any other remedy, but the court must not grant an order for specific performance of the terms of redemption where the company can show that it is unable to meet the cost of redeeming the shares in question out of distributable profits (CA 2006, s 735(3)). Where the company lacks sufficient distributable profits with which

---

[2]   [1944] Ch 6.
[3]   [1991] BCC 638.

to redeem the shares, a remedy which the shareholder could aim for is an injunction to restrain the payment of any dividends to other shareholders until his redeemable shares have been redeemed (this possibility was mentioned in *Re Holders Investment Trust Ltd*[4]).

4.27 The maintenance of the company's capital and the consequential protection of its creditors are the objectives of the prohibition in s 735(2) on the company being liable in damages in respect of any failure on its part to redeem any shares. If such a claim in damages were permissible, it could elevate the rights of the holders of the redeemable shares from rights ranking behind the rights of creditors of the company to rights ranking equally with those creditors. One cannot get round the s 735(2) prohibition by an arrangement which interposes a third party between the company and the holder of the redeemable shares. In *Barclays Bank plc v British & Commonwealth Holdings plc*,[5] the main company, 'B & C', issued in 1987 four tranches of redeemable shares to a corporate shareholder of long standing, 'Caledonia'. The first of these four tranches was redeemable at the end of the year 1988, and the three following tranches were redeemable at the end of the years 1989, 1990 and 1991, respectively. As part of the arrangement relating to the issue of these shares, a third company, Tindalk, granted put options to Caledonia under which Tindalk could be required by Caledonia to buy any of the redeemable shares at the redemption price if B & C failed to redeem them. Tindalk was to be financed for this purpose by six banks, and B & C gave those banks various covenants to the effect that B & C would so conduct its affairs as to be able to redeem Caledonia's redeemable shares on the due dates. Any breach of covenant would give rise to a claim in damages by the banks against B & C. After the first two tranches of shares had been successfully redeemed, B & C got into financial difficulties and was placed in administration. Following B & C's failure to redeem the two remaining tranches of redeemable shares, Caledonia exercised its right to require Tindalk to purchase those shares. Tindalk paid for the shares using money borrowed from the six banks, who then sought to recover their prospectively irrecoverable loans by claiming damages against B & C for breach of covenant.

4.28 The Court of Appeal unanimously upheld the High Court's decision, which included a review of the main authorities on the subject. The following principles can be derived from the judgment:

(a)   Although the actual *ratio decidendi* of *Trevor v Whitworth*[6] was that a limited company did not have the capacity to purchase any of its own shares otherwise than by means of a reduction of capital sanctioned by the court (or now, under the CA 2006, in the case of a private company by means of a reduction of capital supported by a solvency statement), the broader principle on which that decision was based is that it is not competent for a limited company under any circumstances to return any

---

[4]   [1971] 2 All ER 289 at 295b.
[5]   [1995] BCC 1059.
[6]   (1887) 12 App Cas 409.

portion of its capital to any shareholder, except by means of reduction of capital sanctioned by the court (per Lord Macnaghten at 432).

(b)   An agreement is void by reason of *Trevor v Whitworth* if it is an agreement which is only likely to be called upon if the company has no distributable profits and which will, if called upon when the company is insolvent, have the effect of increasing the liabilities of the company by turning rights held by shareholders ranking behind creditors into rights held by a creditor ranking equally with other creditors. Caledonia's right as the holder of two classes of preference shares to have those shares redeemed by B & C purported to have been replaced by the claims of the six banks (as unsecured creditors) for breach of covenant against B & C. That conclusion offended the rule in *Trevor v Whitworth*, with the result that the covenants were, in principle, void. Moreover, it did not make any difference whether the banks' claims were for breach of contract or in the tort of misrepresentation.

(c)   However, on the facts the covenants were saved from being void because in 1987 the entire scheme had (before it was entered into) been sanctioned by the court under CA 1985, s 425 (the predecessor to CA 2006, s 895) (because one element of the scheme, the cancellation of Caledonia's previous shareholding, had involved a reduction of capital). The court's order sanctioning the scheme remained standing (no proper application to set it aside having been made) and rendered the scheme binding on B & C and its administrators.

(d)   An alternative defence raised by B & C to the banks' claim was under the predecessor of CA 2006, s 735, ie that a company is not liable in damages in respect of any failure on its part to redeem any of its shares. This defence failed, on the ground that the banks' claims were 'in respect of' breaches of covenant by B & C and not in respect of B & C's failure to redeem shares, even though the measure of the loss being claimed for the breaches of covenant was derived from B & C's failure to redeem the shares.

4.29   Where any of a company's redeemable shares have not been redeemed before the commencement of the winding up of the company, the terms of redemption may then be enforced against the company, and the sums payable by the company under the terms of redemption must be paid in priority to any amounts due to members in satisfaction of their rights (whether as to capital or income) as members, except in the following circumstances:

(a)   if the terms of redemption provided for the redemption to take place at a date later than the date of the commencement of the winding up; or

(b)   if during the period beginning with the date on which the redemption was to have taken place and ending with the commencement of the winding up the company could not at any time have lawfully made a distribution equal in value to the amount for which the shares were to have been redeemed; or

(c) where other shares carry rights (whether as to capital or as to income) which are preferred to the rights as to capital of the redeemable shares, any amount due in satisfaction of those preferred rights must be paid out first (CA 2006, s 735(4)–(6)).

This provision does no more, in relation to a surplus on a winding up arising after discharging all debts and liabilities of the company (other than any due to members in their character as such), than adjust the rights of the members of the company amongst themselves to what they would have been if the redeemable shares had been redeemed beforehand.

THE LIABILITY OF THE SHAREHOLDER

4.30 Where the procedure for redeeming redeemable shares has been set in motion, there is nothing to prevent the company from enforcing its rights by claiming damages against the redeeming shareholder if he fails to redeem – assuming, of course, that the company would be able to prove that it had suffered a loss. Alternatively, the company should be able to obtain an order for specific performance of the terms of redemption, unless it is unable to meet the cost of redeeming the shares out of distributable profits (see **5.12**). A probably more practical way of enforcing the company's rights is illustrated at para (D)(iii) of the precedent article at **4.19**.

THE BENEFICIAL OWNERSHIP OF THE SHARES

4.31 It is not considered that the shareholder's beneficial ownership of the shares will be affected by the commencement of the procedure for their redemption, unless perhaps he thereby becomes restricted in the manner in which he may deal with the shares (in which case the beneficial ownership may go into suspense). By the same token, the company will not acquire any beneficial interest in the shares, as, by redeeming them, the company will merely be bringing their existence to an end in the manner originally envisaged by the terms of redemption (as in the case of a debenture), and will not be acquiring title to the shares.

NOTICE TO THE REGISTRAR OF COMPANIES

4.32 Within one month after redeeming any redeemable shares, the company is required to give to the Registrar of Companies notice on form SH02, specifying the shares that have been redeemed (CA 2006, s 689(1)). The notice must be accompanied by a statement of capital, stating with respect to the company's share capital immediately following the redemption the total number of shares of the company, the aggregate nominal value of those shares and the amount paid up or unpaid on each share (including by way of premium) and, in respect of each class of share in the company's share capital, the prescribed particulars of the rights and equivalent information concerning the number, aggregate nominal value and paid up or unpaid element of shares of that class (s 689(3)).

DISCLOSURE IN ACCOUNTS

4.33 Where any part of a company's allotted share capital consists of redeemable shares, the company's balance sheet must state the following information (this will usually be done by way of a note):

(a)   the earliest and latest dates on which the company has power to redeem those shares;

(b)   whether those shares must be redeemed in any event or are liable to be redeemed at the option of the company or of the shareholder; and

(c)   whether any (and, if so, what) premium is payable on redemption (Small Companies and Groups (Accounts and Directors' Report) Regulations 2008 (SI 2008/409), para 46(2) of Sch 1; Large and Medium-Sized Companies and Groups (Accounts and Reports) Regulations 2008 (SI 2008/410), para 47(2) of Sch 1).

DIRECTORS' REPORT

4.34 Section 658(1) of the CA 2006 appears, at first sight, to assume that a company 'acquires' shares that it is redeeming. However, for accounting purposes, when it comes to any question of disclosing details of such a redemption in a company's accounts, both para 6(1)(a) of Sch 5 of the Small Companies and Groups (Accounts and Directors' Report) Regulations 2008 (SI 2008/409) and para 8(a) of Part 2 of Sch 7 of the Large and Medium-Sized Companies and Groups (Accounts and Reports) Regulations 2008 (SI 2008/410) omit any reference to a redemption of redeemable shares. Para 8 of Part 2 of Sch 7 of the Large and Medium-Sized Companies and Groups (Accounts and Reports) Regulations 2008 reads as follows:

'This Part of this Schedule applies where shares in a company –

(a)   are purchased by the company or are acquired by it by forfeiture or surrender in lieu of forfeiture, or in pursuance of any of the following provisions (acquisition of own shares by company limited by shares) ...
(iii)   section 659 of the 2006 Act ...'

Para 6(1)(a) of Sch 5 of the Small Companies and Groups (Accounts and Directors' Report) Regulations 2008 is in substantially similar terms.

4.35 Such wording appears to have been carefully chosen, as the only type of own share acquisition which may be done 'in pursuance of section 659' is, very arguably, the one described in the opening words of s 659(1), ie:

> 'A limited company limited may acquire any of its own fully paid shares otherwise than for valuable consideration.'

The Regulations therefore impose no requirement to disclose in the directors' report details of any redemption by the company of any of its redeemable shares. Instead, they require the disclosure in the directors' report of information about shares in which the company has had a beneficial interest at some time during the relevant financial year. As explained at **4.31**, a company which redeems any of its redeemable shares does not thereby acquire any beneficial interest in them; conversely, a company which *purchases* any of its shares will often acquire a beneficial interest in them (see **5.15**), as will a company which acquires shares in itself by way of forfeiture, surrender, gift, or where any of the other circumstances referred to in para 6(1)(b) and (c) of Sch 5 of the Small Companies and Groups (Accounts and Directors' Report) Regulations 2008 or para 8(b) and (c) of Part 2 of Sch 7 of the Large and Medium-Sized Companies and Groups (Accounts and Reports) Regulations 2008 applies.

4.36 However, it does not necessarily follow that the directors' report can remain silent about a redemption by a company of any of its redeemable shares. At least in the case of larger or public companies, para 7(1)(a) of Part 2 of Sch 7 of the Large and Medium-Sized Companies and Groups (Accounts and Reports) Regulations 2008 requires the directors' report to contain:

> '(a) particulars of any important events affecting the company which have occurred since the end of the financial year.'

If shares are redeemed before the date when the previous year's accounts are finalised, it is a matter of judgment whether or not that redemption is an 'important event'.

Chapter 5

A COMPANY'S POWER TO PURCHASE ITS OWN SHARES

5.1   The provisions of the CA 2006 dealing with the purchase by a company of its own shares are now contained in Chapter 4 of Part 18 of the Act, which came into force on 1 October 2009.

THE POWER TO PURCHASE

5.2   Section 690(1) of the CA 2006 confers, subject to the ensuing provisions of Chapter 4, power on a company limited by shares or limited by guarantee and having a share capital to purchase its own shares (including any redeemable shares), subject to any restriction or prohibition in its articles.

5.3   Prior to the CA 2006 coming into force, limited companies required specific authority in their articles in order to purchase their own shares. For companies incorporated under the CA 1985 to 1989, such a power was contained in reg 35 of the 1985 Table A as set out in the Companies (Tables A to F) Regulations 1985, SI 1985/805. Following the introduction of the CA 2006, the company's articles may have a negative effect in restricting or prohibiting an own share purchase. A company that was incorporated prior to the coming into force of the CA 1981 (at a time when own share purchases were not legally permissible), would now be able to purchase its own shares in reliance upon the statutory permission even if it had not altered its articles to introduce such a power before 1 October 2009 and provided it is not subject to any other restriction or prohibition in its articles.

5.4   The drafting of the CA 2006 has considerably simplified the identification of the terms and conditions upon which a company's powers to exercise its own shares may be exercised. Under the CA 1985, it was necessary to cross-reference the provisions concerning an own share purchase with the terms and conditions applicable to a redemption of shares. Now the principal provisions for a redemption and an own share purchase are contained in distinct chapters of the Act (Chapters 3 and 4 of Part 18) and are effectively independent of each other. The provisions concerning a private limited company redeeming or purchasing its shares out of capital overlap and are dealt with together in Chapter 5 of Part 18.

THE CONDITIONS

5.5   The power of a company to purchase its own shares is exercisable subject to the following conditions.

(a)   A company may not purchase its own shares unless they are fully paid (CA 2006, s 691(2)).

(b)   The terms subject to which the shares are purchased must provide for payment to be made on purchase (CA 2006, s 691). This provision should not prevent a single contract from specifying separate completion dates for different shares, as long as payment in full is made on each completion date for the shares then being purchased. It is to be contrasted with the position in relation to the redemption of shares where the price payable on redemption might be deferred by agreement between the company and the member concerned.

(c)   A company may not purchase its shares if as a result of the purchase there would no longer be any member of the company holding shares other than redeemable shares or shares held as treasury shares (CA 2006, s 690(2)). The aim of the legislation is to prevent the occurrence or exacerbation of a state of affairs in which a company's only issued shares are redeemable shares (which might then be redeemed) or treasury shares (which might later be cancelled), in either case leaving it with no issued shares at all.

(d)   There are various rules governing the internal procedure which the company must adopt. These are dealt with in Chapter 6.

(e)   There are restrictions as to the source (within the company's accounts) of the payment which the company makes for the purchase of its own shares. These are considered in Chapter 7.

5.6   These conditions may be significantly modifed by the Companies Act 2006 (Amendment of Part 18) Regulations 2013, currently laid before Parliament. Those Regulations may, if approved in their original form, alter the requirement on private limited companies to pay in full the purchase price of shares in cases where the buy-back is for an employees' share scheme (thus allowing payments to be made in instalments), alter the requirments for shareholder authorisations concerning buy-back contracts to an ordinary resolution and permit a private limited company to hold its shares in treasury and deal with such shares as treasury shares. The commentary in this book does not reflect such possible prospective amendments.

THE EFFECT OF AN OWN SHARE PURCHASE

5.7   The effect of a purchase by a company of its own shares is that, upon completion of the purchase, the shares are treated as cancelled, and the amount of the company's issued share capital is diminished by the nominal value of the shares purchased (CA 2006, s 706(b)(i) and (ii)). The only exception to this is where (in the case of a public limited company) the shares are to be held as treasury shares (see Chapter 8) (CA 2006, s 706(a)).

THE LIABILITY OF THE COMPANY

5.8 Where a company has agreed to purchase any of its own shares, the company cannot be made liable in damages in respect of any failure on its part to purchase any of the shares (CA 2006, s 735(1), (2)). An aggrieved shareholder may sue the company for any other remedy, but it is provided that the court must not grant an order for specific performance of the contract where the company can show that it is unable to meet the cost of purchasing the shares in question out of distributable profits (CA 2006, s 735(3)). Where the company lacks sufficient distributable profits with which to purchase the shares, a remedy which the shareholder could aim for is an injunction to restrain the payment of any dividends to other shareholders until his shares have been purchased. The predecessor to s 735 (s 178, CA 1985) was considered in the context of a redemption of redeemable shares in *Barclays Bank plc v British & Commonwealth Holdings plc*[1] (see **4.27**).

5.9 Where a company has agreed to purchase any of its own shares and the purchase of any of those shares has not been completed by the commencement of the winding up of the company, the terms of the contract may then be enforced against the company, and the purchase price payable by the company must be paid in priority to any amounts due to members in satisfaction of their rights (whether as to capital or income) as members, except in the following circumstances:

(a) if the share purchase contract provided for the purchase to take place at a date later than the date of the commencement of the winding up; or

(b) if during the period beginning with the date on which the purchase was to have taken place and ending with the commencement of the winding up the company could not at any time have lawfully made a distribution equal in value to the price at which the shares were to have been purchased; or

(c) where other shares carry rights (whether as to capital or to income) which are preferred to the rights as to capital of the shares which are the subject of the contract, any amount due in satisfaction of those preferred rights is paid out first (CA 2006, s 735(4)–(6)).

This provision does no more, in relation to a surplus on a winding up arising after discharging all debts and liabilities of the company (other than any due to

---

[1] [1995] BCC 1059.

members in their character as such), than adjust the rights of the members of the company amongst themselves to what they would have been if the share purchase had been completed beforehand.

THE LIABILITY OF THE VENDOR

5.10 Where a company has agreed to purchase any of its own shares, there is nothing to prevent the company from being awarded damages against the vendor. Since an award of damages for breach of contract is a legal and not an equitable remedy, the fact that the company cannot be sued for damages for breach of its own obligation to purchase the shares (see **5.8**) should not prevent the company from obtaining damages in respect of the vendor's breach. This does assume, of course, that the company would be able to prove that it had suffered a loss.

5.11 Perhaps more importantly, the company will often be able to obtain specific performance of the vendor's obligation to sell his shares. In *Vision Express (UK) Ltd v Wilson*,[2] there was an agreement under which the company was to purchase the defendant's shares in the company. This agreement was in the form of a Tomlin order, designed to settle an employment and shareholder dispute. Although the agreement was entered into without it having been previously approved by special resolution (see **6.5**), the court held that it was an implied term of the agreement that the obligation to purchase was:

> 'subject (in so far as necessary) to compliance with statutory provisions for the purchase by the company of its own shares.'

This was by way of application of the general principle (illustrated in *Brady v Brady*[3]) that where an agreement can be performed in two alternative ways, one lawful and one unlawful, it is to be presumed that the parties intend to carry it out in the lawful and not the unlawful manner. Accordingly, the court ordered specific performance of the agreement.

5.12 One instance where the company might not be granted an order for specific performance is where the vendor can show that the company is unable to meet the cost of purchasing the shares in question out of distributable profits. In such a situation, the vendor himself would be unable to obtain an order for specific performance against the company (see **5.8**), with the result that the court will not grant the company an order for specific performance against the vendor unless the court can be persuaded that such an order would be neither unjust nor unfair to the vendor (*Price v Strange*[4]). Where the shares are quoted and freely available on the market (so that a contract for their purchase would *prima facie* not be specifically enforceable), it is considered that the company might obtain an order for specific performance if it can show that

---

2   [1998] BCC 173.
3   [1998] 2 All ER 617.
4   [1977] 3 All ER 371.

damages are not an adequate remedy (e g where the company's main object was to purchase a particular large shareholding).

5.13   It also follows that, if the company were unable to obtain an order of specific performance, it would not be able to obtain an injunction, if the effect of the injunction would be the same as that of a grant of specific performance; e.g. if the vendor expressly agreed to sell the shares to the company and not to anybody else, and the purchase price was to be funded mainly out of capital, the company would not be able to restrain him by injunction from selling to a third party if the effect would be to sterilise the vendor's right to deal with his shares (e g *Page One Records Ltd v Britton*[5]).

5.14   The articles may provide a more practical way of enforcing the company's rights. One such approach is illustrated at para (F) of the precedent article at **9.5**.

BENEFICIAL INTERESTS IN THE SHARES

5.15   Once a company duly enters into an unconditional contract to purchase its own shares, it will acquire a beneficial interest in those shares in any case where the company would be entitled to an order for specific performance of the contract (*Parway Estates Ltd v IRC*[6]). The vendor will, pending completion of the contract, hold the shares subject to the company's interest in them and will, to that extent, be a trustee of them (*Lake v Bayliss*[7]). In cases where the remedy of specific performance is not available, it is doubtful whether the company acquires any beneficial interest when an unconditional contract for the sale of the shares is entered into; the vendor's possible liability to damages for breach of contract is unlikely to be sufficient to cause a beneficial interest in the shares to pass from the vendor to the company, especially as the company may have difficulty in proving that it has suffered a loss. By the same token, where the contract which the company enters into is an option contract (a 'contingent purchase contract', as referred to by ss 694(3) and 705(1)(a) CA 2006), the beneficial ownership of the shares will normally remain with the shareholder at least until the option is exercised (*J Sainsbury plc v O'Connor*[8]).

PURCHASES BY PUBLIC COMPANIES

5.16   Where a public company purchases any of its own shares in compliance with Chapter 4 of Part 18 of the CA 2006 and in consequence the nominal value of the company's allotted share capital falls to below the authorised minimum provided in s 763 (namely, £50,000 or the euro equivalent prescribed by the Secretary of State, currently €57,100), there is nothing in the legislation

---

[5]   [1967] 3 All ER 822.
[6]   (1958) 45 TC 135.
[7]   [1974] 2 All ER 1114.
[8]   [1991] STC 318.

requiring the company to issue new shares or to re-register as a private company. In particular, there is nothing to that effect in s 662 of the CA 2006, where one might have expected to find such a requirement. Accordingly, scope exists for a public limited company to carry on business quite lawfully with an issued share capital whose nominal value is far less than the authorised minimum, as there is no general provision requiring the issued share capital of a public limited company to be maintained at or above that level at all times. However, in such a case, the aggregate of the nominal value of the company's issued share capital and the amount which would have had to have been credited to the capital redemption reserve would be bound to be not less than the authorised minimum (see **7.10**), and this can be said to be equivalent, as far as the distribution of profits is concerned, to the company having an issued share capital of not less than the authorised minimum. It seems that the Secretary of State could, by relying on the wide-ranging powers conferred by s 737 of the CA 2006, modify the provisions of Chapter 4 of Part 18 of the CA 2006, introduce a provision requiring a public company to re-register as private where, in consequence of an own share purchase, the nominal value of the company's allotted share capital falls to below the authorised minimum.

THE MEANING OF THE WORD 'PURCHASE'

5.17 The word 'purchase' is not defined in Chapters 4 and 5 of the CA 2006; therefore, it must bear its ordinary legislative meaning unless the context suggests otherwise. A 'purchase' is the other half of a sale transaction. The ordinary legislative usage of the word 'sale' denotes a transfer of property for cash and not for any other forms of property (*Re Westminster Property Group plc*[9]). The context of Chapters 4 and 5 of the CA 2006 supports the view that the word 'purchase' has its ordinary meaning, eg the close juxtaposition of the words 'price', 'amount' and 'sum' in ss 692(3), 692(4), 701(3), 701(7), 705, 707(4), 710(1) of the CA 2006. In addition, it could well be difficult to operate the rules (such as in s 692(2), (3) of the CA 2006) for determining how an own share purchase is to be financed if the purchase 'price' or 'payment' could include a non-cash consideration without at the same time there being included in the legislation some provision regulating the manner in which that consideration was to be valued for these purposes. It follows that the word 'purchase' in Chapters 4 and 5 of the CA 2006 must bear its ordinary meaning of acquiring property for cash.

CONTRAST WITH AN EXCHANGE

5.18 An exchange is a single transaction under which each of the two parties to it transfers a non-monetary asset to the other on terms that that other should receive some title to the asset transferred. Because an exchange is different from a purchase, a company cannot 'purchase' its own shares in consideration of the transfer to the 'vendor' of a non-cash asset, such as shares

---

[9]   [1985] 2 All ER 426 at 432a and 433g.

in another company, or land. Any such arrangement can only, if at all, be validly achieved *by means of a single transaction* if it takes the form of a reduction of capital, whether confirmed by the court under ss 645–649 of the CA 2006 or, in the case of a private company limited by shares, by a special resolution supported by a solvency statement. In *Ex p Westburn Sugar Refineries Ltd*,[10] the House of Lords confirmed that in a reduction of capital a company may pay off share capital by transferring to the shareholders assets, even where the market value of those assets exceeds the amount by which the share capital is reduced. Alternatively, such an arrangement could be achieved by splitting the transaction into two separate sale transactions; for example, the shareholder could sell his shares to the company, and the company could sell some land to the shareholder. As long as the valuation placed on the non-cash asset is a *bona fide* one, there appears to be no valid basis upon which the two transactions could be re-characterised as a single transaction of exchange. In *BDG Roof-Bond Ltd v Douglas*,[11] a shareholder agreed to sell his 50% shareholding to the company for £135,000, and at the same time agreed to buy from the company some land for £65,000 and a car for £10,000. The shareholder had clearly sold his share to the company for £135,000, even though what he actually received was the land and the car, plus £60,000 in cash. Applying the principle in *Spargo's Case*,[12] that a *bona fide* set-off of one debt against another constitutes payment of both debts, the company had paid the shareholder a total of £135,000.

5.19 It also seems reasonably clear that a company cannot achieve a purchase of its own shares falling within Chapters 4 and 5 of the CA 2006 where the consideration for the purchase takes the form of a debenture issued by the company itself – a 'debenture' meaning any acknowledgement of indebtedness, including a promissory note, loan stock, etc. A sale of shares with the purchase price left outstanding would infringe the requirement of s 691(2) of the CA 2006 that payment must occur on completion of the contract. Although it can be argued (on the basis of *BDG Roof-Bond Ltd v Douglas*[13]) that the word 'payment' in s 691(2) can include the transfer of a non-cash consideration which the company could distribute by way of dividend, that case does not go so far as to suggest that 'payment' could be achieved by the issue of a debenture. The context of Chapters 4 and 5 of the CA 2006 not only indicates that a cash consideration is intended, but also suggests that the intention of s 691(2) would be frustrated if all that the company needed to do to comply with it was to issue a debenture in satisfaction of the purchase price – in reality, that would amount to the company deferring payment beyond the contract's completion date. Even if the company does not issue any debenture, s 691(2) also prevents the vendor shareholder from agreeing to lend the purchase price back to the company on the completion date, with a view to the company avoiding the need to find the money. There is, however, nothing to prevent the vendor shareholder from lending money back to the company after he has

---

10 [1951] AC 625.
11 [2000] BCC 770.
12 (1873) 8 Ch App 407.
13 [2000] BCC 770.

received from the company the sale price of his shares, provided that this is pursuant to an independent transaction.

CONTRAST WITH A REDUCTION OF CAPITAL

5.20 A company's power to purchase its own shares in accordance with Chapter 4 of Part 18 of the CA 2006 is an exception to the rule that a company may not acquire its own shares (CA 2006, s 658(1)). Under the CA 2006, a company's power to reduce its share capital in accordance with Chapter 10 of Part 17 is identified as a quite separate matter that falls outside the CA 2006's regulation of company own share acquisitions.

5.21 An own share purchase involves the acquisition by the company of shares in itself pursuant to a contract of purchase freely entered into by each member concerned. Conversely, a reduction of capital is nowadays concerned mainly with the extinguishment or discharge of liability attaching to partly paid-up share capital, the cancellation of shares without making any repayment in respect of them, or the repayment of any paid-up share capital (CA 2006, s 641(4)) – see also **2.15**; and although a reduction of capital needs to be effected by a special resolution confirmed by the court or (in the case of a private company) by a special resolution supported by a solvency statement, it is not necessary that *every* member whose shares are affected by the reduction of capital should assent to it (e g *Scottish Insurance Corporation Ltd v Wilsons & Clyde Coal Co Ltd*[14]); although the court will not confirm a reduction of capital if the company has not satisfied a requirement in its articles for a reduction of the capital paid up on shares of some class to be sanctioned by a resolution passed at a separate class meeting (as in *Re Northern Engineering Industries plc*,[15] where it was also confirmed that 'reduction' includes a reduction to nil). A contract between a company and a member to pay off part of the nominal value of his shares clearly falls under the heading of a reduction of capital; but if the contract provided for the payment to the shareholder by the company of a sum equal to the nominal value of his shares and for the cancellation of those shares, it appears that the form adopted by the contract will govern which category it falls into. If the contract provided for a *repayment* or *paying off* of the nominal value of the shares, it would probably comprise a reduction of capital; but if instead the contract provided for the *purchase* of the shares by the company at a price which happened to be equal to their nominal value, the validity or otherwise of the transaction would probably be determined by the provisions relating to own share purchases. It follows that, in a number of cases, questions of form – and not of substance – will determine which category the transaction falls into, and that generally, where the parties wish that a transaction be treated as an own share purchase and not as a reduction of capital, they should do everything to ensure that the transaction bears the formal hallmarks of a purchase.

---

[14] [1949] AC 462.
[15] [1994] BCC 618.

Chapter 6

THE PROCEDURE FOR AN OWN SHARE PURCHASE

THE STATUTORY PROCEDURAL REQUIREMENTS

6.1   The CA 2006 has grafted, onto the basic principle that a company may enter into a contract for the purchase of its shares, certain procedural requirements, which differ according to whether the own share purchase is what the Act describes as a 'market purchase' or an 'off-market purchase' (these are dealt with in this chapter), and also, in the case of a private company, according to whether or not any part of the purchase price is to be paid out of capital (those are dealt with in Chapter 7).

AN 'OFF-MARKET PURCHASE'

6.2   A purchase by a company of its own shares is an 'off-market purchase' if either:

(a)   the shares are purchased otherwise than on a recognised investment exchange; or

(b)   the shares are purchased on a recognised investment exchange, but neither:

    (i)   are the shares listed on that investment exchange, nor
    (ii)   has the company been afforded facilities for dealings in those shares to take place on that investment exchange without prior permission for individual transactions from the authority governing that investment exchange and without limit as to the time during which those facilities are to be available (CA 2006, s 693(1), (2)).

As regards the London Stock Exchange, the AIM market (formerly the Alternative Investment Market) falls within (ii). A 'recognised investment exchange' is defined as a recognised investment exchange, within the meaning of Part 18 of the FSMA 2000 (CA 2006, s 693(5)). Under the FSMA 2000, a 'recognised investment exchange' is a body corporate or unincorporated association recognised for the time being as such by the Financial Services Authority (FSMA 2000, ss 285 and 287).

INTERACTION BETWEEN 'OFF-MARKET PURCHASE' AND 'UNQUOTED COMPANY' DEFINITIONS

6.3 The fiscal result of an own share purchase may depend on whether or not the company in question falls within the description of an 'unquoted company'. An 'unquoted company' (see **13.5**) can only make an 'off-market purchase', unless it effects an own share purchase through AIM. Conversely, a 'quoted company' can, in principle, choose whether to make a 'market purchase' or an 'off-market purchase'. An 'unquoted company' may be either a 'public' company or a 'private' company as a matter of company law, but a 'quoted company' must be 'public'.

A 'MARKET PURCHASE'

6.4 A purchase by a company of its own shares is a 'market purchase' if it is made on a recognised investment exchange and it is also not an 'off-market purchase' (CA 2006, s 693(4)).

AUTHORITY FOR AN 'OFF-MARKET PURCHASE'

6.5 A company may only make an off-market purchase of its own shares in pursuance of a contract the terms of which have been approved and authorised by a special resolution of the company before the contract is entered into or the contract must provide that no shares may be purchased in pursuance of the contract until its terms have been authorised by a special resolution of the company (CA 2006, s 694(1), (2)). If an own share purchase agreement is entered into without prior approval, it may be possible to construe the agreement as being subject to an implied term that it is not to be effective until immediately after that approval is given (see **5.11**).

AUTHORITY FOR A 'CONTINGENT PURCHASE CONTRACT'

6.6 The expression 'contingent purchase contract' is not expressly defined by the CA 2006, although, from the reference that is made to that expression in s 705, CA 2006, it is clear that it means a contract of a type falling within s 694(3), CA 2006, namely a contract entered into by a company and relating to any of its shares:

(a) which does not amount to a contract to purchase those shares, but

(b) under which the company may (subject to any conditions) become entitled or obliged to purchase those shares (CA 2006, s 694(3)).

One of the main types of contract falling within the scope of this definition is a contract whereby an option (whether 'put' or 'call' or both) for the purchase of a company's shares is to be granted and/or taken. For an illustration of a so-called 'contingent purchase contract', see **10.10**.

6.7   A company may only make a purchase of its own shares in pursuance of a contingent purchase contract if the contract is approved in advance by a special resolution of the company before the contract is entered into or the contract provides that no shares may be purchased in pursuance of such a contract until its terms have been authorised by a special resolution of the company and such approval has been obtained (CA 2006, s 694(2), (3)).

THE PROCEDURE FOR PASSING THE SPECIAL RESOLUTION

6.8   As noted above, the terms of the contract must either be authorised in advance by way of a special resolution or the contract must provide that no shares may be purchased in pursuance of it until its terms have been authorised by a special resolution of the company.

6.9   The normal rule is that the special resolution (authorising either an 'off-market purchase' or a 'contingent purchase contract') must be passed at a duly convened meeting of the members of the company at which a quorum is present. However, by way of exception, a private company may pass the resolution by way of a written resolution in accordance with Chapter 2 of Part 13 of the CA 2006, which has been approved by members representing not less than 75% of the total voting rights, other than the shareholder who is selling (CA 2006, ss 283, 288 and 695(2)).

A special resolution passed at a general meeting

6.10   A special resolution to confer the required authority is 'not validly passed' unless (if the proposed contract is in writing) a copy of the contract or (if not in writing) a written memorandum of its terms (including the names of the members holding shares to which the contract relates) is available for inspection by members of the company, both:

(a)   at the registered office of the company for at least 15 days ending with the date of the meeting at which the resolution is passed; and

(b)   at the meeting itself (CA 2006, s 696(2)).

A copy of a draft written contract so made available must have annexed to it a written memorandum specifying the names of any members holding shares to which the contract relates if and to the extent that such names do not appear in the contract itself (CA 2006, s 696(4)). Similarly, a memorandum of contract terms so made available must include the names of the members holding shares to which the contract relates (CA 2006, s 696(3)).

6.11 These requirements (of CA 2006, s 696(2)) are in addition to the normal requirements as to notices for convening a meeting at which the passing of a special resolution is to be proposed (CA 2006, s 283(6)). The notice convening the meeting should itself set out at least the substance of the proposed contract, and preferably the full terms (*Normandy v Ind Coope & Co Ltd*;[1] *Re Moorgate Mercantile Holdings Ltd*[2]).

6.12 A point relating to the interpretation of s 696(2) is that although it is clear that the fifteenth day may be the day on which the meeting is held at which the special resolution is passed, it appears that the first of the 15 days must be a full day and not just part of a day: *Chambers v Smith*;[3] *Re Hector Whaling Ltd*.[4]

6.13 It is a general principle of company law that all the corporators, acting together but without actually meeting each other, can do anything which is *intra vires* the company, including the passing of special resolutions or the transacting of business which would normally require the passing of such a resolution. The cases of *Re Duomatic Ltd*,[5] *Re MJ Shanley Contracting Ltd (in voluntary liquidation)*,[6] *Cane v Jones*,[7] and *Re Barry Artist Ltd*[8] all record that principle. However, the principle is restricted to enabling the unanimous assent of the shareholders to override procedural requirements which are for the sole benefit of current shareholders.

6.14 However, as noted, s 696 set out a number of requirements that are each expressed in mandatory terms, concluding that the 'resolution is not validly passed if the requirements of this section are not complied with'. Such language is similar in terms (and, it is submitted, to the same in effect) as the language used in CA 1985 s 164(5) which provided that the resolution was not 'effective' unless the statutory requirements over the resolution were met. Over time, the courts have wrestled with how far such requirements are capable of being waived by the unanimous consent of shareholders.

6.15 In *Re RW Peak (Kings Lynn) Ltd*,[9] a purported own share purchase was held to be void where the contract had not been approved in advance by the relevant shareholder and there was no purported resolution to authorise or record the purchase. Nevertheless, Lindsay J went on to consider whether the principle in *Re Duomatic Ltd* could permit departure from strict adherence to the requirements of the statute operate, considering whether such requirements were simply for the benefit of current members or could be said to involve the

---

[1] [1908] 1 Ch 84.
[2] [1980] 1 All ER 40.
[3] (1843) 12 M & W 2.
[4] [1936] 1 Ch 208.
[5] [1969] 2 Ch 365.
[6] (1979) 124 SJ 239.
[7] [1981] 1 All ER 533.
[8] [1985] PCC 364.
[9] [1998] BCC 596.

interests of future members or some wider class of persons (such as the creditors of the company). He concluded that:

> 'Any given purchase by a company of its own shares affects the members who remain as members, the members who sell their shares and possibly the creditors.'

and:

> '... there may well be a public interest served by the machinery of [the relevant part of the CA 1985] which extends beyond protection of the interest of the current registered holders of shares.'

As such, it was said, it was not open to present members of a company to waive compliance with the statutory formalities.

6.16　Later cases have adopted a more relaxed approach, at least in relation to the disclosure requirements in s 696. In *BDG Roof-Bond Ltd v Douglas*,[10] Park J concluded that the equivalent of what is now s 696(2) was a provision designed solely for the benefit of shareholders and that there was no element of creditor protection in it. In *Kinlan v Crimmin*,[11] Sales J followed *BDG Roof-Bond* and held that the contract inspection requirement now found in s 696(2)(b) was for the exclusive benefit of the current shareholders rather than for a wider class of persons. As such, the *Duomatic* principle could operate to waive the statutory requirement for a 15 day inspection period. Similarly, it mattered not that the resolution as headed as an 'ordinary resolution' rather than a 'special resolution', when it was approved by all shareholders.

6.17　In *Dashfield v Davidson*,[12] the deputy judge went even further and held, contrary to the view expressed in *Peak*, that the *Duomatic* principle could even overcome a failure to approve the own share purchase contract before entering into it, because all the shareholders had approved a resolution to alter the articles of the company that also, so it was held, comprised the contract pursuant to which the shares were to be bought; this was a provision for the benefit of existing members of the company and there was no wider interest that was protected by insisting upon a minimum interval of time between the approval of the contract and its execution.

6.18　That said, there are clearly other provisions that are clearly for the protection of creditors and cannot be waived by the unanimous consent of the company's members. The requirements as to the financing of any repurchase are clearly matters that intrude upon creditor interests and cannot be 'waived' by members. Similarly, the details of the contract and memorandum of contract terms (s 696(3)–(4)) are also matters that might impact upon both creditors and future members.

---

[10]　[2000] BCC 770.
[11]　[2007] BCC 106.
[12]　[2008] BCC 222.

6.19 It should be noted that a special resolution to confer the required authority is also 'not effective' if any member of the company holding shares to which the resolution relates exercises the voting rights (whether he votes on a poll or on a show of hands) carried by any of those shares in voting on the resolution and the resolution would not have been passed had he not done so (CA 2006, s 695(3)–(4)). Votes attaching to shares that are not the subject of the resolution may therefore be cast by that member (in contrast to the position if the matter had been sought to be dealt with by way of a written resolution, where such a member would not be an 'eligible member' (CA 2006, s 695(2)). For this purpose, notwithstanding anything in the company's articles, any member may demand a poll on the question whether the resolution should be passed, and votes and demands for a poll may be cast or made by proxy (CA 2006, s 695(4)). Thus, although a member whose shares are to be purchased may exercise the voting rights attaching to those shares on the special resolution, it will normally be prudent for such a member to abstain from voting on the resolution. It follows that where contracts for the purchase of shares from several members are to be approved at the same meeting, it may prove desirable for the purchase of each proposed vendor's shares to be the subject of a separate resolution, so that he is able to vote on the resolutions concerning the other proposed vendors; it all depends on the particular shareholding position.

A resolution passed as a written resolution

6.20 This procedure is only available to a private company, and not to a public one (even though 'public' companies may, and sometimes do, have only one shareholder). For these purposes, a 'written resolution' means a resolution proposed and passed in accordance with Chapter 2 of Part 13 of the CA 2006 (CA 2006, s 288). For the purposes of authorising an own share purchase contract, a written resolution, of which no prior notice is required, means a resolution stated to be proposed as a special resolution and approved by a majority of members (who at the circulation date of the resolution would be entitled to vote on the resolution) holding not less than 75% of the total voting rights of eligible members (CA 2006, ss 283(2)–(3), 289); though, for the purposes of a resolution authorising an own share purchase, a member holding shares to which the resolution relates is not regarded as a member who would be entitled to attend and vote (CA 2006, s 695(2)). The CA 2006 is likely to increase the use of written resolutions by private companies by removing the pre-existing requirement for a written resolution to receive the unanimous assent of all the members.

6.21 The resolution is treated as being passed when the resolution is approved by the required majority of eligible members signifying their agreement to it (CA 2006, s 296(4)). The members may signify their agreement by the return of an 'authenticated document' identifying the resolution to which it relates and indicating his agreement to the resolution.

6.22 If a company has auditors then they are entitled, under CA 2006, s 502(1) to receive all communications relating to a written resolution as must be supplied to a member. Although there is no provision regulating the time when such communications must be received (cf CA 2006, s 381B), it appears prudent to ensure that a copy of all communications relating to a written resolution are sent to the company's auditors at the same time as they are sent to members.

6.23 The requirement in s 696(2)(b) of the CA 2006 obviously does not apply in the case of a written resolution. Instead, a copy of the contract (or a memorandum setting out its terms) must be sent or submitted to every eligible member at or before the time at which the proposed resolution is sent or submitted to him (CA 2006, s 696(2)(a)). Failure to comply with this requirement means that the resolution is 'not validly passed', (CA 2006, s 696(5)), subject to any possible application of the *Duomatic* principle.

6.24 Similarly, s 695(3) does not apply in the case of such a written resolution (s 695(3) renders provides that a resolution 'is not effective' if passed only by virtue of the exercise of the voting rights attaching to the shares which are to be purchased; see **6.19**). However, this is addressed by providing that, in the case of a written resolution, a member who holds shares to which the resolution relates is not an 'eligible member' (CA 2006, s 695(2)). The effect of this is that the written resolution must be signed by or on behalf of the requisite majority of members other than the member whose shares are to be purchased. A question which this raises is whether it is possible for a company with only a single member to purchase some of that member's shares. Although the answer to that question is not entirely clear-cut, in the author's view, a single member company is not prevented from purchasing some of its shares on the authority of a written resolution signed by the member, in reliance upon CA 2006, s 38; at worst, any purported written resolution would appear to take effect as a decision 'as if agreed by the company in general meeting' (s 357(2)(b)) and it would therefore be appropriate to provide a copy of that decision to the company to ensure it took effect as such and to avoid even the possible commission of an offence (s 357(3)). A precedent for the introductory wording of the written resolution is included in Appendix E.

6.25 The company is required to keep a record of the written resolution in a book in the same way as minutes of general meetings (CA 2006, s 355). Any such record purporting to be signed by a director or the company secretary is evidence of the passing of that resolution and, where there is a record of a written resolution of a private company, the requirements of the CA 2006 with respect to the passing of the resolution are deemed to have been complied with (CA 2006, s 356(2), (3)).

6.26 The procedure for passing a written resolution may be summarised as follows:

(a) Identify the members who have to receive the resolution. In the common case of a company with a single class of ordinary shares, the members who have to receive the resolution will be all the members except for the member(s) whose sale of shares is to be authorised by the resolution.

(b) Give a copy of the draft purchase contract to every member who has to receive the resolution.

(c) If the company has auditors, give them a copy of the draft resolution and any documents relating to it.

(d) Arrange for the resolution to be circulated to all eligible members and approved by the requisite majority of eligible members (with an authenticated document being received back by the company from them to demonstrate their approval to it).

With the co-operation of all members, it is possible for the whole procedure to be implemented in a single day. A copy of the written resolution must be delivered to the Registrar of Companies within 15 days after it becomes effective (CA 2006, s 30). Appendix B sets out a precedent for a written resolution.

THE FORM OF THE SPECIAL RESOLUTION

6.27 Usually, the most convenient form for the special (or written) resolution to adopt is for it to identify unequivocally the draft contract but without incorporating it into the resolution itself. This allows a standard form of resolution to be used and ensures that all the terms of the proposed contract are authorised. It also obviates the need to include a copy of the contract with the formal copy of the special resolution which the company is required (as in the case of any other special resolution passed by the company) to deliver to the Registrar of Companies within 15 days after it is passed (CA 2006, s 30). Suitable wording for such a special resolution, to be passed by a *private* company only, is the following:

> THAT the terms of the proposed contract, whereby the Company may become entitled and obliged to purchase, from Mr _____, _____ of its own Ordinary shares of £1 each, and of which a copy is produced to the Meeting and initialled for the purpose of identification by the Company Secretary, be and are hereby approved, and any director of the Company be and is hereby authorised to enter into the contract on behalf of the Company and to fulfil all obligations of the Company thereunder.

A precedent for a notice of a general meeting incorporating such wording is to be found in Appendix A. The contract needs to be in its final draft form by the time that the notices to convene the meeting are sent out.

6.28   In the case of a *public* company, the special resolution must additionally specify a date on which the authority is to expire, and that date must be not later than 5 years after the date on which the resolution is passed (CA 2006, s 694(5)). In the specimen wording at **6.27** above, one need merely insert the words (and date) 'at any time before _____ 20__' after the words 'on behalf of the Company'. This requirement applies to a resolution renewing a previous authority in the same way as to a resolution giving an authority for the first time. The 'authority' that s 694(5) refers to is the authority to enter into the contract. The contract itself may, however, provide for the completion date or dates to occur at any time. In particular, s 694(5) does *not* prevent a public company from entering into a 'contingent purchase contract' (see **6.6**) under which options may be exercised many years after the contingent purchase contract is entered into, as long as that contract itself is entered into within 5 years of when its terms are authorised by special resolution. Equally, s 694(5) does not prevent a public company from entering into an unconditional own share purchase contract under which the completion date (or, if more than one, any of the completion dates) is more than 5 years after the contract is entered into. A purchase can be completed in pursuance of either type of contract without the need for any further sanction from the shareholders in general meeting.

ALTERATIONS OF THE CONTRACT

6.29   If the company wishes to vary the terms of the contract or release its rights under the contract, or to vary, revoke or renew the authority to enter into the contract, it may only do so with the authority of another special resolution subject to the same type of procedural requirements as the original one (CA 2006, ss 694(4)–700). In the case of a variation of an existing contract, a copy of the proposed variation (if it is in writing) or a written memorandum giving details of the proposed variation, the original contract or (if it is not in writing) a memorandum of its terms, together with any variations previously made to such original contract or memorandum, must each be available for inspection for a 15-day period ending with the date of the meeting and at the meeting itself, in accordance with s 699(2)–(3)). Any copy of the proposed variation to be made so available must have annexed to it a written memorandum specifying the names of the members holding shares to which the variation relates which do not appear in the variation itself (s 699(5)). Similarly, a memorandum of the proposed variation must also include the names of the members holding shares to which the variation relates (s 699(4)). Given that s 697(1) provides that a company 'may only' agreed to a variation of a contract if the contract is approved in advance, a failure to comply with the requirements for a variation would render the purported variation void. Where it is sought to release a company's rights under a contract for off-market purchase, the terms of the proposed agreement must be approved in advance by way of a special resolution before the agreement is entered into (and may then be varied, revoked or from time to time renewed by way of a special resolution) (s 700(2)–(3)). The requirements of ss 698 and 699 as to voting rights and disclosure of the proposed release agreement are incorporated and apply in the case of such a release of the company's rights. Without such authority, any purported release by the company of its rights under an authorised contract is expressly stated to be void (CA 2006, s 700(1)).

AUTHORITY FOR A 'MARKET PURCHASE'

6.30 The following two numbered paragraphs describe the statutory requirements for making a 'market purchase', as laid down in the CA 2006. However, reference should also be made to the requirements of:

(a) the Financial Services Authority; these are contained in *The Listing Rules*, relevant parts of which are set out in Appendix C; and

(b) the Association of British Insurers, whose suggestions are reproduced in Appendix D.

6.31 A company may not make a 'market purchase' of its own shares unless the purchase has first been authorised by ordinary resolution of the company in general meeting (CA 2006, s 701(1)). The resolution must:

(a) specify the maximum number of shares authorised to be acquired;

(b) determine both the maximum and the minimum prices which may be paid for those shares; this may be done either by specifying a particular sum, or by providing a basis or formula for calculating the amount of the price in question, though without reference to any person's discretion or opinion (CA 2006, s 703(3), (7)); and

(c) specify a date on which the authority is to expire, that date being not more than 5 years after the date on which the resolution is passed (CA 2006, s 701(5)). However, completion of the purchase after the specified date will be valid if the contract was concluded before then and the terms of the authority permitted the company to make a contract of purchase which would or might be executed wholly or partly after that date (CA 2006, s 701(6)).

Subject to those three points, the authority conferred by the resolution may be either conditional or unconditional, and general or limited to the purchase of shares of any particular class or description (CA 2006, s 701(2)). It is noteworthy that, in contrast to the case of an 'off-market' purchase, there is no need for the resolution to approve the terms of any actual draft contract. A printed copy of the resolution must be forwarded to the Registrar of Companies within 15 days of its passing (CA 2006, ss 30, 701(8)). An illustration of the wording for such a resolution is the following:

THAT the Company be and is hereby authorised to enter into, at any time before _____ 20__ ('the Expiry Date'), contracts for market purchases (within the meaning of section 693(4) of the Companies Act 2006) of up to an aggregate of _____ Ordinary shares of 10p each in the capital of the Company at a price per share which, in the case of any such contract, is:

(a) no higher than 5 per cent above the average of such a share's middle market quotations derived from the Daily Official List of the London Stock Exchange for the five days immediately preceding the date when the contract is entered into, being days on which the London Stock Exchange is open for the transaction of business, and

(b) no lower than ___p,

and so that the Company may complete any such purchase after the Expiry Date if the contract of purchase was entered into before the Expiry Date.

6.32 If the company wishes to vary, revoke or renew the authority, it may only do so with the authority of another ordinary resolution (CA 2006, s 701(4); s 281(3)).

INALIENABILITY OF THE COMPANY'S CONTRACTUAL RIGHTS

6.33 Once a resolution has been duly passed authorising a contract for the purchase by a company of its own shares, whether it be a 'market purchase' or an 'off-market purchase', or authorising a 'contingent purchase contract', and the contract has been entered into, it is expressly provided that the rights of the company under the contract are not capable of being assigned (CA 2006, s 704).

ACCESS TO SHARE PURCHASE CONTRACTS

6.34 Where a company, having been duly authorised to do so, enters into a contract for the purchase of any of its shares, or enters into a 'contingent purchase contract', it must keep at its registered office (or a place specified pursuant to CA 2006, s 1136 and notified to the Registrar of Companies under CA 2006, 702(5)) a copy of the contract (if it is in writing) or (if the contract is not in writing) a memorandum of its terms, including a copy or memorandum of any variation of the contract, from the conclusion of the contract until the end of the period of 10 years beginning with the date on which the purchase of all the shares in pursuance of the contract is completed or (as the case may be) the date on which the contract otherwise determines (CA 2006, s 702(1)–(4)). Those written terms must be open to inspection without charge:

(a) by any member of the company; and

(b) if the company is a public company, by any other person (CA 2006, s 702(6)).

Since 1 October 2009, reg 4 of the Companies (Company Records) Regulations 2008, SI 2008/3006, requires a private company:

(i)   to make the document available for such inspection on a 'specified day', which must be a working day of which the required notice is given to the company – such notice being at least two working days (if the notice is given during the period of notice for a general meeting or class meeting or during the period within which a proposed written resolution is effective and, in each case, the period of notice both begins and ends during the relevant period) and otherwise 10 working days; and

(ii) to make the document available for not less than two hours beginning with the time to be notified by the person seeking to inspect in their notice of the 'specified day', which must itself be between 9 am and 3 pm on that day.
      In the case of a public company, it must make the document available for inspection for at least 2 hours between 9 am and 5 pm on each working day (reg 5 of the Companies (Company Records) Regulations 2008).
      Both a private company and a public company, must permit a person inspecting the document to copy any information made available for inspection although this does not require the company to assist that person in making a copy of that record or to present information in that record in a different order, structure or form from that set out in the record.

6.35 If a company fails to comply with its obligation to keep such a contract or memorandum at its registered office (or another place notified to the Registrar of Companies under s 702(5)), or if an inspection of those documents is wrongfully refused, the company and every officer in default is liable to a fine and, for continued contravention, to a daily default fine. In addition, if such an inspection is wrongfully refused, the court may make an order compelling an immediate inspection (CA 2006, s 703(1)–(3)).

COMPLETION

6.36 Except where all or part of the purchase price is being drawn from capital (see **7.32**), there are no restrictions as to the date on which the parties may choose to complete the purchase. Completion will normally consist of the vendor delivering to the company a stock transfer form and any relevant share certificate, assuming the shares are (as is usual) registered shares. In the unusual case of bearer shares ('share warrants' to bearer; CA 2006, s 779), the vendor will merely deliver his share certificate. There need not in fact exist any share certificates for registered shares if the terms of issue of the shares make provision to that effect (CA 2006, s 769(1)–(2)); but there must be a proper instrument of transfer delivered to the company in order that the company may lawfully register the transfer (CA 2006, s 770(1)). A 'proper instrument of transfer' has been interpreted to mean an instrument which will attract stamp duty (*Re Paradise Motor Co Ltd*;[13] *Nisbet v Shepherd*[14]); although, in the case of an own share purchase, no stamp duty will in fact arise on the transfer itself (see **17.16** et seq), though duty will be payable on form SH03, which has to be submitted to the Registrar of Companies (see **6.41**).

6.37 A different view is that no transfer is required for the purpose of completing an own share purchase of registered shares, and that all that need be done by the vendor–shareholder is for him to deliver his share certificate to the company for cancellation. However, it is considered that there is no real support for this view in the Act, and that it is contrary to principle in the following two respects:

(a)   The Act draws a clear distinction between a company purchasing its own shares and a company redeeming its redeemable shares. This stands out clearly in s 162(1), where the Act expressly acknowledges that a company may *purchase* its own redeemable shares. When redeemable shares are *redeemed*, the terms of redemption will normally require the shareholder to deliver up or surrender his certificate relating to the shares that are being redeemed. If, where shares are being *purchased* by the company, all that the shareholder were required to do was to deliver up or surrender his share certificate, it would lead to the conclusion that there is no real conceptual difference between an own share purchase and a redemption of shares; all shares would, in a general sense, be redeemable, the only distinction being that shares that were 'redeemable' for the purposes of the Act could only be such if the terms of their redemption were embodied in the articles of association when they were first issued, whereas shares that were 'redeemable' in the general sense could only be redeemed by being 'purchased' for the purposes of the Act pursuant to a contract existing outside the articles. If the draftsman of the Act had wished to bring about such a result, he could have done so expressly. Besides, if all shares could be said to be redeemable, the tax consequences for taxpayers in general would be unfortunate, as every issue of bonus shares could then be regarded as being a taxable 'distribution' (CTA 2010, s 1000(1)(C)). The view that all shares are not redeemable depends significantly on the validity of the assertion that there *is* an intrinsic and conceptual difference between an own share purchase and a redemption of shares.

(b)   It is elementary to state that a share in a company is a *chose in action*; and a *chose in action* cannot be transferred or disposed of simply by handing over a piece of paper evidencing or creating the terms of the *chose*, unless it is made out to bearer. It is one of the terms of the existence of a redeemable share that the occurrence of some event is capable of bringing

---

[13]   [1968] 1 WLR 1125 at 1141.
[14]   [1994] 1 BCLC 300.

to an end the life of the share, prior to the winding up of the company. No transfer of the redeemable share is required when it is being redeemed, because its life is being brought to an end in accordance with its terms of redemption. Conversely, although where a share is purchased by the company the share will normally suffer the same fate as a redeemable share that it redeemed, that fate is not pre-planned from the date of the share's issue, and the share being purchased cannot actually reach that stage until the purchase has been completed; and it is of the very nature of a purchase of a registered share that one cannot complete it merely by handing over the share certificate – assuming, which is not always the case, that a certificate exists.

6.38 It is submitted, therefore, that the view that a transfer *is* required fits in with the scheme of the Act as whole. The principle underlying the provisions of the CA 2006 dealing with own share purchases is the same as that which applies to any other purchase of shares:

(a)   there must be a contract for the sale of the shares; and

(b)   that sale must be completed by a transfer of the shares.

Brett MR stated the general principle in *Skinner v City of London Marine Insurance Corporation*:[15]

> '[There arises] the question what is the ordinary contract by the seller on a bargain and sale of registered shares of a company. It seems to me that the only contract in such a case is that the seller shall execute a valid transfer of the shares and hand the same over to the transferee, and so do all that is necessary to enable the transferee to insist with the company on his right to be registered as a member in respect of such shares.'

6.39 It is considered that there is nothing in the CA 2006 to prevent this general principle from applying in the case of a company purchasing its own shares. The following provisions of the Act are relevant to this question:

(a)   Section 658(1) of the CA 2006 provides:

> 'A limited company must not acquire its own shares, whether by purchase, subscription or otherwise, except in accordance with the provisions of this Part.'

This wording acknowledges that a purchase by a company of its own shares amounts to an acquisition of those shares by the company, and makes it difficult to argue that, because the shares bought by the company have to be cancelled upon completion of the purchase, the company acquires no asset in the form of the shares purchased. It is only when the acquisition has been completed that the cancellation of the shares occurs;

---

[15]   (1885) 14 QBD 882 at 887.

and it is difficult to see how a company can 'acquire' its own shares pursuant to a contract of purchase otherwise than by means of a transfer.

(b) Section 701(3)(a) of the CA 2006 contains a further reference to shares which are the subject of an own share purchase being 'acquired'.

(c) Section 707(1) of the CA 2006 uses different terminology:

> 'Where a company purchases shares under this Chapter, it must deliver a return to the registrar within the period of 28 days beginning with the date on which the shares are delivered to it.'

The reference to the shares which the company has purchased being 'delivered' to it appears curious, as the word 'delivered' is apt to describe a transfer of possession of a chattel but is inappropriate to describe the transfer of a registered share (though a share warrant to bearer may be transferred by 'delivery' of the warrant; CA 2006, s 779). However, the wording appears less strange when one considers that the effect of s 707(1) is that the 28-day period for submitting the statutory return to the Registrar of Companies begins to run from the date when the company (represented by its officers or agents) receives physical possession of whatever documents relating to the shares the vendor has agreed to give to it upon completion of the purchase. The receipt of the documents by the company will usually be accompanied by payment of the purchase price to the vendor and will represent the commercial completion of the deal. It can be said to be reasonable that the 28-day period should begin to run from this time. If, instead, s 707(1) had required the 28-day period to run from the date when the shares are 'transferred' to the company, it would have been possible for the company lawfully to delay substantially its obligation to submit the statutory return simply by delaying the registration of the transfer. It is therefore submitted that there is nothing in s 707(1) to support the proposition that no formal transfer of shares is required when they are purchased by the company.

(d) In s 702(3) of the CA 2006, the Act caters in the same sub-section for the likelihood that 'the conclusion of the contract' will occur before 'the date on which the purchase of all the shares in pursuance of the contract is completed'.

(e) The Act makes constant reference to the 'purchase' by a company of its own shares, and the word 'purchase' may be contrasted with different terminology which the Act might have used instead. Instead, of adopting the same terminology, a clear distinction is drawn between the concept of shares being redeemable and the concept of shares being purchased – as in s 690(1) of the CA 2006, which provides:

> 'A limited company having a share capital may purchase its own shares (including any redeemable shares), subject to–

(a) the following provision of this Chapter; and

(b) any restriction or prohibition in the company's articles.'

6.40 Whilst the provisions referred to above support the use of a stock transfer form in completing an own share purchase, there is a positive advantage to be gained from doing so:

(a) the stamping, or certification as exempt, of a stock transfer form provides a complete defence for the company against any charge to stamp duty reserve tax in respect of the transaction (see **17.26**), and

(b) by giving the transaction one of the formal hallmarks of a purchase, one is making it a little more difficult for someone (e.g. a future liquidator of the company) to allege that what purports to be an own share purchase is in fact an unsanctioned reduction of share capital (which would be void, as well as being unlawful (see **5.21**)).

RETURN TO REGISTRAR

6.41 Within 28 days beginning with the date on which any shares purchased by a company are delivered to it, the company must submit a return on prescribed form SH03 to the Registrar of Companies, stating the number, class and nominal value and date of delivery of the shares so delivered (CA 2006, s 707(3)). By 'shares ... delivered', it is considered (see **6.36** and **6.39**(c)) that the Act means, in the case of an ordinary registered share, the delivery of a stock transfer form and of any relevant share certificate, and, in the case of bearer shares, it means delivery of just the warrant (or certificate). The 28-day period therefore begins to run from the date the company receives the documents, and not from the (often later) date when the company registers the transfers and cancels the shares. In the case of a public company, the return must also state the aggregate amount paid by the company for the shares and the maximum and minimum prices paid in respect of shares of each class purchased (CA 2006, s 707(4)); however, because the FA 1986 requires the return to be stamped (see **17.17**), the return submitted by a private company is required to state the aggregate amount paid for the shares. Particulars of shares delivered to the company on different dates and under different contracts may be included in a single return (CA 2006, s 707(5)) – although, of course, those dates must all fall within the period of 28 days beginning with the date of the first delivery of shares and ending with the date of the submission of the return to the Registrar. If default is made in submitting any such return, every officer of the company who is in default is liable to a fine and, for continued contravention, to a daily default fine (CA 2006, s 707(6)–(7)).

CANCELLATION OF THE SHARES

6.42 Once the company has, upon completion of the purchase contract, received the stock transfer form and share certificate (if any) in respect of the shares which it is purchasing, the shares 'are treated as cancelled' (CA 2006, ss 706) – unless the company is a public company acquiring the shares as treasury shares (see **8.6**). It is considered that the existence of this statutory obligation, framed in the present tense, means that there can be no need for the board of directors to meet and pass the transfer, before the transfer can be registered; the company secretary or registrar may set about registering the transfer once he has been presented with the documents delivered by the vendor and a copy of the contract of purchase.

6.43 The cancellation must take place when the transfer is entered in the register of members, as, by virtue of ss 112(2) and 113(2)(c) of the CA 2006, the vendor remains a member of the company during the interval between the receipt of the documents by the company and the entry of the transfer in the register of members. During that interval, the vendor will hold his share as a bare trustee for the company; and where an accounting period of the company comes to end before the transfer is registered, it is considered that the balance sheet should show the issued share capital as remaining what it was prior to the purchase but must be accompanied by a note explaining the position fully (it is noteworthy that the obligation to make a transfer to the capital redemption reserve arises only 'on cancellation' of the shares being purchased; CA 2006, s 773(2)). The page in the register of members on which the vendor's details are entered should show him as transferring to the company the number of shares which the company is purchasing, and, on a separate page on which the company's details as a member are entered, the shares should be shown as having been acquired by the company from the vendor and immediately 'cancelled in accordance with ss 706(b) of the CA 2006'. Although a company may remain a member of itself if it acquires shares otherwise than for valuable consideration (see **2.7**), where a company acquires shares pursuant to a valid own share purchase it does not (except for treasury shares) have the right to be a member of itself in respect of those shares for more than a fraction of a second.

DIRECTORS' REPORT

6.44 Where a company purchases any of its own shares, the directors' report, with respect to the financial year of the company during which the purchase occurs, must state the number and nominal value of the shares purchased, the aggregate amount of the consideration paid by the company for such shares, and the reasons for their purchase. Where the report states the number and nominal value of shares of any particular description, there must also be stated the percentage of the called-up share capital which shares of that description represent (Small Companies and Groups (Accounts and Directors' Report) Regulations 2008, SI 2008/409, Sch 5, para 6; Large and Medium-Sized Companies and Groups (accounts and Reports) Regulations 2008, SI 2008/410,

Sch 7, paras 8 and 9). For details of the Listing Rules' requirements regarding the annual report and accounts of listed companies, see Appendix C.

6.45   The following is an illustration of wording which could be used in the directors' report of an unquoted company:

> During the year, the company purchased a total of ____ Ordinary shares of £1 each in the capital of the Company, for a total consideration of £_____ . At the time when the duly approved purchase contract was signed by both parties, the shares being purchased represented _____ per cent of the called-up share capital. Once all formalities relating to the purchase were completed, the shares were cancelled in accordance with section 706 of the Companies Act 2006. The shares were purchased in order to enable their holder to realise his investment in the company.

INFRINGEMENT

6.46   The sanction for non-compliance with the statutory procedure for an own share purchase lies in s 658(2) of the CA 2006 (see **2.4**): the share purchase will be illegal and the purported acquisition of shares void. The shares purportedly purchased will therefore remain in issue and the purported vendor will remain their holder. The consequences of this could be far-reaching, e.g. where an intended consequence of the purchase was that the company should become the 75% subsidiary of another company so as to make the two companies part of the same 'group' for corporation tax purposes; or if the company at a later stage went into members' voluntary liquidation having meanwhile made large profits, the surplus in the winding up would have to be shared between *all* the members in accordance with their rights under the articles.

6.47   The other consequences of non-compliance with the statutory procedure for an own share purchase relate to the payment made by the company to the purported vendor. These consequences are likely to become particularly relevant if the company becomes insolvent and goes into liquidation. The payment will fall to be treated as a 'distribution' within the meaning of s 829(1) of the CA 2006, but s 847(2) of the CA 2006, which sets out in part the consequences of an unlawful distribution, is expressly excluded from applying to any payment made by a company in respect of the redemption or purchase by the company of shares in itself (CA 2006, s 847(4)(b)). Accordingly, the consequences as far as the payment is concerned are determined by reference to the common law principles applicable to the unlawful declaration of a dividend. The directors are liable to make good to the company the amount unlawfully paid (*Flitcroft's Case*[16]), although they will have a right of indemnity against shareholders who receive it with knowledge of the facts that render the distribution unlawful (*Moxham v Grant*[17]). By the same token, a

---

[16]   (1882) 21 Ch D 549.
[17]   [1900] 1 QB 88.

shareholder who, with full knowledge of the material facts, receives an unlawful dividend cannot maintain an action against the directors to compel them to reimburse the company for the total amount of the improper dividend, even if (so it seems) he repays his own share of it before commencing the action (*Towers v African Tug Co*[18]). However, a liquidator of the company will not be prevented from recovering by the mere fact that all the shareholders assented to the making of the unlawful distribution (*Precision Dippings Ltd v Precision Dippings Marketing Ltd*[19]). But where a shareholder, and probably also a director, receives or makes the distribution without knowledge of the facts that render the distribution unlawful, no recovery can be made from him (*Re Denham & Co*,[20] where the controlling shareholder and director was, together with the company's book-keeper, perpetrating a fraud on the other shareholders and directors). Also, if proceedings are brought against a director, he may escape liability if he is able to satisfy the court that he acted honestly and reasonably, and that having regard to all the circumstances of the case, he ought fairly to be excused (CA 2006, s 1157(1)).

6.48 Where, before a company is even contemplating going into liquidation, the discovery is made that a purported own share purchase by the company is void, the question may arise as to what, if anything, should be done to remedy the matter. This is a question which admits of no universally applicable answer, but consideration of the following relevant factors should assist in reaching an answer:

(a) whether the parties are willing to co-operate or not;

(b) whether the purchase price is sufficiently large in absolute terms to warrant a future liquidator suing for it;

(c) whether the continued existence of the shares purportedly purchased has *other* unwelcome repercussions for the company.

If the answer to (a) and either (b) or (c) is 'Yes', then an approach which may commend itself (as being the lesser of two evils) is for the procedure for making the own share purchase to be started all over again, this time being implemented correctly, but with the previous purported purchase price being treated by resolution of the shareholders as a dividend, and with the new purchase price of the shares being expressed to be something small, like 1p per share. If this is done, the shares will be duly purchased and later cancelled, the directors will probably have reduced substantially their risk of being sued in respect of their breach of duty or of having misfeasance proceedings taken against them by a future liquidator of the company in respect of this particular affair, and the vendors of the shares will get slightly more than what they will have anticipated. Although there is a possible risk of the vendors being treated for tax purposes as selling their shares at an undervalue, it is not clear that they

---

[18]   [1904] 1 Ch 558.
[19]   [1985] 3 WLR 812.
[20]   (1883) 25 Ch D 752.

would be prejudiced thereby even if the risk did materialise, and this approach enables the parties to achieve most of what they had intended to achieve in the first place.

Chapter 7

THE SOURCE OF THE PAYMENT FOR A PURCHASE OR REDEMPTION

7.1 The CA 2006 lays down various restrictions as to the source of the payment which the company may make for a purchase or redemption of its own shares. The 'sources' referred to here are sources within the company's own accounts, and should not be confused with the company's bank account on which a cheque for the actual money might be drawn. There are three permissible sources from which the purchase or redemption money may come (assuming it is paid prior to the commencement of the winding up of the company).

(a) Out of distributable profits. This is considered at **7.2**.

(b) The proceeds of a fresh issue of shares. This is considered at **7.8**.

(c) In the case of a private company only, out of capital. The many ramifications (including requirements as to publicity and safeguards for creditors) of a payment being made from this source are considered at **7.15**.

These restrictions do not apply where the terms of the purchase or redemption are being enforced after the commencement of the winding up of the company (CA 2006, ss 687(6) and 692(5)) (see **5.9**).

OUT OF DISTRIBUTABLE PROFITS

7.2 As a general principle, a company must use its 'distributable profits' to finance a purchase or redemption of its own shares (CA 2006, ss 687(2) and 692(2)). In practice, this is the most commonly used source.

7.3 By way of exceptions, the legislation allows in certain circumstances all or part of the money to be drawn from the proceeds of a fresh issue of shares or from 'capital'. Notwithstanding those exceptions, in the following circumstances (which, in practice, occur only seldom) any payment made by the company *must* be made out of its distributable profits, and no part of it may be drawn from capital or the proceeds of a fresh issue of shares:

(a)   a payment made by the company in consideration of acquiring any right with respect to the purchase of its own shares in pursuance of a duly approved contingent purchase contract for the off-market purchase of its shares (see **6.6**);

(b)   a payment made by the company in consideration of the variation of a duly approved contingent purchase contract or contract for an off-market purchase of its own shares; or

(c)   a payment made by the company in consideration of the release of any of the company's obligations with respect to the purchase of any of its own shares under a duly approved contingent purchase contract or contract for either a market or an off-market purchase of its own shares (CA 2006, s 705(1)).

Section 705(2) of the CA 2006 specifies the consequences if this requirement is breached. If the breach relates to a payment falling within (a) above, no purchase by the company of any of its own shares in pursuance of the contract is lawful; in the case of a payment falling within (b) above, no such purchase following the variation is lawful; and in the case of a payment falling within (c) above, the purported release is void.

7.4   The expression 'distributable profits' of a company means, in relation to any payment made by the company, those profits out of which it could lawfully make a 'distribution' equal in value to that payment (CA 2006, s 736) – the word 'distribution' having the meaning given by ss 829–830 of the CA 2006. In effect, it means profits legally available for distribution by way of dividend. Section 830(2) of the CA 2006 lays down the general rule that a company's profits available for distribution are its accumulated, realised profits, so far as not previously utilised by distribution or capitalisation, less its accumulated, realised losses, so far as not previously written off in a reduction or reorganisation of capital duly made. Additional restrictions apply to distributions by public companies, which can only lawfully be made if:

(a)   the amount of the company's net assets is not less than the aggregate of its called up share capital and undistributable reserves; and

(b)   if and to the extent that the distribution does not reduce the amount of those assets less than that aggregate (s 831).

7.5   Generally, the amount of a company's distributable profits must be determined by reference to the company's last annual accounts, properly prepared in accordance with the CA 2006 or prepared subject only to matters that are not material for determining whether a distribution could lawfully be made (CA 2006, s 836(2)). Exceptionally, reliance may be placed either on 'interim accounts', if the company's last annual accounts show a figure which is less than the amount of some proposed distribution; or on 'initial accounts', if the company has not been in existence for long and has not yet produced statutory accounts in respect of its first accounting period. Interim or initial accounts are those that 'enable a reasonable judgment to be made as to' the company's profits, losses, assets, liabilities, provisions, share capital and reserves (including undistributable reserves) (CA 2006, ss 838(1), 839(1)).

7.6   A potential pitfall arises where the company's last annual accounts have been audited and the auditors' report contains a qualification as to whether the accounts have been properly prepared in accordance with the Act. In this case, those qualified accounts may not be relied upon to justify a proposed distribution unless the auditors state in writing (either at the time of their report or subsequently) whether, in their opinion, the matter in respect of which their report is qualified is material for determining the sufficiency of profits for the purposes of some proposed distribution or distributions in general (CA 2006, s 837(4)). However, the requirements for an audit report do not apply where the company's accounts are exempt from audit and have therefore not been audited (CA 2006, s 837(3)). But where the accounts have been audited, and the audit report is qualified, and the auditors do not give any written statement regarding the materiality of their qualification to the level of the company's distributable profits, then if the company purports to purchase some of its own shares out of distributable profits determined on the basis of those qualified accounts, the own share purchase will not comply with s 736 of the CA 2006 and will therefore be void – as occurred in *BDG Roof-Bond Ltd v Douglas*.[1]

7.7   In determining the sufficiency of a company's distributable profits for the purposes of a proposed purchase or redemption, regard must be had merely to the price at which the shares are to be purchased or redeemed, and one should ignore consequential costs such as professional fees and stamp duty (and, before 1999, Advance Corporation Tax (ACT)). If a company has distributable profits of $£X$, it may purchase shares in itself up to a total price of $£X$, irrespective of consequential costs. The reasoning that leads to this conclusion is as follows:

(a)   The context of the word 'redeemed' which occurs in s 687(2)(a) as part of the phrase:

'redeemable shares in a limited company may only be redeemed out of –

(a)   distributable profits of the company, or
(b)   the proceeds of a fresh issue of shares ...'

indicates that it is only referring to redemption at the redemption price. The word 'purchase' is defined in a similar fashion in s 692(2).

(b)   Section 710(2) defines the payment which may (if all due procedures are gone through) be made by a private company out of capital in respect of a redemption or purchase of its own shares as an ascertainable part (which

---

[1]   [2000] BCC 770.

may include all) of 'the price of redemption or purchase'. That price must mean either the redemption price ascertained from the terms on which the redeemable shares were issued or the purchase price ascertained from the relevant purchase contract. The word 'price' has a much narrower scope than, for example, the word 'cost'. It follows that if a private company has no distributable profits and is not making any fresh issue of shares, then the 'permissible capital payment' for a purchase of its own shares will be equal to the contract price and nothing more.

In the case of a purchase completed before 6 April 1999 (the date when the ACT rules were abolished), an own share purchase would often give rise to a liability to account for ACT. This ACT was a purely consequential cost, because the very essence of ACT was that it was *not* an amount which was deducted from a dividend or other distribution payment, but rather that (as far as the company making the distribution was concerned) it was a separate liability which:

(i)   accrued to the company 14 days after the end of the ACT quarter in which the distribution was made (ICTA 1988, Sch 13, paras 1(3) and 3(1)); and

(ii) arose only to the extent that the franked payment of which the ACT formed a part exceeded any available franked investment income (ICTA 1988, s 241); and

(iii) was calculated as a specified fraction of the distribution payment (ICTA 1988, s 14(3)).

WHERE A FRESH ISSUE OF SHARES IS MADE

7.8   A company may purchase or redeem its own shares, up to the amount of their nominal value, out of the proceeds of a fresh issue of shares made for the purpose of the purchase or redemption (CA 2006, ss 687(2) and 692(2)). Ordinarily, any premium payable on the redemption or purchase of shares must be paid out of distributable profits (CA 2006, ss 687(3) and 692(2)(b)).

7.9   However, where the shares being purchased or redeemed by the company were issued at a premium, any premium payable on their purchase or redemption may be paid out of the proceeds of a fresh issue of shares made for the purposes of the purchase or redemption, up to an amount equal to:

(a)   the aggregate of the premiums received by the company on the issue of the shares being purchased or redeemed; or

(b)   the current amount of the company's share premium account (including any sum transferred to that account in respect of premiums on the new shares), whichever is the lower (ss 687(4) and 692(3)). Any such payment of premium made out of the proceeds of the issue of the new shares reduces the company's share premium account by a corresponding amount (CA 2006, ss 687(4) and 692(3)). It can be seen that this provision, if it is to be taken advantage of, requires one to be able to identify particular shares, and therefore renders it desirable that all companies should give distinguishing numbers to their shares even where (as commonly occurs) there is no legal obligation to do so by virtue of s 543 of the CA 2006 (i.e. where all shares of the company, or shares of the same class, are fully paid up and rank equally with each other for all purposes).

Examples

1. One hundred ordinary £1 shares, originally issued at par, are to be purchased for £1,100. The whole of the £1,000 'premium' element of this price must be paid out of distributable profits. All or part of the remaining £100, representing the nominal value of the shares, may be paid out of the proceeds of a fresh issue of shares.

2. One hundred ordinary £1 shares, originally issued for £5 each (i.e. at a premium of £4 each), are to be purchased for £1,100. The current level of the share premium account is £4,000. Of the £1,100 purchase price, the following is the maximum that may be paid out of the proceeds of a fresh issue of shares:

    (a) £400 out of the premium element; and
    (b) the £100 representing the nominal value.

The remaining £600 must be paid out of distributable profits.

In each of the above examples, if the company is a private company and has either no or insufficient distributable profits, it may be feasible to have resort to capital instead (see **7.15**).

The capital redemption reserve

7.10 Whenever a company purchases or redeems any of its own shares *wholly* out of the company's profits, an amount corresponding to the nominal value of those shares must, on their cancellation, be transferred to a reserve called 'the capital redemption reserve' (CA 2006, s 733(2)). This is the new name given, originally by the CA 1981, to 'the capital redemption reserve fund' which a company was obliged to establish under s 58 of the CA 1948 (repealed long ago) upon the redemption of redeemable preference shares. The capital redemption reserve may only be dealt with in either of the following two ways:

(a) it may be applied by the company in paying up unissued shares of the company to be allotted to members of the company as fully paid bonus shares; or

(b) it may be reduced pursuant to Chapter 10 of Part 17 of the CA 2006 as if it were share capital (CA 2006, s 733(6)).

As can be seen, the object of the capital redemption reserve is to maintain a company's capital where it purchases or redeems any of its own shares otherwise than out of capital.

7.11 A transfer must also be made to the capital redemption reserve in any of the following circumstances, where a company purchases or redeems any of its own shares:

(a) wholly out of the proceeds of a fresh issue, or partly out of the proceeds of a fresh issue and partly out of distributable profits, then if the aggregate amount of the proceeds of the fresh issue is less than the aggregate nominal value of the shares purchased or redeemed, the amount of the difference must be transferred to the capital redemption reserve (CA 2006, s 733(3));

(b) wholly out of capital (see **7.15**), or partly out of capital and partly out of distributable profits, then if the payment out of capital is less than the aggregate nominal value of the shares purchased or redeemed, the amount of the difference must be transferred to the capital redemption reserve (CA 2006, s 734(1), (2));

(c) partly out of capital and partly out of the proceeds of a fresh issue of shares, then (whether or not the purchase or redemption is also financed in part out of distributable profits) if the aggregate of the payment out of capital and the proceeds of the fresh issue is less than the aggregate nominal value of the shares purchased or redeemed, an amount corresponding to the difference must be transferred to the capital redemption reserve (CA 2006, s 734(4)).

7.12 Conversely, where a private company makes a payment out of capital which exceeds the nominal amount of the shares purchased or redeemed:

(i) the amount of any capital redemption reserve, share premium account or fully paid share capital of the company; and

(ii) any amount representing unrealised profits of the company for the time being standing to the credit of any revaluation reserve maintained by the company,

may be reduced by a sum not exceeding (or by sums not in the aggregate exceeding) the amount by which the payment out of capital exceeds the nominal amount of those shares (CA 2006, s 734(3)). For this purpose, where, in conjunction with a payment out of capital, a payment is also made out of the proceeds of a fresh issue, the amount of those proceeds is added to the amount of the payment out of capital (CA 2006, s 734(4)).

7.13 The following example illustrates the rules as to the source of a payment for a purchase or redemption of shares and the effect on the capital redemption reserve:

Example

A Ltd has an issued share capital of 100,000 ordinary shares of £1 each. It is to purchase 15,000 of these shares from *Mr X* for £30,000. *Mr X*'s shares were originally issued to him at par. The following different permutations give rise to correspondingly different methods of financing the purchase and their effects on the capital redemption reserve and (where relevant) the share premium account:

(i)   *A Ltd* has £30,000 or more in distributable profits. The whole of the purchase price may be paid out of distributable profits, in which case £15,000 must be transferred to the capital redemption reserve:

	Before purchase	After purchase
	£	£
Share capital	100,000	85,000
Capital redemption reserve (CRR)	Nil	15,000

(ii) Ten thousand new shares are issued for the purposes of the purchase at an issue price of £2 each. Because the shares being purchased were originally issued at par, only £15,000 of the proceeds of the new issue may be used to pay for the purchase (£15,000 being the total nominal value of the shares being purchased). The remaining £15,000 should come out of distributable profits:

	Before purchase	After purchase
	£	£
Share capital	100,000	95,000
CRR	Nil	Nil
Share premium A/c	Nil	10,000
Total		105,000

(iii) *A Ltd* has only £8,000 in distributable profits, all of which is 'available'. Up to £15,000 of the purchase price may be paid out of the proceeds of any fresh issue of shares, and the balance must be paid, first, using the available profits, and, secondly, out of capital (see **7.15** and **7.32**). Assume that 3,000 new shares are issued at a price of £2 each, and the entire proceeds are used in part payment of the purchase price. The remaining £24,000 must be paid, first, by using up the £8,000 of distributable profits, and only the balance of £16,000 may come from capital:

	Before purchase	After purchase
	£	£
Share capital	100,000	88,000
CRR	Nil	Nil
Share premium A/c	Nil	Nil

It is noteworthy that the aggregate of the payment out of capital (£16,000) and the proceeds of the fresh issue (£6,000) is greater than the nominal value of the shares being purchased (£15,000). Although the share premium account would fall to be credited with £3,000 following the new issue of shares, the share premium account may be reduced by an amount not exceeding £16,000 + £6,000 – £15,000 = £7,000 (see **7.9**); hence, the share premium account may be reduced back to nil by absorbing £3,000 of the aforementioned £7,000. The remaining £4,000 of that amount may be applied in reduction of any revaluation reserve.

(iv) *A Ltd* has only £20,000 in distributable profits, all of which is 'available'. Three thousand new shares are issued at a price of £2 each, and the entire proceeds are used in part payment of the purchase price. The remaining £24,000 must be paid, first, by using up the £20,000 of distributable profits, and only the balance of £4,000 may come from capital:

	Before purchase	After purchase
	£	£
Share capital	100,000	88,000
CRR	Nil	5,000
Share premium A/c	Nil	3,000
Total		96,000

It is noteworthy that the aggregate (£10,000) of the payment out of capital (£4,000) and the proceeds of the fresh issue (£6,000) is less than the nominal value of the shares being purchased (£15,000). The amount of the difference must be transferred to the capital redemption reserve (see **7.11(c)**); and the £3,000 credit made to the share premium account following the new issue of shares has to stay there.

7.14   In one instance (not involving a payment out of capital) it is considered that there is no need to make a transfer to the capital redemption reserve sufficient in amount to maintain the company's capital. This is where the shares being purchased or redeemed were originally issued at a premium and are being purchased or redeemed at a premium which is paid as far as permissible out of the proceeds of a fresh issue of shares.

Example

A Ltd issued 100 ordinary shares of £1 each at a premium of 50p each. *A Ltd*'s total amount of undistributable capital in respect of these shares is therefore £150, consisting of £100 in share capital and £50 in the share premium account. *A Ltd* wishes to purchase 50 of these shares at a premium of £1 each (ie a total purchase price of £2 each), and at the same time to make an issue of 25 new ordinary £1 shares also at a premium of £1 each. £25 out of the £50 received by *A Ltd* for the new issue can be used to pay part of the premium of £50 on the 50 shares being bought by *A Ltd*, thereby maintaining the share premium account at £50 (ie £50 + £25 − £25) (see **7.9**). The remaining £75 of the purchase price comes as to £25 from the nominal value of the newly issued shares and as to £50 from distributable profits. *A Ltd* is now left with share capital of £75 and a share premium account of £50, having effectively diminished its capital by £25. Nothing needs to be transferred to the capital redemption reserve, as the aggregate amount of the proceeds of the fresh issue (£50) is *not* less than the aggregate nominal value of the shares purchased (£50) (see **7.11**(a)).

OUT OF CAPITAL

7.15   A private company limited by shares or limited by guarantee and having a share capital may, subject to any restriction or prohibition in its articles, make a payment for the purchase or redemption of its own shares out of capital (CA 2006, ss 687(1), 692(1), 709(1)). The company must actually have auditors, if such a payment is to be lawful and valid (see **7.21**). A 'payment out of capital' for this purpose means a payment otherwise than out of 'available profits' or out of the proceeds of a fresh issue of shares (CA 2006, s 709(1)). However, any payment made by such a company for the purchase or redemption of its own shares must first use up any 'available profits'; and if the company chooses to make a fresh issue of shares for the purposes of the purchase or redemption, the payment it makes for the purchase or redemption must use up the proceeds of that issue before drawing on 'capital' (CA 2006, s 710(1)). The amount that the company might lawfully use by way of a 'payment out of capital' is referred to as the 'permissible capital payment' (s 710(2)). The expression 'available profits' is explained at **7.32**.

7.16 If a payment out of capital for the purchase or redemption of a private company's own shares is to be lawful, the following procedural requirements must be observed (CA 2006, s 713(1)). There are basically five steps to be completed.

Step 1

7.17 Accounts for the company must be drawn up and be capable of being relied upon by the directors for the purposes of the share purchase or redemption. If less than three months have passed since the end of the company's last accounting period before the date of the directors' statement referred to below, it may be possible to use the company's ordinary annual accounts for this purpose; otherwise, it will be necessary to produce a set of accounts specially for the purpose. The accounts must enable a reasonable judgment to be made as to the amounts of the company's profits, losses, assets, liabilities, share capital, reserves (including undistributable reserves) and provisions as identified in s 712(2) (CA 2006, s 712(6)).

Step 2

7.18 Within three months from the end of the period covered by the company's accounts upon which reliance is to be placed for the purposes of the share purchase or redemption, the directors must make a statement specifying the amount of the 'permissible capital payment' which is to be paid for the shares in question and stating that, having made full inquiry into the affairs and prospects of the company, they have formed the opinion:

(a)   as regards its initial situation immediately following the date on which the payment out of capital is proposed to be made, that there will be no ground on which the company could then be found to be unable to pay its debts; and

(b)   as regards its prospects for the year immediately following that date, that, having regard to their intentions with respect to the management of the company's business during that year and to the amount and character of the financial resources which will in their view be available to the company during that year, the company will be able to continue to carry on business as a going concern (and will accordingly be able to pay its debts as they fall due) throughout that year (CA 2006, s 714(3)).

7.19 Further regulations for the content of the directors' statement are contained in reg 5 of the Companies (Shares and Share Capital) Order 2009 (SI 2009/388). The statement must:

(a)   be in writing;

(b)   indicate that it is a directors' statement made under s 714; and

(c)   be signed by each of the company's directors.

It must also state whether or not the company's business includes that of a banking company or of an insurance company. While not addressed by the regulations or the CA 2006, provided that each copy of the directors' statement has annexed to it a copy of the auditor's report, there is no reason to suppose that the directors' statement cannot be signed in identical counterparts, although they should each be signed on the same day.

7.20 In forming their opinion with regard to the company's initial situation, the directors must take into account all of the company's liabilities (including prospective and contingent liabilities) (CA 2006, s 714(4)). The directors must only sign the statement after due inquiry, if it is to be properly made (cf *Re In a Flat Envelope Co Ltd*[2]).

7.21 The directors' statement must have annexed to it a report addressed to the directors by the company's auditors, stating that:

(a)   they have inquired into the company's state of affairs;

(b)   the amount specified in the statement as the permissible capital payment for the shares in question is in their view properly determined in accordance with ss 710 and 712; and

(c)   they are not aware of anything to indicate that the opinion expressed by the directors in their statement is unreasonable in all the circumstances (CA 2006, s 714(6)).

It follows that a company must actually have auditors if it is to be able to make a purchase out of capital.

7.22 Any director who makes declaration statement under s 714 without having reasonable grounds for the opinion expressed in it commits a criminal offence, punishable by imprisonment of up to two years or a fine or both (CA 2006, s 715(1), (2)).

Step 3

7.23 On the same day as the directors make their statement, or within the week immediately following, the company in general meeting must pass a special resolution approving the proposed payment out of capital (CA 2006, s 716(1)). This special resolution is in addition to the special resolution which, in the case of an off-market purchase, the company must pass authorising the making of the share purchase contract (see **6.5**), although there is no reason why they cannot both be passed at the same meeting. Where the meeting is to consider a single own share purchase, suitable wording for the special resolution approving the payment out of capital is the following:

---

[2]   [2004] 1 BCLC 64.

THAT there be and is hereby approved the proposed payment of £_____ out of 'capital' (within the meaning of section 709 of the Companies Act 2006) to be made in pursuance of the proposed agreement under which the Company may become entitled and obliged to purchase _____ of its own Ordinary shares of £1 each and the terms of which have been approved by special resolution passed previously at this meeting.

The special resolution approving the proposed payment out of capital can be passed at a duly convened meeting of the members of the company at which a quorum is present or by way of a written resolution. In Appendix E, there is a precedent for a case where the two resolutions (ie the resolution approving the contract and the resolution approving the payment out of capital) are to be passed as written resolutions.

7.24 In the case of resolution proposed at a general meeting of the company, a copy of the directors' statement and the auditor's report must be available for inspection by members of the company at the meeting (s 718(2)(b)). Failure to comply with this requirement renders the resolution 'not effective' (s 718(3)). The resolution is 'ineffective' if any member of the company holding shares to which the resolution relates exercises the voting rights (whether on a poll or on a show of hands) carried by any of those shares in voting on the resolution and the resolution would not have been passed had he not done so (CA 2006, s 717(3)). For this purpose, any member may demand a poll on the question whether the resolution should be passed, and votes and demands for a poll may be cast or made by proxy (CA 2006, s 717(4)(b), (c)). Thus, although a member whose shares are to be purchased may exercise the voting rights attaching to those shares on the special resolution, it will normally be prudent for such a member to abstain from voting on the resolution. Where a resolution only relates to part of a member's shareholding, that member is entitled to exercise on a poll the votes attached to the shares which are not being bought back or redeemed.

7.25 However, in the case of a written resolution, a member who holds shares to which the resolution relates is not an eligible member (s 717(2)). As such, in the case of a proposed purchase or redemption of part of a member's interest, it may be highly significant whether the resolution is proposed at a general meeting (where the member concerned could look to vote the shares that were not being purchased on a poll) or by way of a written resolution (where that member would not be regarded as an eligible member). If the written resolution route is used, a copy of the directors' statement and the auditor's report must be sent or submitted to every eligible member at or before the time at which the proposed resolution is sent or submitted to them (s 718(2)(a)). If this is not done, the resolution is 'ineffective' (s 718(3)).

7.26 Even though s 718(3) of the CA 2006 specifies the consequences for the resolution of a failure to observe the requirements of s 718(2) it appears that a 'resolution' could nevertheless be saved by the unanimous consent of the members to its terms in accordance with the *Duomatic* principle (see **6.13** et seq), as the requirements of s 718(2) might fairly be regarded as protections for the benefit of the company's members rather than necessarily to its creditors (compare *Wright v Atlas Wright (Europe) Limited*[3]).

7.27   Written resolutions also present some timing issues. Ordinarily, a written resolution lapses if not passed within 28 days of the circulation date (s 297). As the resolution approving the payment out of capital must be passed within one week of the directors' statement, it is sensible to make the resolution conditional upon the requisite approval having been given before that one week period expires. The special resolution approving a payment out of capital must be filed with the Registrar of Companies within 15 days of it being passed (ss 29–30).

Step 4

7.28   Within the week immediately following the date of the special resolution, the company must cause to be published in the *London Gazette* (or, where the company is registered in Scotland, the *Edinburgh Gazette*) a notice:

(a)   stating that the company has approved a payment out of capital for the purpose of acquiring its own shares by redemption or purchase or both (as the case may be);

(b)   specifying the amount of the permissible capital payment for the shares in question and the date of the special resolution;

(c)   stating that the directors' statement and the auditor's report are available for inspection; and

(d)   stating that any creditor of the company may at any time within the five weeks immediately following the date of the special resolution apply to the court under s 721 of the CA 2006 (see **7.36**) for an order preventing the payment (CA 2006, s 719(1)).

Within the same week, the company must also either cause a notice to the same effect to be published in a newspaper circulating throughout England and Wales (or throughout Scotland, in the case of a company registered in Scotland), or give notice in writing to that effect to each of its creditors (CA 2006, s 719(2), (3)). A precedent for such a notice appears in Appendix E.

7.29   By the date on which the company first publishes any such notice, or (if earlier) the date on which such a notice is first given to any creditor, the company must deliver to the Registrar of Companies a photocopy of the directors' statement and auditor's report (CA 2006, s 719(4)). Also, starting on that date and ending five weeks after the date of the special resolution for payment out of capital, the directors' statement and the auditor's report must be kept at the company's registered office or at an alternative inspection location notified to the Registrar of Companies under regulations made

---

[3]   (1999) BCC 163.

pursuant to s 1136, CA 2006 (at present, the Companies (Company Records) Regulations 2008 (SI 2008/3006)) (s 720(2)). Notice must be given to the Registrar of Companies of any change in such a place, unless they have at all times been kept at the company's registered office (s 720(3)). At all times, the directors' statement and the auditor's report must be open to the inspection of any member or creditor of the company without charge (CA 2006, s 720(4)). Since 1 October 2009, regs 4 and 5 of the Companies (Company Records) Regulations 2008, SI 2008/3006, requires:

(i)   a private company, to make documents available for inspection for at least 2 hours starting from a time (between 9 am and 3 pm) and upon a date that have each been specified by the person seeking to inspect the records, provided both that the specified day is a working day and at least 10 days' notice of the wish to inspect has been provided (reg 4); and

(ii)   a public company, to make the documents available for such inspection for not less than two hours during the period between 9 am and 5 pm on each working day (reg 5).

In the case of both a public and a private company, the company need not present information in that record in a different order, structure or form from that set out in the record (reg 6(1)). A company must permit a person inspecting the documents to copy any information made available for inspection, though this does not require the company to provide any facilities to assist that person in making a copy of that record (reg 6(2)).

7.30   If such an inspection is refused, the company and every officer in default is liable to a fine and, for continued contravention, to a daily default fine, and the court may make an order compelling an immediate inspection (CA 2006, s 720(6), (7)).

Step 5

7.31   The payment out of capital must be made not earlier than five nor more than seven weeks after the date of the special resolution approving the payment out of capital (CA 2006, s 723(1)).

Available profits

7.32   The expression 'available profits', referred to at **7.15**, means the profits of the company available for distribution, as determined in accordance with s 712 of the CA 2006 rather than in accordance with ss 836–842 (see s 711). The accounts that are to be used in order to determine the amount of the available profit must be accounts prepared as at a date within 3 months before the date of the directors' statement and must enable a reasonable judgment to be made as to the amounts of the items by reference to which 'available profits' are determined.

7.33 The first stage involves determining the 'profits' of the company by reference to the following items as stated in the relevant accounts:

(a)   profits, losses, assets and liabilities;

(b)   provisions:

   (i)   where the relevant accounts are Companies Act accounts (within the meaning of ss 395(1)(a) and 403(2)), that are specified for the purposes of s 712(2) by either Schedule 7 of the Small Companies and Groups (Accounts and Directors' Report) Regulations 2008 (SI 2008/409) or Schedule 9 of the Large and Medium-sized Companies and Groups (Accounts and Reports) Regulations 2008 (SI 2008/410); or

   (ii)   where the relevant accounts are IAS accounts (within the meaning of ss 395(1)(b), 403(1), (2)(b)), of any kind;

(c)   share capital and reserves (including any undistributable reserves).

7.34 The second stage involves reducing this amount of 'profits' by:

(a)   the amount of any distribution lawfully made by the company,

(b)   any financial assistance lawfully given by the company out of its distributable profits to some other person for the acquisition of any of the company's shares,

(c)   any payment lawfully made out of distributable profits by the company for the purchase of any of its other shares, and

(d)   any payment lawfully made by the company (necessarily out of distributable profits) within s 705(1) of the CA 2006 (see **7.3**),

being in any such case a payment made at any time after the date to which the relevant accounts are drawn and ending on the date when the directors make their statement (CA 2006, s 712(3), (4)).

7.35 The net figure following these two stages is the amount of 'available profits' (s 712(5)).

Objections by members or creditors

7.36 Within five weeks of the date on which a private company passes a special resolution approving any payment out of capital for the purchase or redemption of any of its shares:

(a)   any member of the company other than one who consented to or voted in favour of the resolution, and

(b) any creditor of the company,

may apply to the court for the cancellation of the resolution (CA 2006, s 721(1), (2)). The application may be made on behalf of the persons entitled to make the application by such one or more of their number as they may appoint in writing for the purpose (CA 2006, s 721(2)(b)).

7.37 If any such application is made, the applicant must immediately give notice of that fact to the Registrar of Companies (s 722(1)). Upon being served with such an application, the company must immediately notify the Registrar of Companies of the fact using Form SH17 (s 722(2)). Within 15 days of the court making any order on the hearing of the application, or such longer period as the court may by order direct, the company must deliver an office copy of the order to the Registrar (CA 2006, s 722(3)). Default in complying with the requirements imposed on the company renders the company and every officer of the company who is in default liable to a fine and, for continued contravention, to a daily default fine (CA 2006, s 722(5)). There is no similar criminal offence committed by an applicant who fails to give notice to the Registrar of Companies that the application has been made.

7.38 Upon hearing the application, the court may, if it thinks fit, adjourn the proceedings in order that an arrangement may be made to the court's satisfaction for the purchase of the interests of dissentient members or for the protection of dissentient creditors, and the court may give such directions and make such orders as it thinks expedient for facilitating or carrying into effect any such arrangement (CA 2006, s 721(3)). Subject to that power to adjourn, the court is obliged to make an order on such terms and conditions as it thinks fit, either confirming or cancelling the resolution (CA 2006, s 721(4)). Where the court confirms the resolution, it may, in particular, by order alter or extend any date or period of time specified in the resolution or in any provision of ss 709–723 of the CA 2006 which applies to the purchase or redemption of shares to which the resolution relates (CA 2006, s 722(5)). The court's order may provide for the purchase by the company of the shares of any members of the company and for the reduction accordingly of the company's capital, and may make such alterations in the articles of the company as may be required in consequence of that provision. The court order may require the company not to make any, or any specified, alteration in its articles, without the leave of the court (CA 2006, s 721(7)).

Liability of past shareholders and directors

7.39 Where the winding up of a private company commences within one year after the date when it makes a payment out of capital in respect of the purchase or redemption of any of its shares, then if the aggregate of the amount of its assets and the amounts paid by way of contribution to its assets is (apart from these provisions) not sufficient for payment of its debts and liabilities and the expenses of the winding up, the following persons are liable to the following extent in respect of that insufficiency:

(a) Each person from whom the shares were purchased or redeemed is liable to contribute to the assets of the company an amount not exceeding the amount paid to him by the company out of capital in respect of his shares.

(b) Every director of the company who signed the relevant statement is jointly and severally liable with each person from whom the shares were purchased or redeemed and to the same extent, except a director who shows that he had reasonable grounds for forming the opinion set out in the statement (Insolvency Act 1986, s 76(1)–(3), as amended by the Companies Act 2006 (Consequential Amendments and Transitional Provisions) Order 2011 (SI 2011/1265)).

7.40 A person who has contributed any amount to the assets of a company in pursuance of s 76 may apply to the court for an order directing any other person jointly and severally liable in respect of that amount to pay to him such amount as the court thinks just and reasonable (Insolvency Act 1986, s 76(4)).

7.41 Any person who could be made liable to contribute as a past shareholder or director is given *locus standi* to petition the court for the winding up of the company under s 122(1)(f) or (g) of the Insolvency Act 1986 (where the company is unable to pay its debts, and on the 'just and equitable' ground) (Insolvency Act 1986, s 124(3)). Such a power might be used by a former shareholder to prevent the company's fortunes, which have turned bad within the year following the share purchase, from becoming even worse.

Chapter 8

TREASURY SHARES

THE POWER TO PURCHASE TREASURY SHARES

8.1   This chapter considers in detail the circumstances in which a limited company may purchase its own shares and then continue to hold them ('in treasury'), instead of having to cancel them. Provisions concerning the holding of treasury shares were introduced into the CA 1985, with effect from 1 December 2003, by the Companies (Acquisition of Own Shares) (Treasury Shares) Regulations 2003 (SI 2003/1116). Further amendments were made by the Companies (Acquisition of Own Shares) (Treasury Shares) No 2 Regulations 2003 (SI 2003/3031), with effect from 18 December 2003. These changes followed a period of public consultation on the subject. The present provisions are now contained in Chapter 6 of Part 18 CA 2006 (ss 724–732). The most significant change from the CA 1985 is the removal of the 10 per cent limit on the proportion of shares that might be held by a company as treasury shares. The analysis of the requirements of the CA 2006 is greatly simplified by the drafting, which now separates out the provisions dealing with the disposal and cancellation of treasury shares. Further changes to the position of private companies and their ability to hold (and deal with) treasury shares may, in due course, be made by the Companies Act 2006 (Amendment of Part 18) Regulations 2013, which are currently only in draft.

Quoted shares only

8.2   It is not possible for a private company to purchase its own shares and hold them as treasury shares. This opportunity is only available to a company which is a public company, because 'treasury shares' must be shares which are quoted in any of the following ways:

(a)   the shares are included in 'the official list', in accordance with Part 6 of the FSMA 2000;

(b)   they are traded on the Alternative Investment Market established under the rules of London Stock Exchange plc;

(c)   they are officially listed in a European Economic Area (EEA) State; or

(d)   they are traded on a regulated market established in an EEA State which is a regulated market as set out in Directive 2004/39/EC of the European Parliament and Council on markets in financial instruments or, in relation to an EEA State that has not implemented that Directive, then as set out in Council Directive 93/22/EEC on investment services in the securities field (CA 2006, ss 724(2), 1173(1); FSMA 2000, s 103(1)).

8.3   The purchase must generally be in accordance with the other procedural requirements of the Act (CA 2006, s 724(1)). It is for the public limited company to decide whether any shares in itself which it buys are to be bought for the purpose of being held as treasury shares, or whether such shares are to be cancelled upon the completion of their purchase (in accordance with the normal rules). Such purchases may also be restricted by the provisions of the company's articles, which might require repurchased shares to be cancelled, such that they cannot be held as treasury shares.

The purposes

8.4   The main stated purpose of allowing public limited companies to hold treasury shares is to give them greater flexibility to adjust their share capital, by reducing their costs of doing so, and thereby to stimulate investment. By being able to sell treasury shares through a broker, the company can raise new capital whilst avoiding the costs of a new issue of shares. A secondary purpose is to bring British company law more into line with the company laws of the UK's major trading partners.

The source of the payment

8.5   If shares are to be capable of being held as treasury shares, the public limited company purchasing them must do so only out of distributable profits (see **7.2**), and, therefore, not out of the proceeds of a fresh issue of shares (CA 2006, s 724(1)(b)).

Holdings of treasury shares

8.6   Treasury shares are shares which have been held by the company continuously following a lawful own share purchase of them (CA 2006, s 724(5)). The company must be entered in the register of members as the member holding those shares, in accordance with s 113 of the CA 2006 (CA 2006, s 724(4)). Accordingly, treasury shares cannot be registered in the name of a nominee.

Maximum holdings

8.7   The requirement set out in s 725 of the 1985 Act that the aggregate nominal value of shares held as treasury shares should not at any time exceed 10% of the nominal value of the issued share capital (or, where the share capital is divided into different classes, of shares in that class), came into force on 1 October 2009 and was immediately repealed. This was done with savings for existing obligations by the Companies (Share Capital and Acquisition by

Company of its Own Shares) Regulations 2009.[1] As such, there is no now limit on the proportion of shares of the company, or a class of shares of the company, that can be held as 'treasury shares'.

Limited rights

8.8 The company must not exercise any right in respect of the treasury shares, including any right to attend or vote at shareholders' meetings; any purported exercise of such a right is void (CA 2006, s 726(2)). No dividend may be paid, and no other distribution (whether in cash or otherwise) of the company's assets (including any distribution of assets to members on a winding up) may be made, to the company in respect of the treasury shares (CA 2006, s 726(3)). However, the company is not prevented from receiving:

(a) an allotment of shares as fully paid bonus shares in respect of the treasury shares (any such bonus shares must be treated as if they were purchased by the company at the time they were allotted, and thenceforth held as treasury shares); or

(b) the payment of any amount payable on the redemption of the treasury shares, if they are redeemable shares (CA 2006, s 726(4), (5)).

8.9 If the company actually issues any new shares at a time when it already holds some treasury shares, any statutory pre-emption rights relating to that share issue do not apply in favour of the treasury shares (CA 2006, s 561(4)).

DEALINGS WITH TREASURY SHARES

8.10 As an alternative to continuing to hold treasury shares, the company may at any time:

(a) sell the shares (or any of them) for a cash consideration (CA 2006, s 727(1)(a);

(b) transfer the shares (or any of them) for the purposes of, or pursuant to, an employees' share scheme (CA 2006, s 727(1)(b)); or

(c) cancel the shares (or any of them) (CA 2006, s 729).

8.11 The definition of 'cash consideration' is slightly wider than the definition of 'cash' that had been provided for by CA 1985, s 162D(2), in particular by the introduction of a new subsection contained in CA 2006, s 727(2)(e). For the purposes of a sale of treasury shares, 'cash consideration' means:

(a) cash (including foreign currency) received by the company; or

---

[1]   SI 2009/2022.

(b)   a cheque received by the company in good faith which the directors have no reason for suspecting will not be paid; or

(c)   a release of a liability of the company for a liquidated sum; or

(d)   an undertaking to pay cash to the company on or before a date not more than 90 days after the date on which the company agrees to sell the shares; or

(e)   payment by any other means giving rise to a present or future entitlement (of the company or a person acting on the company's behalf) to a payment, or credit equivalent to payment, in cash (including foreign currency) (CA 2006, s 727(2)), including where shares are allotted or paid up using the CREST settlement system, the obligation which arises on the part of the settlement bank to make payment (Companies (Shares and Share Capital) Order 2009 (SI 2009/388), reg 4(3)).

8.12   A sale or transfer of treasury shares does not involve an allotment of shares for the purposes of the statutory pre-emption rights conferred by s 551 of the CA 2006. However, statutory pre-emption rights will arise under s 561 on the sale of treasury shares (s 560(3)). If the company is to avoid having to offer the treasury shares to the other shareholders, those pre-emption rights must be disapplied (either by the articles or by special resolution) (CA 2006, s 570). The wording of any such resolution must either specifically refer to sales of treasury shares or be sufficiently wide to include such sales.

8.13   The only other limit on the company's power to sell or transfer treasury shares is where the company has received a notice under s 979 of the CA 2006 (right of offeror to buy out minority shareholders) that a person desires to acquire any of the shares. In this case, the company must not sell or transfer the shares to which the notice relates except to that person (CA 2006, s 727(4)).

8.14   If a company cancels any treasury shares, the amount of the company's share capital is reduced accordingly by the nominal amount of the shares cancelled (CA 2006, s 729(4)). It is for the directors to decide on the procedure to adopt for cancelling the shares. This may involve nothing more than a board resolution followed by an appropriate entry in the register of members; it does not require any resolution of the shareholders or any application to court for approval as in the case of a reduction of share capital under s 645 of the CA 2006 (CA 2006, s 729(5)). An amount corresponding to the nominal amount of the cancelled treasury shares must be transferred to the capital redemption reserve (CA 2006, s 733(4)).

8.15   If shares held as treasury shares cease to be quoted at all in any of the ways described at **8.2**, the company must forthwith cancel the shares (CA 2006, s 729(2)). For these purposes, shares are not to be regarded as ceasing to be so quoted by virtue only of:

(a)   the suspension of their listing in accordance with the applicable rules in the EEA State in which the shares are officially listed; or

(b)   the suspension of their trading in accordance with:

    (i)   in the case of shares traded on the Alternative Investment Market, the rules of London Stock Exchange plc; and

    (ii)   in any other case, the rules of the 'regulated market' on which they are traded, ie a regulated market as set out in Directive 2004/39/EC of the European Parliament and Council on markets in financial instruments or, in relation to an EEA State that has not implemented that Directive, then as set out in Article 16 of Council Directive 93/22/EEC on investment services in the securities field (CA 2006, s 729(3)).

Proceeds of sale

8.16   Where shares held as treasury shares are sold, the proceeds of sale are to be treated for accounting purposes as a realised profit of the company, up to and including the amount of the purchase price previously paid by the company for the shares. Any amount by which the proceeds of sale exceed the purchase price paid by the company for the shares must be transferred to the company's share premium account. The purchase price paid by the company for the shares must be determined by the application of a weighted average price method. For these purposes, where the shares were allotted to the company as fully paid bonus shares, the purchase price paid for them must be treated as being nil (CA 2006, s 731).

8.17   If a company contravenes any provision of ss 724–732 of the CA 2006, the company and every officer of it who is in default is liable to a fine (CA 2006, s 732(1), (2)).

RETURNS TO COMPANIES HOUSE

8.18   If a company purchases some of its own shares as treasury shares and decides to cancel some or all of these shares forthwith after the date on which the documents relating to those shares are delivered to the company (so that the company does not actually hold or deal with the shares as treasury shares), the company must include particulars of those cancelled shares on Form SH03 (the form to be used for reporting normal own share purchases), to be delivered to the Registrar of Companies within 28 days (CA 2006, ss 707, 708; and see **6.41** regarding Form SH03).

8.19   Where a company has purchased some of its own shares as treasury shares and then subsequently cancels them, the company must deliver to the Registrar of Companies Form SH05 within the period of 28 days after the cancellation. The form must state, with respect to the shares of each class that are cancelled, the number and nominal value of the shares and the date on which they were cancelled (s 730(2)). Such a notice must be accompanied by a statement of capital (s 730(4), (5)).

8.20 Within the period of 28 days beginning with the date on which a company sells or transfers any treasury shares for the purposes of or pursuant to an employees' share scheme, the company must deliver to the Registrar of Companies a Form SH04, stating the number and nominal value of the shares of each class disposed of and the date of cancellation or disposal (CA 2006, s 728(1), (2)). Such details must be provided separately for each class of share disposed of (s 728(2)). It is not necessary for the notice to be accompanied by a statement of capital.

ACCOUNTING TREATMENT

8.21 The Accounting Standards Board's Urgent Issues Task Force (UITF) Abstract 37 (adopted by the Financial Reporting Council which took over responsibility for the setting up of accounting standards from 2 July 2012) to some extent undermines the status of treasury shares by requiring (at para 4) that:

> 'An entity's purchase of its own shares gives rise to a reduction in the entity's ownership interest, not an asset. This principle is reflected in FRS 4 "Capital Instruments" (paragraph 39), which states "Where shares are repurchased or redeemed, shareholders' funds should be reduced by the value of the consideration given". Transactions in own shares do not give rise to gains or losses in the issuing entity's profit and loss account or statement of total recognised gains and losses.'

The full text of Abstract 37 is reproduced in Appendix F.

8.22 If a company holds treasury shares, the company's accounts must include a statement of the number and aggregate nominal value of those treasury shares and, where shares of more than one class have been allotted, the number and aggregate nominal value of the shares of each class held as treasury shares (para 47(1) of Sch 1 of the Large and Medium-Sized Companies and Groups (Accounts and Reports) Regulations 2008, SI 2008/410).

Chapter 9

OWN SHARE PURCHASES AND THE ARTICLES

9.1   The purpose of this chapter is to consider what provisions a company may place in its articles with a view to achieving something more than just prohibiting or restricting the statutory power of a limited company to purchase its own shares. Here, we are looking at ways in which the articles can be used to bring about an own share purchase. It is necessary to begin by considering the legal constraints placed upon this general idea.

THE NEED FOR A SEPARATE CONTRACT

9.2   It is a pre-requisite to a company making any purchase of its own shares that a resolution of the company's shareholders needs to be passed beforehand; in the case of an off-market purchase (see **6.5**), the resolution must approve the terms of the proposed purchase contract; and in the case of market purchases (see **6.31**), the resolution must authorise the making of such contracts within specified limits. The tenor of the legislation does not readily accommodate the idea that the company's own articles could constitute that contract. Instead, it envisages the company entering into particular contracts with named members and in respect of specified shares – a different relationship from the general contract which the articles are deemed to constitute between the members and the company by s 33(1) of the CA 2006, which provides:

> 'The provisions of a company's constitution bind the company and its members to the same extent as if there were covenants on the part of the company and of each member to observe those provisions.'

9.3   However, on this point it should be noted in *Dashfield v Davidson*,[1] the court was willing to treat the signature of all the members of a company to a resolution altering the articles (to provide a mechanism under which the company might become entitled to purchase their shares), as also constituting a duly approved contract by each of those shareholders to sell their shares in the company on such terms. This was achieved in reliance upon the principle in *Re Duomatic Ltd*[2] and the fact that all the shareholders in the company had expressly approved the articles.

---

[1]   [2008] BCC 222.
[2]   [1969] 2 Ch 365.

9.4   *Dashfield* should, it is suggested, be treated with some caution and viewed as based on its somewhat unusual facts. The same result may have been achieved, perhaps more easily, by the implication of a term into the articles as adopted that each member or his executors or personal representatives would cooperate in approving, so far as they were able or required to do so, a separate contract providing for the shares repurchase, on the other terms set out in the articles. Until the point is resolved by a higher court, good practice will always be to rely upon a separate contract. Of course, as already suggested above, there is nothing to prevent a company's articles from setting out a standard set of terms and conditions upon which own share purchase may be made, with those terms then forming part of the actual contract separate from the articles.

THE SCOPE OF ARTICLES DEALING WITH OWN SHARE PURCHASES

9.5   It is not possible, therefore, for the procedural requirements of s 694 of the CA 2006 (relating to off-market purchases) to be circumvented by the company being given, under a transfer pre-emption clause in its articles, pre-emption rights which could by themselves obligate the company to purchase, and any of the members to sell, shares to the company itself; each purchase contract has to be authorised by special resolution and must come into being outside the articles. However, by framing transfer pre-emption clauses in such a way as to cater for the possibility of the shares being transferred to the company, one may seek to achieve the following useful purposes.

(a)   To spell out the extent to which, if at all, the pre-emptive rights enjoyed by members do not apply in cases where shares are to be purchased by the company itself.

(b)   To build into the pre-emption clause's timetable a provision to enable an extraordinary general meeting to be convened for the purpose of considering a special resolution to approve a proposed own share purchase contract; or to enable such a resolution to be passed as a written resolution.

9.6   In cases where a transfer pre-emption article requires or deems a member to offer to sell his shares in certain circumstances (eg if he ceases to be an employee of the company), it is also possible to build in a provision imposing certain disabilities on that member's shares if he refuses to sign an own share purchase contract proffered to him by the company.

9.7   The following precedent transfer pre-emption clause illustrates these points, in relation to a private company otherwise subject to the Model Articles for Private Companies Limited by Shares (as set out in Sch 1 to the Companies (Model Articles) Regulations 2008). Paragraphs (A)(ii) and (F) are of particular relevance to the question of the company being given the opportunity to purchase its own shares from a willing or semi-willing vendor. Paragraphs (K), (L) and (M) are provisions which impose obligations on shareholders who cease to be employees of the company. None of these provisions can be used to force a sale from a vendor who refuses absolutely to co-operate.

TRANSFER OF SHARES

(A)   The Directors shall register the transfer of any Share:

  (i)   to any person other than the Company, if the transfer has been assented to in writing by the holders for the time being of not less than 95 per cent of the issued Shares; or

  (ii)   to the Company itself, if the transfer is made in completion of any purchase of the Share in accordance with Part 18 of the Act.

(B)   The Directors shall register the transfer of any Share to any other Member.

(C)   Notwithstanding the provisions of paragraphs (D) onwards of this Article, but subject to paragraphs (A) and (B) of this Article, the Directors may in their absolute discretion decline to register any transfer:

  (i)   of any Share on which the Company has a lien; or

  (ii)   which is to be made pursuant to paragraph (J) of this Article, whether or not the Share is fully paid; or

  (iii)   unless it is lodged at the Office or at such other place as the Directors may appoint and is accompanied by any certificate for the Shares to which it relates and such other evidence as the Directors may reasonably require to show the right of the transferor to make the transfer; or

  (iv)   unless it is in respect of only one class of Shares; or

  (v)   if it is in favour of more than four transferees.

Article 26 of the Model Articles for Private Companies Limited by Shares shall not apply to the Company.

(D)   Except where a transfer is to be made under paragraph (A) or (B) of this Article, any person (a 'Proposing Transferor') proposing to transfer any Share or any beneficial interest in it must give a notice in writing (a 'Transfer Notice') to the Company stating the number of Shares he wishes to transfer. The Transfer Notice may also specify the price per Share at which he is willing to sell; but where the Transfer Notice either:

  (i)   fails to specify any such price, or

  (ii)   states that the Proposing Transferor wishes to sell at a fair value determined by the Valuer, or

  (iii)   is a deemed Transfer Notice,

the price shall be determined under paragraph (G) of this Article. The Transfer Notice makes the Company the agent of the Proposing Transferor for the sale of the Share in accordance with this Article and at whichever is the lower of any price specified in the Transfer Notice and the fair value of the Share if determined under paragraph (G) of this Article. If the Transfer Notice relates to more than one Share, the Company is only authorised to sell all those Shares and not just any part of them, unless either the Proposing Transferor states to the contrary in writing or paragraph (F) of this Article is invoked. A Transfer Notice shall not be revocable except with the sanction of the Directors.

(E)   The Shares included in a Transfer Notice must be offered by notice in writing (an 'Option Notice'), no later than 7 days after the Company receives the Transfer Notice, to all the Members except the Proposing Transferor and any other Proposing Transferor, and as closely as possible in proportion to the number of Shares held by each of them (in the case of a deemed Transfer Notice, the date of its receipt is deemed to be the date when the Directors have notice of the act or omission which results in the Transfer Notice being deemed to be given). The Option Notice shall additionally:

(i)   specify the date when the Company received the Transfer Notice and any price specified in it or, if no such price was specified or in the case of a deemed Transfer Notice, shall state that the price will be determined under paragraph (G) of this Article; and

(ii)   invite each Member in his reply to state how many (if any) Shares in excess of his proportion he wishes to purchase; and

(iii)   impose a time limit, of not less than 21 nor more than 42 days, within which the offer may be accepted, the starting date of the time limit being expressed to be either the date of the Option Notice or the date of any certificate of valuation under paragraph (G) of this Article, whichever alternative produces the longer period.

If any Member does not before the expiry of that time limit (the 'Acceptance Date') claim by notice in writing (an 'Acceptance Notice') any Shares offered to him, they shall be used to satisfy any claims for excess Shares in proportion to the existing Shares held by the claimants respectively, but so that no such claimant shall be bound to take more excess Shares than he shall have applied for. If any Shares cannot, without fractions, be offered to the Members in proportion to their existing holdings or be used to satisfy a Member's claim for excess Shares, those remaining Shares shall be allocated among the Members, or some of them, in such proportions or in such a way as may be determined by lots drawn in such manner as the Directors think fit. Any Member who gives an Acceptance Notice is hereinafter called a 'Purchaser'. If the Transfer Notice specified a sale price, any potential Purchaser may, not later than 7 days after receiving his Option Notice, by notice in writing to the Company require that the fair value of the Shares be determined under paragraph (G) of this Article.

(F)   If Purchasers are not found under paragraph (E) of this Article for all the Shares comprised in the Transfer Notice, the Directors may, no later than 7 days after the Acceptance Date, convene a general meeting of the Company in accordance with section 694 of the Act, such meeting to be held no later than 30 days after the date on which it is convened, for the purpose of considering and, if thought fit, passing a special resolution to authorise the terms of a contract for the purchase by the Company of any of the Shares comprised in the Transfer Notice at a price per Share equal to the lower of any price specified in the Transfer Notice and any price already determined under paragraph (G) of this Article. If such a meeting is convened, all references hereinafter to the 'Acceptance Date' shall be construed as references to the seventh day after the due date of the meeting. If such a resolution is passed and the Company is in all other respects able and willing to purchase the Shares to which the contract relates in accordance with Part 18 of the Act, the Proposing Transferor shall not be bound to accept an offer by the Company in the terms of the contract so authorised, but if, by the Acceptance Date, he fails to accept such an offer in respect of all the Shares for which Purchasers have not been found under paragraph (E) of this Article, he may not transfer in pursuance of the Transfer Notice the Shares to which that offer relates but shall be deemed to have authorised the Company to sell the number of Shares for which Purchasers have been found under paragraph (E) of this Article, and shall not be entitled to give any other Transfer Notice under paragraph (D) of this Article for a period of 6 months commencing immediately after the Acceptance Date, Provided always that:

(i) during that 6-month period nothing here shall prevent a Transfer Notice from being deemed or required to be given under paragraphs (L), (M) or (O) of this Article; and

(ii) where the Transfer Notice was deemed or required to be given under any of paragraphs (L), (M), or (O) of this Article, a further Transfer Notice (in respect of the Proposing Transferor's remaining Shares) shall be deemed to be given under that same paragraph of this Article immediately upon the expiry of that 6-month period, and that further deemed Transfer Notice shall be deemed to specify a sale price per Share equal to the same price as that under the offer which was made pursuant to this paragraph (F) and which the proposing Transferor failed to accept.

If such a contract is entered into between the Company and the Proposing Transferor, the Company shall hereinafter be included in the expression 'Purchaser', and the sale of the Shares to which the contract relates shall be completed in accordance with the terms of the contract, but, subject thereto, the following provisions of this Article shall apply in relation to that sale.

(G) Where the fair value or the price of a Share has to be determined under this paragraph (G), then if the Valuer shall, as at any date in the period beginning three months after the end of the Company's most recently completed accounting reference period and ending with the date of the Transfer Notice, have certified in writing the fair value of a Share in accordance with the following provisions of this paragraph, the value so certified shall be deemed to be the fair value of the Share which is the subject of the current Transfer Notice, unless the Directors resolve that that would for any reason (including any material difference in the sizes of the two relevant shareholdings) be manifestly unjust. Otherwise, the Valuer shall certify the fair value or price of the Share in writing in accordance with the following provisions of this paragraph. In so certifying, the Valuer shall pay due regard to the total number of Shares included in the Transfer Notice in question and the percentage of the issued Shares of the same class represented by those Shares; and he may take into account any other factors which, in his discretion, he considers relevant. The sum so certified shall be the sum which is in his opinion the fair value of the Share as at the date of the Transfer Notice. All costs incurred in making any valuation shall be borne by the Company, unless the Proposing Transferor served (or was deemed to have served) another Transfer Notice less than 12 months before the date when the current Transfer Notice was given or deemed to be given, in which event those costs shall be borne as to half by the Company and as to half by the Proposing Transferor. In certifying the fair value of a Share, the Valuer shall be considered to be acting as an expert and not as an arbitrator, and accordingly any provisions of law or statute relating to arbitration shall not apply.

(H) If one or more Purchasers are found for all the Shares included in any Transfer Notice (or for any lesser number of those Shares which the Proposing Transferor has, or is deemed to have, authorised the Company to sell), the Company shall within 7 days after the Acceptance Date give notice (a 'Sale

Notice') to the Proposing Transferor specifying the Purchasers of such Shares and the applicable price per Share, which shall be the lower of any price specified in the Transfer Notice and any fair value determined under paragraph (G) of this Article. The Proposing Transferor shall, upon payment in full of the applicable price, transfer the Shares to the Purchasers, and the Directors shall register every such transfer.

(I)   If the Proposing Transferor, after having become bound as aforesaid, makes default in transferring any Share included in a Sale Notice, the Company may receive the purchase money on his behalf and may authorise some person to execute a transfer of the Share in favour of the Purchaser, who shall thereupon be registered as the holder thereof. The receipt of the Company for the purchase money shall be a good discharge to the Purchaser. The Company shall account to the Proposing Transferor for the purchase money and shall be deemed to be his interest-free debtor, and not a trustee for him in respect of the same. Pending payment of the purchase money to the Proposing Transferor, the Directors may employ such money in the Company's business or invest it in such investments as they may from time to time think fit.

(J)   If the Company fails to give a Sale Notice to the Proposing Transferor in respect of any particular Share included in the Transfer Notice he may, no later than 30 days after the Acceptance Date and subject to paragraphs (C) and (F) of this Article, sell and transfer that Share or any beneficial interest in it to any person and at any price; Provided that, unless the Proposing Transferor in his Transfer Notice authorised the Company to act as his agent for the sale of any and not just all of the Shares included in the Transfer Notice, he may not, under this paragraph, transfer only some (and not all) of the Shares (or any beneficial interest in them) included in his Transfer Notice.

(K)   For the purposes of the following paragraphs of this Article, an 'Employee-shareholder' means an individual who is, or holds a right or interest whereby he may become, a Member, and who is a director or employee of the Company and/or any other company under the 'control' (within the meaning of section 840 of the Income and Corporation Taxes Act 1988) of the Company; and the reference in paragraph (L) of this Article to an individual ceasing to be an Employee-shareholder shall be construed as a reference only to the case where such individual ceases to hold all directorships or employments by virtue of which he would otherwise be an Employee-shareholder.

(L)   Upon any Employee-shareholder ceasing to be such (otherwise than on death):

(i)   he must, no later than 30 days after that cessation, give a Transfer Notice in respect of all the Shares (if any) then held by him, unless during that 30-day period the Directors resolve that he is exempt from this requirement; and

(ii)   if, after such cessation, he or any other person acquires Shares in pursuance of rights or interests obtained by him, he or that other person (as the case may be) must, no later than 30 days after such acquisition, give a Transfer Notice in respect of all the Shares so acquired, unless during that 30-day period the Directors resolve that this requirement does not apply;

and if the Employee-shareholder or that other person does not comply with that requirement he shall, immediately upon the expiry of that 30-day period, be deemed to have given the Company a Transfer Notice under paragraph (D) of this Article in respect of all the Shares in question.

(M)   Upon the death of any Member or Employee-shareholder:

   (i)   his personal representatives must, no later than three months after the death, give a Transfer Notice in respect of all the Shares (if any) held by the deceased individual, unless during the period of 28 days beginning with the date when the Company receives notice of the death the Directors resolve that the personal representatives are exempt from this requirement; and

   (ii)   if the personal representatives or any other person after the death acquire Shares in pursuance of rights or interests obtained by the deceased individual, they or that other person (as the case may be) must, no later than 30 days after that acquisition, give a Transfer Notice in respect of all the Shares so acquired, unless during that 30-day period the Directors resolve that this requirement does not apply;

and if the personal representatives or that other person do not comply with that requirement they shall, immediately upon the expiry of that three month or 30-day period (as the case may be), be deemed to have given the Company a Transfer Notice under paragraph (D) of this Article in respect of all the Shares in question.

(N)   The Company shall give forthwith to a Proposing Transferor a copy of, or notice of the contents of, every Option Notice given by the Company under paragraph (E) of this Article. Whenever the fair value of a Share falls to be determined under paragraph (G) of this Article as a result of a request from a potential Purchaser, the Company shall immediately inform of such request both the Proposing Transferor and also every Member to whom an Option Notice has been given; and the Company shall give to the Proposing Transferor and every Member to whom an Option Notice has been given a copy of the certificate of valuation as soon as it is received by the Company.

(O)   The Directors may demand such evidence as they think fit for the purpose of securing compliance with paragraphs (D) and (J) of this Article. If the Directors become aware that any Member has, without the sanction in writing of every other Member, declared himself a nominee in respect of any Share or has otherwise assigned or created any beneficial interest in such Share in favour of any other person, the Directors may by notice in writing given to such Member require him forthwith to give a Transfer Notice in respect of such Share, and thereafter the Member shall (unless he gives a Transfer Notice beforehand) be deemed to give such a Transfer Notice 7 days after the date of such notice.

(P)   Where a Transfer Notice is deemed to be given under any paragraph of this Article, the other paragraphs of this Article shall, where the context permits, but subject to any changes required by that context, apply in the same way to any such deemed Transfer Notice as they apply to an actual Transfer Notice.

9.8   It has been assumed that the above draft article would be supplemented by straightforward definitions of 'the Company', 'Director', 'Member', 'Office' and 'Share'. Paragraph (A)(ii) is sufficiently broad to include the case where an own share purchase is approved by means of a written resolution.

9.9   A separate agreement between shareholders may enable one to achieve more than that which is permissible under the articles alone. For example, a company with a small number of shareholders has granted share options to some senior employees. Upon the termination of the employment of such an employee, the terms of the share option scheme give the board of directors a discretion as to whether the share option may be exercised during a limited period. The director-shareholders are content that the option be exercised, provided that the resulting shares are immediately purchased by the company, without any uncertainty in the matter. This objective can be achieved by the directors requiring the departing employee initially to sign and hand over to the board:

(a)   an agreement whereby the departing employee undertakes to the shareholders (or to holders of at least 75% of the voting shares) that he will sell his shares to the Company for £X each, in return for the shareholders agreeing to persuade the board of directors to exercise its discretion to allow him to exercise his share option. For the purpose of securing that obligation and protecting the shareholders' interests, the agreement (which must be in the form of a deed) should include an irrevocable power of attorney in favour of one of the shareholders, entitling him to sign on behalf of the departing employee any contract for the purchase of that employee's shares by the Company at £X a share which may be approved by written (or special) resolution of the shareholders;

(b)   an undated stock transfer form;

(c)   an undated transfer notice (conforming with the articles). This would be used only if, for some unexpected reason, the proposed own share purchase turned out not to be feasible (the shares could then be offered to the other shareholders).

Following the exercise of the option and the issue of the shares, a separate draft own share purchase contract (between the employee and the company) would be approved by written (or special) resolution of the shareholders. The employee (or his attorney) and the company then sign that contract and complete the deal. This transfer of shares would be authorised under para (A) in the draft article at **9.7**.

Chapter 10

OWN SHARE PURCHASE CONTRACTS

10.1 The purpose of this chapter is to set out and comment upon forms of own share purchase contract which are capable of being used in an off-market purchase.

A STRAIGHTFORWARD AND IMMEDIATE PURCHASE

10.2 The following is a simple form of unconditional contract for a purchase and sale which is to be completed immediately (or very shortly) after the contract is entered into. The vendor is to sell his entire shareholding to the company, and the purchase price is to be financed wholly out of distributable profits.

THIS AGREEMENT is made the _____ day of _____ 201__

BETWEEN: (1) _____ LIMITED (registered in England under number _____ and hereinafter called 'the Company'), whose registered office is at _____, and

(2) _____ (hereinafter called 'the Vendor') of
_____

WHEREAS:

(A) The Vendor is the holder and beneficial owner of ____ fully paid up Ordinary Shares of £1 each in the capital of the Company, those shares of the Vendor being hereinafter called 'the Sale Shares';

[either]

(B) The draft terms of this agreement were available for the inspection of the members of the Company at its registered office for the period of 15 days ending with _____ 201__ and were similarly available at the General Meeting of the Company held on that date at which the draft terms of this agreement were authorised by special resolution of the Company in accordance with section 694 of the Companies Act 2006, and such authority has been neither varied nor revoked;

[*or*]

(B)   The draft terms of this agreement have been authorised by a written resolution signed, in accordance with section Chapter 2 of Part 13 of the Companies Act 2006, by all members of the Company except the Vendor, and such authority has been neither varied nor revoked;

(C)   The Company desires to purchase, and the Vendor desires to sell, the Sale Shares on the terms hereinafter appearing.

NOW IT IS HEREBY AGREED as follows:

The Sale and Purchase

1 The Vendor shall sell, and the Company shall purchase, the Sale Shares for the sum of £_____. The Company shall pay that sum out of its 'distributable profits' (within the meaning of section 736 of the Companies Act 2006).

The Vendor's undertakings relating to the Sale Shares

2.1 The Vendor warrants that recital (A) to this Agreement is accurate and that the Sale Shares are free from any lien, charge or encumbrance.

2.2 With effect from the signing of this Agreement, the Vendor shall, for so long as the Vendor remains the holder of any of the Sale Shares, hold them as a bare trustee for the Company.

Completion

3.1 Completion of the purchase of the Sale Shares shall take place not later than 7 days after this Agreement has been signed by both parties, and shall be effected by:

(a)   the Vendor delivering to the Company a stock transfer form sufficient in every respect to transfer to the Company the legal title to all the Sale Shares, together with any and every share certificate which the Vendor may possess representing [or including] all or any of the Sale Shares; and

(b)   the Company delivering to the Vendor a [cheque *or* banker's draft], payable to the Vendor, for the amount of the purchase price mentioned in Clause 1 above.

3.2 As soon as is reasonably practicable after completion has been effected in accordance with Clause 3.1 above, the Company shall alter its register of members so as to show:

(a)   that the Vendor has transferred the Sale Shares to the Company and has thereby ceased to hold those shares; and

(b)   that the Sale Shares have been cancelled in accordance with section 706(b) of the Companies Act 2006.

Costs

4. The Company shall bear all professional costs and charges relating to this Agreement, and shall also pay all stamp duties falling due in respect of the completion of the purchase of the Sale Shares in accordance with this Agreement.

IN WITNESS whereof the parties hereto have hereunto set their hands the day and year first before written.

Signed: _____ for and on behalf of

_____ Limited

Signed: _____ ('the Vendor')

10.3 In the above draft, it is desirable to include whichever version of recital (B) is appropriate, both as a reminder regarding the procedure that must have been gone through before the contract is signed, and also for the purpose of trying to strengthen the presumption that all administrative transactions are presumed to have been implemented correctly (*omnia rite praesumuntur esse acta*).

10.4 If there are a substantial number of shareholders whose shares are to be bought by the company on the same occasion (e g where the company is purchasing all its preference shares), it can be simpler to structure the contract in such a way as to keep all of it the same for all vendors except for an area at the bottom where each vendor's name, address and shareholding are entered. Starting with the precedent at **10.2**, this can be achieved by replacing the description of party (2) and recital (A) with the following:

(2)   the person or persons (hereinafter called 'the Vendor') whose name(s) and address are set out at the foot of this Agreement below where the Vendor signs.

WHEREAS:

(A)   The Vendor holds such number of fully paid up Preference Shares of £1 each in the capital of the Company as is printed near the Vendor's name at the foot of this Agreement, those shares of the Vendor being hereinafter called 'the Sale Shares';

The words 'per share' must be inserted at the end of the first sentence of clause 1, so that that sentence reads:

The Vendor shall sell, and the Company shall purchase, the Sale Shares for the sum of £____ per share.

Finally, immediately below where the vendor signs, one prints:

Name and address   No of Preference Shares held

It is normally feasible to fit this straightforward form of contract onto a single side of A4.

10.5 If the shareholder lives abroad, it may be desirable (for clarity's sake) to include the following clause defining the applicable law:

Applicable law

5.   This Agreement shall be construed and interpreted in all respects in accordance with the law of England to the exclusive jurisdiction of which the parties hereto submit.

A STRAIGHTFORWARD AND CONDITIONAL CONTRACT

10.6   Where it is sought to make the agreement conditional upon subsequent authorisation by a special resolution of the company, the precedent at **10.2** above might be adapted as follows:

(a)   Recital (B) should be replaced with the following:

'The Company and the Vendor agree that none of the Sale Shares will be purchased pursuant to this agreement until its terms have been authorised by a special resolution of the Company.'

(b)   The words 'Subject to clause 5 below' should be inserted at the start of clause 1, so that the first sentence reads:

'Subject to clause 5 below, the Vendor shall sell, and the Company shall purchase, the Sale Shares for the sum of £_____.'

(c)   The opening words of clause 2.2 should reflect the conditional nature of the obligation to purchase the shares and that clause should be replaced with the following:

'Upon authorisation being provided pursuant to clause 5 below, the Vendor shall, for so long as the Vendor remains the holder of any of the Sale Shares, hold them as a bare trustee for the Company.'

(d)   The date for completion of any share purchase should flow from the date of the special resolution and the words 'not later than 7 days after this Agreement' in clause 3.1 should be replaced with the following words:

'not later than 7 days after the date of the passing of the special resolution set out in clause 5 below.'

(e)   There should also be a new clause 5 introducing the conditionality to which such an agreement must be subject:

'*Condition*

5.   The sale and purchase of the shares in accordance with this agreement is conditional on a special resolution of the Company being passed authorising the terms of this agreement. If such authorisation is not provided by _____, this agreement shall cease to have effect.'

PURCHASE AND OPTION CONTRACTS

10.7 This type of contract includes both an immediate purchase by the company of some of the vendor's shares, and the grant of cross-options in respect of the remainder of the vendor's shares. The cross-options form a contingent purchase contract, as identified in s 694(3), CA 2006 (see also s 705(1)(a)). The following purchase and option contract enables the vendor and his wife to spread over three tax years sales of their 2,000 shares (out of a total issued share capital of 10,000 shares). In each of the first two years, his shareholding interest in the company is not 'substantially reduced'.

THIS AGREEMENT is made the _____ day of _____ 201__

BETWEEN:

(1) _____ LIMITED (registered in England under number _____ and hereinafter called 'the Company'), whose registered office is at _____, and

(2) _____ (hereinafter called 'Mr Vendor') of _____, and

(3) _____ (hereinafter called 'Mrs Vendor') of _____.

WHEREAS:

(A) Mr Vendor and Mrs Vendor each hold and beneficially own 1,000 ordinary shares of £1 each in the capital of the Company;

(B) The Company wishes to buy, and Mr and Mrs Vendor wish to sell, 570 out of the total of 2,000 shares held by them, and on the terms hereinafter appearing;

(C) The Company on the one part, and Mr and Mrs Vendor on the other, wish to grant to each other options upon the exercise of which by either of them the other will become bound in instalments to effect a purchase and sale by Mr and Mrs Vendor to the Company of the remaining 1,430 ordinary shares held by Mr and Mrs Vendor in the capital of the Company, and on the terms hereinafter appearing;

[either]

(D) The draft terms of this agreement were available for the inspection of the members of the Company at its registered office for the period of 15 days ending with _____ 201__ and were similarly available at the General Meeting of the Company held on that date at which the draft terms of this agreement were authorised by special resolution of the Company in accordance with section 694 of the Companies Act 2006, and such authority has been neither varied nor revoked;

[*or*]

(D) The draft terms of this agreement have been authorised by a written resolution signed, in accordance with section Chapter 2 of Part 13 of the Companies Act 2006, by all members of the Company except Mr and Mrs Vendor, and such authority has been neither varied nor revoked.

NOW IT IS HEREBY AGREED as follows:

Interpretation

1.1 In this Agreement words and expressions defined above (in the descriptions of the parties) shall have the meanings respectively assigned to them, and the words or expressions below shall have the meanings respectively assigned to them as follows:

'Clause' means a clause of this Agreement, or, where the context so admits or requires, any sub-clause or paragraph of such a clause;

'Distributable Profits' has the same meaning as in section 736 of the Companies Act 2006;

an 'Exercise Notice' means a notice in writing requiring the party upon whom it is served to join in a sale of any shares in accordance with Clause 5;

a 'Seller' means either of Mr and Mrs Vendor.

1.2 References in this Agreement to a Seller owning any particular number of shares shall, if either:

(a) additional shares are issued to that Seller pursuant to a bonus issue, or
(b) the number of shares held by that Seller is varied by reason of any sub-division or consolidation of the Company's share capital,

be deemed to be references to the same proportion of that Seller's shareholding in the Company after the issue, sub-division or consolidation as the proportion represented by the particular number of shares immediately before the issue, sub-division or consolidation.

1.3 References in this Agreement to any statutory provision shall include references to any statutory modification or re-enactment thereof for the time being in force and any statutory instrument or order made pursuant thereto. Where the context permits the singular shall include the plural, and vice versa, and the masculine shall include the feminine. The headings of clauses in this Agreement are for convenience of reference only and shall be disregarded in the interpretation of this Agreement.

1.4 This Agreement shall be construed and interpreted in all respects in accordance with the law of England, to the exclusive jurisdiction of which the parties hereto agree to submit.

The Initial Sales and Purchases

2.1 Mr Vendor hereby sells as beneficial owner, and the Company hereby purchases, 285 of his shares in the Company for the sum of £_____. The Company shall pay that sum out of its Distributable Profits.

2.2 Mrs Vendor hereby sells as beneficial owner, and the Company hereby purchases, 285 of her shares in the Company for the sum of £_____. The Company shall pay that sum out of its Distributable Profits.

2.3 With effect from the signing of this Agreement, each Seller shall, for so long as he remains the holder of any of the shares sold under Clauses 2.1 and 2.2, hold them as a bare trustee for the Company.

2.4 Completion of the purchases of the shares sold under Clauses 2.1 and 2.2 shall take place immediately after this Agreement has been signed by all parties, and shall be effected by:

(a)   each Seller delivering to the Company a stock transfer form sufficient in every respect to transfer to the Company the legal title to the shares he is selling, together with any and every share certificate which the Seller may possess representing or including all or any of those shares; and

(b)   the Company delivering to each Seller a cheque for the amount of the purchase price and made payable to the Seller or as the Seller may direct.

2.5 As soon as is reasonably practicable after completion has been effected in accordance with Clause 2.4, the Company shall alter its register of members so as to show:

(a)   that the Sellers have transferred the shares in question to the Company and have thereby ceased to hold those shares; and

(b)   that the purchased shares have been cancelled in accordance with section 706(b) of the Companies Act 2006.

2.6 After the steps described in Clause 2.5 have been fulfilled, the Company shall supply each Seller with such share certificate as is appropriate to represent that Seller's remaining shareholding in the Company.

The First Options

3.1 At any time after the period of *three* months commencing with the date of this Agreement, each Seller shall be entitled to serve on the Company an Exercise Notice in respect of 200 shares in the Company, requiring those shares to be bought by the Company for the sum of £_____.

3.2 At any time after the period of *three* months commencing with the date of this Agreement, the Company shall be entitled to serve on each Seller an Exercise Notice in respect of 200 shares in the Company, requiring those shares to be sold to the Company for the sum of £_____.

The Second Options

4.1 At any time after the period of *fifteen* months commencing with the date of this Agreement, each Seller shall be entitled to serve on the Company an Exercise Notice in respect of his remaining 515 shares in the Company, requiring those shares to be bought by the Company for the sum of £_____.

4.2 At any time after the period of *fifteen* months commencing with the date of this Agreement, the Company shall be entitled to serve on each Seller an Exercise Notice in respect of his remaining 515 shares in the Company, requiring those shares to be sold to the Company for the sum of £_____.

The exercise of any option

5.1 If any party serves on another party an Exercise Notice in accordance with this Agreement:

(a)   the Seller concerned shall thereby become bound to sell, and the Company shall thereby become bound to purchase, all the shares (and not just any part of them) to which the Exercise Notice in question relates and at the applicable price; and

(b)   the Seller shall, for so long as the Seller remains the holder of any of the shares to which the Exercise Notice in question relates, hold them as a bare trustee for the Company.

5.2 The Company shall pay the price for the shares being purchased out of its Distributable Profits, and shall use its best endeavours to ensure that it retains sufficient Distributable Profits for the purpose.

The Sellers' warranty

6. The Sellers warrant that their shares are free from any lien, charge or encumbrance and will remain free from any lien, charge or encumbrance at all times that are material for the purposes of this Agreement.

Completion following exercise

7.1 If, in accordance with Clause 5, any parties hereto become bound to purchase and sell any shares, completion of that purchase and sale shall take place not later than 7 days following the date when the Exercise Notice is served, or on such later date as may be agreed for the purpose by the parties concerned, and shall be effected by:

(a)   the Seller delivering to the Company a stock transfer form sufficient in every respect to transfer to the Company the legal title to all the shares to which the Exercise Notice in question relates, together with any and every share certificate which the Seller may possess representing or including all or any of those shares; and

(b)   the Company delivering to the Seller a cheque for the amount of the relevant purchase price and made payable to the Seller or as the Seller directs.

7.2 As soon as is reasonably practicable after completion has been effected in accordance with Clause 7.1, the Company shall alter its register of members so as to show:

    (a)   that the Seller has transferred the shares in question to the Company and has thereby ceased to hold those shares; and

    (b)   that those shares have been cancelled in accordance with section 706(b) of the Companies Act 2006.

Costs

8. The Company shall bear all professional costs and charges relating to this Agreement, and shall also pay all stamp duties falling due in respect of the completion of the purchase of the Sale Shares in accordance with this Agreement.

Assignment

9.1 The Company, being prevented by law from assigning its rights under this Agreement, shall not purport to do so.

9.2 A Seller shall neither assign nor purport to assign all or any of such Seller's rights under this Agreement; Provided that if a Seller shall die at any time before the termination of this Agreement in accordance with Clause 10, that Seller's rights and obligations hereunder shall pass to his personal representatives.

Termination

10.1 Subject to Clause 10.2 and to any agreement between the parties hereto to the contrary, this Agreement shall terminate on the sixth anniversary of the date of this Agreement.

10.2 If all possible Exercise Notices shall have been served before the sixth anniversary of the date of this Agreement, this Agreement shall terminate upon the fulfilment of the parties' obligations hereunder.

Notices

11. Any notice or other communication under or in connection with this Agreement may be given by personal delivery (which, in the case of delivery to the Company, shall mean personal delivery to any director of the Company or by delivery to the registered office of the Company) or by sending the same by post to the last known address of the party to be served; and where a notice or other communication is given by first class post, it shall be deemed to have been served 48 hours after it was put into the post properly addressed and stamped.

IN WITNESS *etc.*

10.8 A less straightforward type of purchase and option contract is the following one, which gives to the vendor the benefit of:

(a) selling all but one of his shares immediately for their present market value; and

(b) selling the remaining share at a future date, at a price which will reflect specified future events.

In the following draft, the vendor is, in substance, selling his shareholding to the company on terms that if, within a specified period following the sale, the company is taken over or its shares become publicly quoted, the vendor will be paid a further sum to reflect the increased purchase price he might have obtained had he remained a shareholder and sold his shares either to the take-over bidder or on the Stock Exchange. It is not possible for such an agreement to be entered into in a straightforward manner (ie with the vendor selling *all* his shares for £*X* plus a promise of further payment if a flotation or a take-over occurs), because of the rule (CA 2006, s 692(2)) that payment (in full) must be made on completion of the purchase. The solution is for the vendor to sell for £*X* all of his shares bar one, and for he and the company to grant each other options for the purchase and sale of this remaining share at a price and time determined by future events.

THIS AGREEMENT is made the _____ day of _____ 201__

BETWEEN:

(1) _____ LIMITED (registered in England under number ____ and hereinafter called 'the Company'), whose registered office is at _____, and

(2) _____ LIMITED (registered in England under number _____ and hereinafter called 'the Vendor'), whose registered office is at _____;

WHEREAS:

(A) The Vendor holds _____ fully paid up Ordinary Shares of £1 each in the capital of the Company;

[either]

(B) The draft terms of this agreement were available for the inspection of the members of the Company at its registered office for the period of 15 days ending with _____ 201__ and were similarly available at the General Meeting of the Company held on that date at which the draft terms of this agreement were authorised by special resolution of the Company in accordance with section 694 of the Companies Act 2006, and such authority has been neither varied nor revoked;

[*or*]

(B) The draft terms of this agreement have been authorised by a written resolution signed, in accordance with section Chapter 2 of Part 13 of the Companies Act 2006, by all members of the Company except the Vendor, and such authority has been neither varied nor revoked;

(C) The Vendor desires to sell its aforementioned shares to the Company on the terms and subject to the conditions hereinafter appearing.

NOW IT IS HEREBY AGREED as follows:

Interpretation

1.1 In this Agreement the following words or expressions shall have the meanings respectively assigned to them as follows:

'Accounting Period' means an accounting period of the Company ending on _____ in any year, or on any other date which is for the time being the Company's accounting reference date (within the meaning of sections 391 and 392 of the Companies Act 2006);

'Clause' means a clause of this Agreement, or, where the context so admits or requires, any sub-clause or paragraph of such a clause;

'Distributable Profits' has the same meaning as in section 736 of the Companies Act 2006;

an 'Exercise Notice' means a notice in writing requiring the party upon whom it is served to join in a sale of the Option Share in accordance with Clause 6;

the 'Exercise Period' means any time on or after the earlier of:

(a) the Final Date, and
(b) if a Sale Event occurs before the Final Date, the date on which that Sale Event occurs;

the 'Exercise Price' shall be determined in accordance with Clause 7;

the 'Final Date' means _____ 201__;

the 'Option Share' means one Ordinary Share of £1 in nominal value in the capital of the Company, being a share which is held at the date hereof by the Vendor;

'Ordinary Share' means any issued share (by whatever name called) in the capital of the Company, other than a share which confers on its holder:

(a) a right to a dividend at a fixed rate to the exclusion of any other right to share in the profits of the Company; and
(b) a right in a winding up, or on any reduction of capital involving a repayment of paid up capital, to repayment of the capital paid up thereon, together with a sum equal to any arrears or deficiency of the said fixed rate dividend

(whether earned or declared or not) calculated down to the date of repayment, to the exclusion of any other right to share in the assets of the Company;

the 'Purchase Price' shall be £_____;

'Sale Event' means either of the following:

(a) the admission of any shares in the capital of the Company to the Official List of the Stock Exchange, or the grant by the Stock Exchange of permission for any shares in the capital of the Company to be dealt in on AIM, a sub-market of the Stock Exchange;
(b) the acceptance by or on behalf of holders of the issued Ordinary Shares in the capital of the Company of an offer (which either is when made, or subsequently becomes, unconditional) made to holders of such shares, if as a result of such acceptance the offeror and/or any person controlled by or connected with the offeror holds or becomes entitled to hold more than 75 per cent of the issued Ordinary Shares in the capital of the Company;

the 'Sale Shares' means _____ Ordinary shares of £1 each in the capital of the Company, being shares which at the date hereof are held by the Vendor;

'the Stock Exchange' means London Stock Exchange Group plc.

1.2 The headings of clauses in this Agreement are for convenience of reference only and shall be disregarded in the interpretation of this Agreement.

1.3 References herein to any statutory provision shall include references to any statutory modification or re-enactment thereof for the time being in force. Where the context permits, the singular shall include the plural, and vice versa.

1.4 This Agreement shall be construed and interpreted in all respects in accordance with the law of England to the exclusive jurisdiction of which the parties hereto agree to submit.

The Initial Sale and Purchase

2. The Vendor shall sell as beneficial owner, and the Company shall purchase, the Sale Shares for the Purchase Price. The Company shall pay that sum out of its Distributable Profits.

The Vendor's undertakings relating to the Sale Shares

3.1 The Vendor warrants that the Sale Shares are free from any lien, charge or encumbrance.

3.2 With effect from the signing of this Agreement, the Vendor shall, for so long as it remains the holder of any of the Sale Shares, hold them as a bare trustee for the Company.

Completion of the purchase of the Sale Shares

4.1 Completion of the purchase of the Sale Shares shall take place not later than 7 days after the signing of this Agreement and shall be effected by:

    (a)   the Vendor delivering to the Company a stock transfer form sufficient in every respect to transfer to the Company the legal title to all the Sale Shares, together with any and every share certificate which the Vendor may possess representing or including all or any of the Sale Shares; and

    (b)   the Company delivering to the Vendor a cheque for the amount of the Purchase Price and made payable to the Vendor.

4.2 If the Vendor shall, in accordance with Clause 4.1(a), deliver to the Company any share certificate evidencing the Option Share as well as the Sale Shares, the Company shall on completion deliver to the Vendor a new share certificate evidencing the Option Share.

4.3 As soon as is reasonably practicable after completion has been effected in accordance with Clause 4.1, the Company shall procure the alteration of its register of members so as to show:

(a)   that the Vendor has transferred the Sale Shares to the Company and has thereby ceased to hold those shares; and

(b)   that the Sale Shares have been cancelled in accordance with section 706(b) of the Companies Act 2006.

The Options

5.1 The Vendor shall be entitled at any time during the Exercise Period to serve an Exercise Notice on the Company.

5.2 The Company shall be entitled at any time during the Exercise Period to serve an Exercise Notice on the Vendor.

5.3 The Company shall give to the Vendor not less than 14 days' written notice of the likely occurrence, before the Final Date, of a Sale Event, Provided that, in the case of a Sale Event falling within paragraph (b) of the definition of 'Sale Event' in Clause 1.1, no such advance notice shall be given without the prior consent of the offeror or prospective offeror. If such advance notice is not given of the occurrence of any Sale Event, and without prejudice to any other rights which the Vendor may have pursuant to this Clause in respect of such a default on the part of the Company, the Company shall inform the Vendor by written notice as soon as possible thereafter that a Sale Event has taken or will take place.

The Sale and Purchase of the Option Share

6. If either of the parties hereto serves on the other an Exercise Notice, the Vendor shall thereby become bound to sell, and the Company shall thereby become bound to purchase, the Option Share for the Exercise Price.

The Exercise Price

7.1 The Exercise Price shall be determined in accordance with Clauses 7.2, 7.3 and 7.4.

7.2 Subject to Clause 7.3, the Exercise Price shall be 50 pence.

7.3 If before the Final Date there occurs a Sale Event, the Exercise Price shall, if an Exercise Notice is served during the period of thirty days commencing with the date of the occurrence of the Sale Event or, if later, with the date of receipt by the Vendor of notice (given pursuant to Clause 5.3) of the occurrence of a Sale Event, be determined, subject to Clause 7.4, as follows:

$$£E = \frac{N \times P - [M]}{[D]}$$

Where:

$£E$ = the Exercise Price;

N = the number of Ordinary Shares in issue on the date when the Sale Event occurs;

$P =$

(a) if the Sale Event which has occurred is of a type falling within paragraph (a) of the definition of 'Sale Event' in Clause 1.1, the price per Ordinary Share as shown in the prospectus published in connection with the Sale Event or, if none, the amount per share at which Ordinary Shares were placed in preparation for, and immediately prior to, that Sale Event; or
(b) if the Sale Event which has occurred is of a type falling within paragraph (b) of the definition of 'Sale Event' in Clause 1.1, the price or value offered per Ordinary Share as stated in or derived from the offer to purchase;

[and 'M' and 'D' are numbers to be calculated by reference to the particular facts; see **10.9**.]

Provided always that the Exercise Price shall not be less than 50 pence nor more than the amount of the Distributable Profits of the Company on the date when the Exercise Notice is served.

7.4 If, following the signing of this Agreement, the Company issues any Ordinary Shares otherwise than as bonus shares, any determination of the Exercise Price in accordance with Clause 7.3 shall be adjusted in such manner as the auditors for the time being of the Company shall in their written opinion consider fair and reasonable in the light of the parties' agreed intention that the Vendor should participate in the realisation of any gain which it would have realised on the occurrence of such Sale Event had this Agreement not been entered into and assuming that the Vendor would not, in the period from the date hereof to the occurrence of such Sale Event, have increased or decreased the aggregate nominal value of its shareholding in the Company otherwise than as a result of any bonus issue of shares, and any such opinion, and any adjustment resulting therefrom, shall, save in the case of manifest error, be final and binding on the parties hereto.

7.5 Either party may at any time before the thirtieth day following the Final Date require the auditors for the time being of the Company to state whether in their opinion a Sale Event has occurred and/or to calculate the Exercise Price in accordance with Clauses 7.3 and/or 7.4. Any such opinion or calculation in writing shall be final and binding on the parties hereto.

7.6 When giving any opinion or making any calculation pursuant to Clauses 7.4 or 7.5, the auditors shall be acting as experts and not as arbitrators, and accordingly any provisions of law relating to arbitration shall not apply.

7.7 The Company shall pay the Exercise Price out of its Distributable Profits.

Restrictions on the Company

8.1 The Company shall not, without the prior written consent of the Vendor (such consent not to be unreasonably withheld), at any time prior to the earlier of:

(a)   the Final Date, and
(b)   if a Sale Event occurs before the Final Date, the end of the period of 30 days commencing on the date of the occurrence of the Sale Event or, if later, on the date of receipt by the Vendor of notice (given pursuant to Clause 5.3) of the occurrence of such Sale Event,

do any of the following:

(i)   capitalise any of its Distributable Profits for the time being;
(ii)   declare any dividend in respect of any shares in the Company unless the total amount of such dividends declared at that time, when aggregated with the amount of any other dividends declared in respect of any shares in the Company since the last day of the Company's most recent Accounting Period for which audited accounts exist at that time, does not exceed whichever is the lesser of:

(A)   20 per cent of the aggregate of the amounts for the time being paid up on the shares in the Company; and
(B)   20 per cent of the after-tax profits of the Company for the most recent Accounting Period for which audited accounts exist at that time;

(iii) issue any shares other than Ordinary Shares;
(iv)   enter into or complete any contract under which the Company would or might become entitled and obliged to purchase any of its own shares (other than shares held or owned by the Vendor), if and to the extent that the aggregate of the amounts which would be or might become payable by the Company upon the completion of all such contracts would exceed £_____;
(v)   reduce its share capital or any share premium account or capital redemption reserve in accordance with section 641 of the Companies

Act 2006, unless and to the extent that the amount of the Company's Distributable Profits is not diminished by such reduction.

8.2 The Company undertakes to use its best endeavours to promote and extend the business of the Company until the end of the Exercise Period.

The Vendor's warranty relating to the Option Share

9. The Vendor warrants that the Option Share is free from any lien, charge or encumbrance and that the Option Share will remain free from any lien, charge or encumbrance at all times that are material for the purposes of this Agreement.

Completion of the purchase of the Option Share

10.1 If, in accordance with Clause 6, the parties hereto become bound to purchase and sell the Option Share, completion of the purchase of the Option Share shall take place not later than 7 days after the later of:

(A)   the date on which the Exercise Notice is served, and
(B)   if the auditors for the time being of the Company have been required to perform any function pursuant to Clauses 7.4 or 7.5, the date of the auditors' opinion or calculation given pursuant to either of those Clauses,

or on such later date as may be agreed for the purpose by the parties hereto, and shall be effected by:

(a)   the Vendor delivering to the Company a stock transfer form sufficient in every respect to transfer to the Company the legal title to the Option Share, together with any share certificate which the Vendor may possess representing the Option Share; and
(b)   the Company delivering to the Vendor either:
      (i)   if the Exercise Price shall be 50 pence, a cheque for that amount; or
      (ii)   in any other case, a banker's draft for the amount of the Exercise Price; made payable, in either case, to the Vendor.

10.2 As soon as is reasonably practicable after completion has been effected in accordance with Clause 10.1, the Company shall procure the alteration of its register of members so as to show:

(a)   that the Vendor has transferred the Option Share to the Company and has thereby ceased to hold that share; and
(b)   that the Option Share has been cancelled in accordance with section 706(b) of the Companies Act 2006.

Stamp Duties

11. The Company shall pay all stamp duties falling due in respect of the completion of every purchase of shares in accordance with this Agreement.

Assignment

12. Neither party shall assign or purport to assign all or any of his rights under this Agreement.

No relevant restrictions on transfers

13. The Company shall not, prior to the completion of the purchase of the Option Share and without the consent of the Vendor, make any amendment to its Articles such as would or might impose or vary any restriction of whatsoever description relating to any transfer of shares, unless such restriction is expressly precluded from applying to any purchase by the Company of its own shares.

Notices

14. Any notice or other communication under or in connection with this Agreement may be given by personal delivery to any director of either party or by sending the same by post to the registered office of the party to be served; and where a notice or other communication is given by first class post, it shall be deemed to have been served 48 hours after it was put into the post properly addressed and stamped.

IN WITNESS *etc.*

10.9   The formula in Clause 7.3 is based on the assumption that if £Z is to be paid for Y% of the existing issued ordinary shares, the remaining $(100 - Y)$% may be said to be worth:

$$£Z \times \frac{(100 - Y)}{Y}$$

It appears necessary to make this assumption, because if a sale event occurs, the exercise price must then be calculated as a proportion of 100% of the issued ordinary shares (without any discount resulting from the size of a Y% holding). Moreover, the price which a purchaser would pay for 100% of the remaining issued ordinary shares would inevitably reflect the extent of the contingent liability imposed on the company by the option agreement. The purchaser will therefore be paying less in total than he would be doing if the vendor were still a Y% shareholder; though the selling shareholders should still each receive the same amount as if the vendor were still a Y% shareholder. If the vendor were to remain a Y% shareholder and 100% of the ordinary shares were sold, then if the purchaser were to pay a total of £$A + F$ (accrued value plus future value), out of this total the vendor would get:

$$£\frac{(A + F) \times Y}{100}$$

If the company buys the vendor's Y% holding for £Z and a contingent liability, a 100% holding of ordinary shares in the company will in future be worth:

$$£Z \times \frac{(100 - Y)}{Y} + F - C$$

where C = the contingent liability. C must equal F x $Y/100$, so that the total purchase price, T, may be expressed as:

$$T = £Z \times \frac{(100 - Y)}{Y} + F - F \times \frac{Y}{100}$$

which may be re-written as:

$$F \times \frac{Y}{100} = £Z \times \frac{(100 - Y)}{Y} + F - T$$

However, once Y and Z are known (which they should be by the time the contract is being drafted), it should become possible to re-express the formula in the neater format illustrated at clause 7.3 of the draft agreement.

Example

Suppose the vendor's 25% shareholding is to be purchased for £300,000. If the vendor were to remain a 25% shareholder and 100% of the ordinary shares were sold, the purchaser would pay a total of £1,200,000 + F (F representing future growth in value). Of this total, the vendor would get £300,000 + $F/4$.

If the company buys the vendor's 25% holding for £300,000 and a contingent liability, a 100% holding of ordinary shares in the company will in future be worth:

$$£900,000 + F - C$$

where C = the contingent liability. C must equal $F/4$, so that the total purchase price, T, may be expressed as:

$$T = £900,000 + \frac{3F}{4}$$

From this, $F/4$ may be expressed in terms of T as:

$$\frac{F}{4} = \frac{T - 900,000}{3}$$

If we now replace $F/4$ with $£E$, and replace T with $N \times P$, we end up with a specific version of the formula in clause 7.3:

$$£E = \frac{N \times P - 900,000}{3}$$

The formula would need to be adjusted if a basis of valuation other than a *pro rata* one were adopted for determining the vendor's contingent future payment.

A CONTINGENT PURCHASE CONTRACT

10.10 The following draft contingent purchase contract (as that expression is used in s 705 referring back to s 694, CA 2006) effects the grant of cross-options to and by the company and the widow of one of the director-shareholders. The company is engaged in property development and each of its director-shareholders has been taking charge of a particular project. The terms as to their remuneration have been that each director-shareholder will draw a small salary but hope to receive the bulk of his remuneration by way of a bonus, which will be calculated by reference to the profitability of the project on which he has been engaged. Following the untimely death of one of them, the surviving director-shareholders wish to give his widow the security of having the deceased's shares purchased by the company at a fair price, to be funded from the profits to be derived from the last project which the deceased had managed.

THIS AGREEMENT is made the _____ day of _____201__

BETWEEN:

(1) _____ LIMITED (registered in England under number _____ and hereinafter called 'the Company'), whose registered office is at _____, and

(2) _____ (hereinafter called 'the Vendor') of _____

WHEREAS:

A) On _____ 50,000 ordinary shares of £1 each (such 50,000 shares being hereinafter called 'the Sale Shares') were issued to _____ (who was the husband of the Vendor and is hereinafter called 'the Deceased') for a total consideration of £50,000;

(B) The Deceased died on _____ 201__ and his will was proved on _____;

(C) The Vendor having become entitled to the Sale Shares upon the death of the Deceased, the Vendor was registered as the holder of the Sale Shares on _____;

(D)   The Company and the Vendor desire to grant to each other options upon the exercise of which by either of them the other will become bound to complete a purchase and sale of the Sale Shares by the Vendor to the Company and on the terms hereinafter appearing;

[either]

(E)   The draft terms of this agreement were available for the inspection of the members of the Company at its registered office for the period of 15 days ending with _____ 201__ and were similarly available at the General Meeting of the Company held on that date at which the draft terms of this agreement were authorised by special resolution of the Company in accordance with section 694 of the Companies Act 2006, and such authority has been neither varied nor revoked;

[*or*]

(E)   The draft terms of this agreement have been authorised by a written resolution signed, in accordance with section Chapter 2 of Part 13 of the Companies Act 2006, by all members of the Company except the Vendor, and such authority has been neither varied nor revoked;

NOW IT IS HEREBY AGREED as follows:

Interpretation

1.1 In this Agreement the following words or expressions shall have the meanings respectively assigned to them as follows:

'the Auditors' means the auditors for the time being of the Company;

'Clause' means a clause of this Agreement, or, where

the context so admits or requires, any sub-clause or paragraph of such a clause;

an 'Exercise Notice' means a notice in writing requiring the party upon whom it is served to join in a sale of the Sale Shares in accordance with Clause 3;

the 'Exercise Period' means the period described in Clause 2.3;

the 'Sale Price' means the price determined pursuant to Clause 4;

the 'Sale Shares' means 50,000 Ordinary shares of £1 each in the capital of the Company, being shares which at the date hereof are held and beneficially owned by the Vendor; Provided that if:

(a)   the Vendor ceases to hold some only of the Sale Shares; and/or
(b)   the Vendor comes to hold further shares in the capital of the Company, whether by reason of any bonus or rights issue or otherwise,

this Agreement shall continue to apply as if references to 'the Sale Shares' were references to those shares which the Vendor holds for the time being and to which she is beneficially entitled.

1.2 References in this Agreement to any statutory provision shall include references to any statutory modification or re-enactment thereof for the time being in force and any statutory instrument or order made pursuant thereto. Where the context permits the singular shall include the plural, and vice versa, and the masculine shall include the feminine. The headings of clauses in this Agreement are for convenience of reference only and shall be disregarded in the interpretation of this Agreement.

1.3 In giving any opinion or making any determination under this Agreement, the Auditors shall be deemed to be acting as experts and not as arbitrators, and accordingly all provisions of law relation to arbitration shall not apply. All costs of the Auditors for acting in relation to this Agreement shall be borne by the Company.

1.4 This Agreement shall be construed and interpreted in all respects in accordance with the law of England, to the exclusive jurisdiction of which the parties hereto agree to submit.

The Options

2.1 The Vendor shall be entitled at any time during the Exercise Period to serve an Exercise Notice on the Company.

2.2 The Company shall be entitled at any time during the Exercise Period to serve an Exercise Notice on the Vendor.

2.3 For the purposes of this Agreement, the 'Exercise Period' means the period which:

(a)   begins with the date on which the Company shall complete the sale of its freehold land and premises described in the Schedule to this Agreement, or the second anniversary of the date of this Agreement, whichever shall occur first; and
(b)   ends thirteen weeks after it began.

2.4 If, in accordance with Clause 2.3, the Exercise Period begins before the second anniversary of the date of this Agreement, the Company shall thereupon immediately give notice in writing to the Vendor of that event.

2.5 For the purposes of Clause 2.3(a), the word 'sale' includes the grant of a lease which is due to expire not less than 50 years later.

2.6 The Company shall, if and when requested to do so by the Vendor, submit applications to the Inland Revenue for any appropriate tax clearances that might be considered desirable, but the rights and obligations of the parties hereto shall be in no way affected by the outcome of any such application.

The Sale and Purchase

3 If either of the parties hereto serves on the other an Exercise Notice in accordance with this Agreement:

(a)   the Vendor shall thereby become bound to sell, and the Company shall thereby become bound to purchase, all the Sale Shares (and not just any part of them) at a price per share equal to the Sale Price;

(b)   the Company shall thereupon immediately instruct the Auditors to ascertain and certify the Sale Price in accordance with Clause 4; and

(c)   the Vendor shall, for so long as the Vendor remains the holder of any of the Sale Shares, hold them as a bare trustee for the Company.

The Sale Price

4.1 The Sale Price shall be certified by the Auditors for the time being of the Company as that sum which represents the fair value of the Sale Shares as at the date when the Exercise Notice is given.

4.2 The Auditors may require the Company to provide them with such information as they may think fit for the purpose of fulfilling their obligations under Clause 4.1, and the Company shall comply with any such request for information without unreasonable delay.

4.3 For the purpose of Clause 4.1 above, the Auditors shall be entitled to rely on any information supplied by the Company.

4.4 The Company shall pay the Sale Price out of its 'distributable profits' (within the meaning of section 736 of the Companies Act 2006), and shall use its best endeavours to ensure that it retains sufficient distributable profits for the purpose.

The Vendor's warranties

5.1 The Vendor warrants that the Sale Shares are free from any lien, charge or encumbrance and that the Sale Shares will remain free from any lien, charge or encumbrance at all times that are material for the purposes of this Agreement.

5.2 The Vendor warrants that, for the purpose of enabling the Company to comply with its obligations under Clause 2.6, the Vendor will supply to the Company such information as the Company may reasonably request and that the information so supplied will be accurate and complete.

Completion

6.1 If, in accordance with Clause 3, the parties hereto become bound to purchase and sell the Sale Shares, completion of the purchase of the Sale Shares shall take place not later than 7 days after the date on which the Auditors certify the Sale Price, or on such later date as may be agreed for the purpose by the parties hereto, and shall be effected by:

(a) the Vendor delivering to the Company a stock transfer form sufficient in every respect to transfer to the Company the legal title to all the Sale Shares, together with any and every share certificate which the Vendor may possess representing all or any of the Sale Shares; and

(b) the Company delivering to the Vendor a banker's draft for the amount of the Sale Price and made payable to the Vendor or as the Vendor directs.

6.2 As soon as is reasonably practicable after completion has been effected in accordance with Clause 6.1, the Company shall alter its register of members so as to show:

(a) that the Vendor has transferred the Sale Shares to the Company and has thereby ceased to be a member of the Company; and

(b) that the Sale Shares have been cancelled in accordance with section 706(b) of the Companies Act 2006.

Costs

7. The Company shall bear all professional costs and charges relating to this Agreement, and shall also pay all stamp duties falling due in respect of the completion of any purchase of the Sale Shares in accordance with this Agreement.

Assignment

8.1 The Company, being prevented by law from assigning its rights under this Agreement, shall not purport to do so.

8.2 The Vendor shall neither assign nor purport to assign all or any of the Vendor's rights under this Agreement; Provided that if the Vendor shall die at any time before the termination of this Agreement in accordance with Clause 9, the Vendor's rights and obligations hereunder shall pass to the Vendor's personal representatives.

Termination

9.1 Subject to any agreement between the parties hereto to the contrary, this Agreement shall terminate at the end of the Exercise Period if no Exercise Notice shall have been served beforehand.

9.2 If an Exercise Notice shall have been served before the end of the Exercise Period, this Agreement shall terminate upon the fulfilment of the parties' obligations hereunder.

Notices

10. Any notice or other communication under or in connection with this Agreement may be given by personal delivery (which, in the case of delivery to the Company, shall mean personal delivery to any director of the Company) or by sending the same by post to the last known address of the party to be served; and

where a notice or other communication is given by first class post, it shall be deemed to have been served 48 hours after it was put into the post properly addressed and stamped.

THE SCHEDULE

[*Description of the land and premises*]

IN WITNESS *etc.*

A PURCHASE OUT OF CAPITAL

10.11 The following draft contract can be used where the whole of the purchase price for the shares is to be financed out of 'capital' (see **7.15**).

THIS AGREEMENT is made the _____ day of _____ 201___

BETWEEN:

(1) _____---___ LIMITED (registered in England under number _____ and hereinafter called 'the Company'), whose registered office is at _____, and

(2) _____ (hereinafter called 'the Vendor') of _____

WHEREAS:

(A) The Vendor is the holder and beneficial owner of ____ fully paid up Ordinary Shares of £1 each in the capital of the Company, those shares of the Vendor being hereinafter called 'the Sale Shares';

(B) The Vendor wishes to sell, and the Company wishes to purchase, the Sale Shares on the terms hereinafter appearing;

(C) Accounts have been prepared for the Company in respect of the period ending _____201___
[*a date less than 3 months before the directors make their statement*], and these accounts indicate that the Company has no distributable profits out of which to finance any part of the purchase price for the Sale Shares;

(D) On _____ 201___ the directors of the Company made a statement specifying the amount of the permissible capital payment and otherwise in accordance with section 714 of the Companies Act 2006;

[*either*]

(E) The draft terms of this agreement were available for the inspection of the members of the Company at its registered office for the period of 15 days ending with _____ 201___ ('the Approval Date') and were similarly available at the General Meeting of the Company held on that date at which the draft terms of this agreement were authorised by special resolution of the Company in accordance with section 714 of the Companies Act 2006, and such authority has been neither varied nor revoked;

(F) Also on the Approval Date, the Company passed a further special resolution approving the proposed payment out of capital to be made in pursuance of this Agreement if this Agreement were to be entered into;

[*or*]

(E) The draft terms of this agreement have been authorised by a written resolution signed, in accordance with section Chapter 2 of Part 13 of the Companies Act 2006, by all members of the Company except the Vendor, and such resolution took effect on _____ 201___ ('the Approval Date') and has been neither varied nor revoked;

(F) Also taking effect on the Approval Date is a further written resolution, signed in accordance with section Chapter 2 of Part 13 of the Companies Act 2006, and approving the proposed payment out of capital to be made in pursuance of this Agreement if this Agreement were to be entered into.

NOW IT IS HEREBY AGREED as follows:

The Sale and Purchase

1 The Vendor shall sell, and the Company shall purchase, the Sale Shares for the sum of £_____. The Company shall pay that sum out of 'capital' (within the meaning of section 709 of the Companies Act 2006).

The Vendor's undertakings relating to the Sale Shares

2.1 The Vendor warrants that recital (A) to this Agreement is accurate and that the Sale Shares are free from any lien, charge or encumbrance.

2.2 With effect from the signing of this Agreement, the Vendor shall, for so long as he remains the holder of any of the Sale Shares, hold them as a bare trustee for the Company.

Publicity

3.1 The Company shall forthwith cause to be published such a notice as is required by section 719 of the Companies Act 2006 both in the *London Gazette* and in a newspaper circulating throughout the part of the United Kingdom in which the Company is registered.

3.2 The Company shall forthwith deliver to the Registrar of Companies a copy of the statement of the directors and of the auditors' report required by section 714 of the Companies Act 2006.

3.3 The original of the directors' statement and auditors' report shall be kept at the Company's registered office henceforth until the expiry of the period of five weeks after the Approval Date, and during that period shall be open to the inspection of any member or creditor of the Company without charge.

Completion

4.1 Completion of the purchase of the Sale Shares shall take place on the thirty-fifth day after the Approval Date, or on such later date as the parties may agree if such date is no later than the forty-ninth day after the Approval Date, and shall be effected by:

(a)   The Vendor delivering to the Company a stock transfer form sufficient in every respect to transfer to the Company the legal title to all the Sale Shares, together with any and every share certificate which the Vendor may possess representing [or including] all or any of the Sale Shares; and

(b)   The Company delivering to the Vendor a cheque for the amount of the purchase price mentioned in Clause 1 above and made payable to the Vendor.

4.2 As soon as is reasonably practicable after completion has been effected in accordance with Clause 4.1 above, the Company shall alter its register of members so as to show:

(a)   that the Vendor has transferred the Sale Shares to the Company and has thereby ceased to hold those shares; and

(b)   that the Sale Shares have been cancelled in accordance with section 706(b) of the Companies Act 2006.

Costs

5 The Company shall bear all professional costs and charges relating to this Agreement, and shall also pay all stamp duties falling due in respect of the completion of the purchase of the Sale Shares in accordance with this Agreement.

Interpretation

6.1 References herein to any statutory provision shall include references to any statutory modification or re-enactment thereof for the time being in force. Where the context permits, the singular shall include the plural, and vice versa, and the masculine shall include the feminine.

6.2 This Agreement shall be construed and interpreted in all respects in accordance with the law of England to the exclusive jurisdiction of which the parties hereto agree to submit.

IN WITNESS *etc.*

10.12   It will normally be desirable for the statutory declaration and the two special resolutions to be made and passed all on the same day; the recitals to the above contract are drafted on that premise. It will also usually be desirable for the contract itself to be entered into as soon as the special resolutions have been passed, although there is no actual necessity for such immediate signature. If the parties choose to delay entering into the contract for a short period, clauses 3.1 and 3.2 will need to be either amended or deleted. The recitals to the agreement are also drafted on the premise that the company has no distributable profits at all; if the company has some distributable profits, but not enough to cover the purchase price, suitable amendments will be required. Finally, it has been assumed that the company will not be making any fresh issue of shares for the purpose of financing the purchase.

10.13 If the purchase price for the shares is to be financed partly out of distributable profits and as to the remainder out of 'capital', the following changes to the draft at **10.11** should be made:

(a) *Recital (C)*: replace with:

> (C) [Interim] accounts have been prepared for the Company in respect of the period ending _____ 201__ [*a date less than 3 months before the directors make their statement*], and these accounts indicate that the Company has distributable profits of £_____;

(b) *Clause 1*: replace with:

> 1. The Vendor shall sell, and the Company shall purchase, the Sale Shares for the sum of £_____. For accounting purposes, the first £_____ of that sum shall be set against (and shall thereby extinguish) the Company's distributable profits, and only the balance of £_____ shall be a payment out of 'capital' (within the meaning of section 709 of the Companies Act 2006).

10.14 There is nothing to prevent a wholly owned subsidiary purchasing some of its own shares from its parent company (assuming that the subsidiary has auditors). Where such a purchase is to be financed wholly or in part out of capital, the following changes to the draft at **10.11** should be made:

(a) *Recitals (A) and (B)*: replace with:

> (A) The Vendor is the holder and beneficial owner of *2,000,000* fully paid up Ordinary Shares of £1 each in the capital of the Company, and is the sole member of the Company;
>
> (B) The Vendor wishes to sell, and the Company wishes to purchase, *1,500,000* of its Ordinary Shares of £1 each in the capital of the Company (such *1,500,000* shares being hereinafter called 'the Sale Shares') on the terms hereinafter appearing;

(b) *Recitals (D), (E) and (F)*: replace with:

> (D) On the same date as this Agreement and shortly before this Agreement was signed, the directors of the Company made a statement specifying the amount of the permissible capital payment and otherwise in accordance with section 714 of the Companies Act 2006;
>
> (E) The draft terms of this agreement were authorised by a special resolution approved by the sole member of the Company, and such resolution took immediate effect and has been neither varied nor revoked;

(F)   At the same time as approving the last-mentioned resolution, the sole member of the Company approved a further special resolution, approving the proposed payment out of capital to be made in pursuance of this Agreement if this Agreement were to be entered into.

(G)   The date of this Agreement, being also the date on which the resolution referred to at (F) above was approved, is hereinafter called 'the Approval Date'.

Chapter 11

FINANCIAL ASSISTANCE

11.1 This chapter considers the provisions of ss 677–683 of the CA 2006 which prevent, subject to some significant exceptions, both a public company from giving financial assistance for the acquisition of its own shares or those of its private holding company and, further, any company which is a subsidiary of a public company from giving financial assistance for the acquisition of that parent public company's shares. Broadly stated, the type of transaction envisaged here is not a purchase by the company of its own shares, but the provision by the company to someone else of either the purchase price itself or of some other means of assisting the purchase. The most common example is where a company is being bought; the company's resources should not be used directly or indirectly to assist the buyer financially in making the purchase. These provisions serve to reinforce the protection afforded to a company's creditors and anyone else who has an interest in the maintenance of the company's capital (eg minority shareholders who are not selling). However, even if a transaction does not represent unlawful financial assistance, it may still not be most likely to promote the interests of the company concerned, or might involve an unlawful return of capital or be contrary to the provisions of the Insolvency Act 1986.

THE HISTORY OF THE PROVISIONS

11.2 Since their introduction, these provisions have undergone significant development. The earliest version of these provisions was found in s 16 of the CA 1928, which was enacted to curb the practice which had developed in the 1920s of persons purchasing companies which had substantial cash balances or easily realisable assets and then so arranging matters that the purchased company would advance the cash required to finance the purchase. Upon consolidation, this provision became s 45 of the CA 1929. After amendments made by s 73 of the CA 1947 (extending the scope of the section to cover subscriptions as well as purchases, and also to cover shares in the company's holding company as well as shares in the company itself), the provisions became s 54 of the CA 1948. The subsequent amendments made by para 10 of Sch 3 to the CA 1980 were short-lived, for the whole section was repealed and re-cast in the form of ss 42–44 of the CA 1981 with effect from 3 December 1981, also introducing a detailed procedure that might be followed by a private company to 'whitewash' the giving of financial assistance. Upon consolidation, those provisions became ss 151–158 of the CA 1985, which were amended by the FSA 1986 with effect from 1 December 1987 (SI 1987/1997), by the CA

1989 with effect from dates in 1990 and by the Companies Act 1985 (Electronic Communications) Order 2000, SI 2000/3373, with effect from 22 December 2000. The general scheme of the legislation then prohibited (subject to significant exceptions) any company from giving financial assistance for the acquisition of its own shares or those of its holding company, whether before or after the date of the acquisition, but permitted a private company to undertake a 'whitewash' procedure (set out in ss 155–158 CA 1985) where the acquisition was of shares in that private company or (assuming there was no intervening public company holding company in the group structure) its private company parent company.

11.3 Over the years, there have been consultations and proposals for amending the sections in more substantial ways. In 2002, the DTI-organised Final Report on Modern Company Law proposed the removal of the prohibition on the giving by private companies of financial assistance for the acquisition of their own shares. Upon consolidation of the companies' legislation in the CA 2006, this proposal was brought into effect, with effect in relation to private companies from 1 October 2008, with the repeal of ss 151–158, CA 1985. The repeal of the prohibition against financial assistance by private companies in relation to an acquisition of their own shares or those in a private company parent company was effected by the Companies Act 2006 (Commencement No 5, Transitional Provisions and Savings) Order 2007, SI 2007/3495, with effect from 1 October 2008, which repealed ss 151–153 and 155–158 of the CA 1985 insofar as they concerned the giving of financial assistance by a private company for the purposes of the acquisition of shares in itself or another private company and where the assistance was given on or after 1 October 2008, even if the shares were acquired or liability incurred at an earlier point in time. From 1 October 2009, the relevant provisions are now contained in the CA 2006. The removal of many private company transactions from the scope of the prohibition is significant; that repeal has alone been estimated to bring a saving of transaction costs for private companies of some £20 million per annum (Regulatory Impact Assessment URN 06/2234).

11.4 In relation to public companies, the financial assistance prohibition remains, with ss 677–683 being brought generally into force from 1 October 2009. This reflects the requirements of Article 23(1) of the Second Company Law Directive (77/91/EEC), which provides that, subject to derogations contained in Article 23(2), public companies:

> 'may not advance funds, nor make loans, nor provide security, with a view to the acquisition of its shares by a third party.'

Article 23(3), which provides a further exception from the scope of Article 23(1) in relation to the acquisition of shares by certain investment companies, does not apply in the UK.

Sections 677–683 of the CA 2006

11.5 The current provisions may be divided into:

(a) those which set out the general nature of the prohibition which are, in turn, divided into the prohibitions that apply to an acquisition of shares in a public company (s 678) and the prohibitions that apply to a public company for the acquisition of shares in its private holding company (s 679); these are dealt with in the first part of this chapter; and

(b) those setting out exceptions from these general prohibitions, which are either unconditional (s 681) or conditional (s 682); these are dealt with at **11.31** onwards.

11.6 Whether under s 678 or s 679, there are two sub-rules against the giving of 'financial assistance'; the first applies to present or future share acquisitions (ss 678(1) and 679(1)), and the second in relation to past ones (ss 678(3) and 679(3)). It had been held, when construing a much earlier version of this legislation (CA 1929, s 45), that the word 'purchase' as part of the expression 'purchase of any shares in the company' did not include the acquisition of shares by subscription or allotment – *Re VGM Holdings Ltd.*[1] The present legislation uses the more general word 'acquisition' covering not only purchases of, and subscriptions for, shares, but also contracts where shares are obtained in exchange for a non-cash consideration. The legislation also uses the term 'proposing to acquire shares' in both ss 678(1) and 679(1), making it clear that the provisions may be infringed even if no acquisition of shares ultimately takes place – *Parlett v Guppys (Bridport) Ltd*;[2] *Chaston v SWP Group plc*;[3] *Makram Estafnous v London & Leeds Business Centres Ltd* (point not considered on appeal).[4] It is not enough that the financial assistance is 'in connection with' the acquisition of shares – it must be for the purpose of the acquisition of shares or to reduce a liability that was incurred for the purpose of such an acquisition (*Dyment v Boyden*[5]).

Financial assistance for a present or future acquisition

11.7 CA 2006, s 678 applies to the acquisition of shares in a public company, whether by that company or by any company (whether public or private) that is a subsidiary of the target company. By s 678(1):

> 'where a person is acquiring or is proposing to acquire shares in a public company, it is not lawful for that company, or a company that is a subsidiary of that company, to give financial assistance directly or indirectly for the purpose of reducing or discharging the liability if, at the time the assistance is given, the company in which the shares were acquired is a public company.'

---

[1]   [1942] 1 All ER 224.
[2]   [1996] BCC 299.
[3]   [2003] BCC 140 at 155.
[4]   [2009] EWHC 1308 (Ch).
[5]   [2005] BCC 79.

11.8 CA 2006, s 679 is concerned with the acquisition of shares in a private company, prohibiting the giving of financial assistance by a public company subsidiary of that private company. By s 679(1):

> 'where a person is acquiring or is proposing to acquire shares in a private company, it is not lawful for a public company that is a subsidiary of that company to give financial assistance directly or indirectly for the purpose of the acquisition before or at the same time as the acquisition takes place.'

Financial assistance for a past acquisition

11.9 Both the prohibitions addressed at **11.7** and **11.8** above are supplemented by other provisions that address the question of past acquisitions of shares. Accordingly, s 678(3) of the CA 2006 provides:

> 'Where
>
> (a)   a person has acquired shares in a company; and
> (b)   a liability has been incurred (by that or any other person) for the purpose of the acquisition,
>
> it is not lawful for that company, or a company that is a subsidiary of that company, to give financial assistance directly or indirectly for the purpose of reducing or discharging the liability if, at the time the assistance is given, the company in which the shares were acquired is a public company.'

11.10 Similarly, s 679(3) of the CA 2006 provides:

> 'Where
>
> (a)   a person has acquired shares in a private company; and
> (b)   a liability has been incurred (by that or any other person) for the purpose of the acquisition,
>
> it is not lawful for a public company that is a subsidiary of that company to give financial assistance directly or indirectly for the purpose of reducing or discharging the liability.'

11.11 These prohibitions, through an expanded meaning given to the words 'reducing or discharging', include the giving by the relevant company of financial assistance for the purpose of wholly or partly restoring the other person's financial position to what it was before the acquisition took place (CA 2006, s 683(2)(b)). Also, for these purposes, a person is deemed to 'incur a liability' if he changes his financial position by making an agreement or arrangement (whether enforceable or unenforceable, and whether made on his own account or with any other person), or by any other means (CA 2006, s 683(2)(a)).

11.12 Both ss 678 and 679 apply to companies that are subsidiaries of the target. In contrast to the position under the CA 1985 (which stated that 'it is not lawful for the company or any of its subsidiaries'), the legislative provisions of the CA 2006 now make the extent of the prohibition clear. The term 'company', as defined in s 1 of the CA 2006, means a company formed and registered under the CA 2006 or the other earlier UK legislation referred to in that section. Both ss 678 and 679 use language that make it clear that they are directed towards a 'company' in this specific sense (in s 678, 'public company' and 'a *company* that is a subsidiary of *that company*' and, in s 679, 'private company' and 'a public *company* that is a subsidiary of *that company*', emphasis added), such that a non-UK registered company will not be a 'company' within the meaning used in those sections. While the same conclusion had ultimately been reached on the scope of ss 151–158, CA 1985 in *Arab Bank plc v Mercantile Holdings Ltd*[6] (later applied by the Court of Appeal in *AMG Global Nominees (Private) Ltd v Africa Resources Ltd*[7]), this reasoning was based upon the presumption that domestic legislation does not have extra-territorial effect.

11.13 However, ss 678 and 679 do not prohibit a company incorporated in England and Wales or Scotland from giving financial assistance for the purpose of an acquisition of shares in its holding company if that holding company is incorporated elsewhere. By contrast, s 54 of the CA 1948 did impose such a prohibition.

11.14 It was also held in *Arab Bank plc v Mercantile Holdings Ltd*[8] that the mere giving of financial assistance by a subsidiary does not of itself constitute a giving of such assistance by the parent company. However, if the parent company procures its subsidiary to breach s 678 or s 679, that act of procurement will constitute a breach of the relevant section by the parent. Moreover, if an arrangement involving the use of a foreign subsidiary was simply a sham (for example, a foreign subsidiary had been specially established for the sole purpose of enabling otherwise prohibited financial assistance to be provided), then the use of a foreign subsidiary might well be disregarded and the English parent company itself found to be in breach of the prohibition on financial assistance.

11.15 Further, even though ss 678 and 679 do not apply to financial assistance given by a foreign subsidiary, if an English company subject to the prohibition were to hive down an asset to a foreign subsidiary in order to enable it to be made available to finance a contemplated acquisition of shares in the English company, that would constitute an 'indirect' provision of financial assistance by the English company in breach of the prohibition. Similarly, if an English registered company were to put an overseas subsidiary into a position to give financial assistance (for example, guaranteeing a loan to the foreign subsidiary for the purpose of the overseas subsidiary assisting an otherwise prohibited acquisition), then it is likely that the English registered company will also be found to have engaged in the provision of 'indirect' financial assistance.

---

[6]   [1993] BCC 816.
[7]   [2009] 1 BCLC 281.
[8]   [1993] BCC 816.

'Financial assistance'

11.16 The current legislation, as with the CA 1985, contains a form of definition for the expression 'financial assistance'. It is not a full definition, because the words 'financial assistance' are included in each of the four paragraphs of the definition, thereby requiring one to have regard (particularly in the final paragraph) also to the ordinary meaning of the words; but it nevertheless goes some way towards narrowing down and exposing the meaning of the expression. The following paragraphs consider the particular meanings given by s 677(1) of the CA 2006 to the expression 'financial assistance'.

Financial assistance given by way of gift (s 677(1)(a))

11.17 Any gift, irrespective of its size, can represent financial assistance of this type, even if it does not materially reduce the company's net assets. In addition, a gift by a company may in any event be unlawful as an unauthorised reduction of capital (*Re Lee Behrens & Co;*[9] *Aveling Barford Ltd v Perion Ltd*[10]) or as some other misappropriation of the company's assets, e g payments purporting to be bonuses but bearing no relation to remuneration or performance, which were made for the purpose of enabling the recipients to pay calls made on the company's partly paid shares (*Re a Company (No 008126 of 1989)*[11]); or a payment of clearly excessive remuneration, as a term of an agreement to transfer shares in the company which was to pay that remuneration (*Parlett v Guppys (Bridport) Ltd*[12]); or an arrangement which seeks to achieve a distribution of assets, as if on a winding up, without making proper provision for creditors (*MacPherson v European Strategic Bureau Ltd*[13]); or the purchase of assets by a company at an inflated price (see Aldous LJ in *Barclays Bank plc v British & Commonwealth Holdings plc*[14]). An example of an otherwise lawful corporate gift falling within paragraph (a) would be where the issued shares in a company are to be sold on terms that the acquirer will also acquire additional shares by way of subscription for cash, which will then be paid by the company into its pension fund, of which the vendors of the shares are the main beneficiaries.

Financial assistance given by way of guarantee, security or indemnity, other than an indemnity in respect of the indemnifier's own neglect or default, or by way of release or waiver (s 677(1)(b))

11.18 In *Barclays Bank plc v British & Commonwealth Holdings plc*[15] (for the facts, see **4.27**), it was held that the words 'guarantee', 'security', 'indemnity',

---

9   [1932] 2 Ch 46.
10   [1989] PCC 370.
11   [1992] BCC 542 at 552.
12   [1996] BCC 299.
13   [2002] BCC 39.
14   [1996] 1 BCLC 1 at 41.
15   [1995] BCC 1059.

'release' and 'waiver' were all used in the statutory predecessor to what is now paragraph (b) as legal terms of art. Applying the view of Pearce LJ in *Yeoman Credit Ltd v Latter*[16] that:

'An indemnity is a contract by one party to keep the other harmless against loss.'

it was held that the covenants for the breach of which the banks were suing did not contain any indemnity as such, with the result that no 'financial assistance' within the meaning of paragraph (b) had been given. The term 'guarantee' will therefore be given its ordinary legal meaning of:

'a contract to answer for the debt, default or miscarriage of another who is to be primarily liable to the promisee.'

11.19 An example of a giving of 'security' which falls within paragraph (b) is where a subsidiary is indebted to its parent company on an unsecured basis, and a third party offers to buy the subsidiary on terms that the subsidiary's indebtedness will be paid off over a period of time after completion of the sale. If the parent now wishes to secure its future position by taking a charge over assets of the subsidiary, the giving by the subsidiary of that charge will constitute a giving of financial assistance for the purpose of the proposed acquisition of its shares. However, where a company has indebtedness that it is already obliged to repay on demand, the grant by the company of security in order to borrow monies to repay that indebtedness does not involve any financial assistance (*Anglo Petroleum Ltd v TFB (Mortgages) Ltd*;[17] *Gradwell (Pty) Ltd v Rostra Printers* Ltd;[18] *Re Wellington Publishing Co Ltd*[19]).

11.20 In order for financial assistance to be given by way of security, it has been held that all that is required to make the financial assistance effective is that the lender should believe the security to be valid and on the strength of it make the loan (*Heald v O'Connor*,[20] doubting *Victor Battery Co Ltd v Curry's Ltd*,[21] where it had been held that an invalid debenture could not give any financial assistance).

---

[16]   [1961] 1 WLR 828 at 831.
[17]   [2008] 1 BCLC 185.
[18]   1959 (4) SA 419.
[19]   [1973] 1 NZLR 133.
[20]   [1971] 2 All ER 1105 at 1109g.
[21]   [1946] 1 All ER 519.

Financial assistance given by way of a loan or any other agreement under which any of the obligations of the person giving the assistance are to be fulfilled at a time when in accordance with the agreement any obligation of another party to the agreement remains unfulfilled, or by way of the novation of, or the assignment of rights arising under, a loan or such other agreement (s 677(1)(c))

11.21   As with the giving of a guarantee or an indemnity, financial assistance by way of 'loan' should be viewed as being given when the company enters into the relevant commitment rather than at the time when it is actually performed.

11.22   An example of such an 'other agreement' is where a vendor, V, agrees to sell his shares in P on condition that P causes its wholly owned subsidiary S to pay to V an amount sufficient to discharge P's pre-existing indebtedness to V, as occurred in *Armour Hick Northern Ltd v Armour Trust Ltd*.[22] P would not be providing financial assistance if it were to use its own resources to discharge its indebtedness to V. However, if (because P is impecunious) S pays V and thereby discharges P's debt to V, S is voluntarily making available its money to V for the benefit of P and is thereby providing assistance for the purpose of the acquisition of P's shares. In these latter circumstances, if at least one of P or S is a public company, it will be caught by the financial assistance prohibitions. Similarly, an agreement between V, P, S and the buyer that S would pay to V the amount owed by P to V would be an agreement under which an obligation of S (the person providing financial assistance) would be fulfilled at a time when, in accordance with the agreement, there would remain unfulfilled P's newly acquired indebtedness towards S.

11.23   An example of a novation of a loan falling within paragraph (c) is where a buyer borrows money for the purpose of buying shares in the company, and the company then buys from the lender the right to repayment of the loan.

Any other financial assistance given by a company the net assets of which are reduced to a material extent by the giving of the assistance or which has no net assets (s 677(1)(d))

11.24   'Net assets' here means the aggregate of the company's assets, less the aggregate of its liabilities. It is the actual value of the assets and liabilities at the time of the relevant transaction that needs to be considered, not merely their book value (*Hill v Mullis & Peake*;[23] *Parlett v Guppy's (Bridport) Ltd*[24]). For this purpose, 'liabilities' includes, where the company draws up Companies Act individual accounts, any provision of a kind specified for the purposes of s 677(3) under s 396 of the CA 2006 and, where the company draws up IAS individual accounts, any provision made in those accounts (CA 2006, s 677(3)).

11.25   The words 'any other financial assistance' in paragraph (d) would include the case where the company buys an asset from someone who then uses

---

[22]   [1980] 3 All ER 833.
[23]   [1999] BCC 325 at 332A.
[24]   [1996] BCC 299.

the proceeds of sale to acquire shares in the company. However, such a transaction will only fall within paragraph (d) as a whole if the purchase causes the company's net assets to be reduced to a material extent or if the company has no net assets. Whether a reduction is 'material' or not is a question of fact and degree (*Parlett v Guppy's (Bridport) Ltd*[25]). Both the relative percentage reduction and the total amount involved should be considered. As a rule of thumb, a percentage reduction in net assets of 1 per cent or less might be sensibly said, of itself, not to involve a material reduction, although, in the case of a company with very substantial net assets, the total amount involved might, quite independently, be viewed as reducing the company's net assets to a material extent.

11.26 Where a company purchases an asset at an overvalue, this will cause a reduction in its net assets; whereas if the purchase is at a proper commercial price, the company's net assets should not be reduced to a material extent, if at all. In this respect, it is considered that the scope of ss 678–679 of the CA 2006 (and what was s 154 of the CA 1985) are narrower than that of s 54 of the CA 1948, the most relevant part of the wording of which was the following:

'... it shall not be lawful for a company to give, whether directly or indirectly, and whether by means of a loan, guarantee, the provision of security *or otherwise*, any financial assistance for the purpose of or in connection with a purchase or subscription made or to be made by any person of or for any shares in the company ...'

It was on the scope of s 54 of the CA 1948 that the following view was expressed in *Belmont Finance Corp Ltd v Williams Furniture Ltd (No 2)* by Buckley LJ:[26]

'If A Ltd buys something from B without regard to its own commercial interests, the sole purpose of the transactions being to put B in funds to acquire shares in A Ltd, this would, in my opinion, clearly contravene the section [CA 1948, s 54], even if the price paid is a fair price for what is bought ... If A Ltd buys something from B at a fair price, which A Ltd could readily realise on a resale if it wished to do so, but the purpose, or one of the purposes, of the transaction is to put B in funds to acquire shares in A Ltd, the fact that the price was fair might not, I think, prevent the transaction from contravening the section, if it would otherwise do so, though A Ltd could very probably recover no damages in civil proceedings, for it would have suffered no damage.'

Although the legislation now no longer applies to the acquisition of shares in a private company (except where the financial assistance would be given by a public limited company that was a subsidiary of that private company), it is considered that the transactions so described by Buckley LJ would not now (if references to A Ltd in the above quotation were replaced with references to A plc) contravene s 678 of the CA 2006 and would not constitute 'financial

---

[25] [1996] BCC 299.
[26] [1980] 1 All ER 393 at 402f.

assistance', provided that the company has some net assets. Otherwise, if the company has no net assets, such transactions would be capable of contravening s 678.

11.27   It can be seen that whereas paras (a)–(c) of the definition of 'financial assistance' in s 677(1)(a)–(c) are worded in such a way that one does not have to rely to any material extent on the ordinary meaning of the words 'financial assistance' with which each of those paragraphs begins, para (d) makes the whole definition of 'financial assistance' somewhat open-ended by requiring one to have regard to the ordinary meaning of those words. This renders directly relevant to s 677 such case-law as there is relating to the meaning of the words 'financial assistance' under s 54 of the CA 1948, which did not attempt any definition of those words, as well as the subsequent case-law in relation to s 152 of the CA 1985 (which is materially identical to the language now contained in s 677). Thus, in *Charterhouse Investment Trust Ltd v Tempest Diesels Ltd*,[27] Hoffmann J held (in relation to s 54) that the words 'financial assistance' had no technical meaning and had to be interpreted in the light of the language of ordinary commerce. The commercial realities of each transaction had to be examined to determine if it could properly be described as involving the giving of financial assistance, but bearing in mind that the section was a penal one and should not be strained to cover transactions which were not fairly within it. In the case in question, there was a composite transaction under which the company which was to be sold both received benefits and assumed burdens; it was necessary to look at the transaction as a whole and decide where the net balance of financial advantage lay. On the facts, the judge held that as this balance appeared to lie in favour of the company, it had not been proved that the company had given financial assistance by agreeing to surrender its tax losses to a company which was in the same group as its holding company immediately prior to the sale of the shares in the company to the purchaser. There was no evidence as to what value, if any, the tax losses had at the time when the agreement was entered into; that value appeared speculative, as it depended on the ability of the purchaser to restore the company to profitability. The 'commercial realities' approach of Hoffmann J was approved by the Court of Appeal in *Barclays Bank plc v British & Commonwealth Holdings plc*,[28] in *Chaston v SWP Group plc*[29] and in *Corporate Development Partners LLC v E-Relationship Marketing Ltd*.[30]

11.28   If a potential buyer of the shares in a company insists upon a due diligence exercise being carried out and that the costs of that exercise must be met by someone else, and the potential sellers then cause the company itself (or a subsidiary) to meet those costs, the company (or its subsidiary) will thereby be giving financial assistance for the purpose of the proposed acquisition – such costs being the normal commercial responsibility of the buyer and/or the

[27]   [1986] 1 BCLC 1.
[28]   [1995] BCC 1059 at 1071.
[29]   [2003] BCC 140 at [32].
[30]   [2009] BCC 295 at [29]–[35].

seller (*Chaston v SWP Group plc*[31]). In the *Chaston* case, after buying the company, the buyer successfully sued a former director and major shareholder for damages for breach of fiduciary duty for having procured, or connived in, the giving of this financial assistance by a subsidiary of the company, the net assets of which had been thereby reduced to a material extent.

Interpretation

11.29 When construing documents and considering transactions, the court is required to bear in mind the fact that the prohibition on the giving of financial assistance is a penal provision (see **11.30**), so as not to bring within the prohibition a transaction which can fairly be thought to fall outside it (*per* Harman J in *Barclays Bank plc v British & Commonwealth Holdings plc*,[32] whose decision was approved by the Court of Appeal). Where a document is capable of two different interpretations, one involving a breach of the prohibition and the other not, the presumption of legality will influence a court into preferring the interpretation that does not involve any breach (*Neilson v Stewart*;[33] *Lawlor v* Gray;[34] *Parlett v Guppys (Bridport) Ltd*;[35] *Grant v Lapid Developments Ltd*[36]) and, where possible, that will be presumed to have been the company's intention (cf *Re John Willment (Ashford) Ltd*[37]).

Infringement

11.30 Superficially, the only sanction for infringement of the prohibition on the giving of financial assistance would appear to be contained in s 680, which provides that contravention of the section renders the company liable to a fine and every officer (which includes, a director, manager or secretary) in default liable to a fine or up to two years' imprisonment or both. Such an officer will be 'in default' if they authorise or permit or participate in, or fail to take reasonable steps to prevent, a contravention (s 1121(3), CA 2006). However, the more significant sanction for infringement lies in its civil law consequences; it is established that an infringing agreement is illegal and unenforceable, and renders void any security that breaches the section (*Selangor United Rubber Estates Ltd v Cradock (No 3)*;[38] *Heald v O'Connor*[39]). The ramifications of this illegality include the following:

(a)   Directors of the company providing the assistance will be in breach of their fiduciary duties to the company and may be accountable for losses suffered by the company even if they were ignorant of the prohibition (*Re*

---

[31]   [2003] BCC 140.
[32]   [1995] BCC 19 at 38.
[33]   [1991] BCC 713.
[34]   (1980) 130 NLJ 317.
[35]   [1996] BCC 299.
[36]   [1996] BCC 410.
[37]   [1980] 1 WLR 73.
[38]   [1968] 2 All ER 1073 at 1149–1154.
[39]   [1971] 2 All ER 1105.

VGM Holdings Ltd;[40] *Selangor United Rubber Estates Ltd v Cradock (No 3)*;[41] *Steen v Law*[42]); and, if the company becomes insolvent, they may also be vulnerable to becoming the subjects of disqualification orders under s 6 of the Company Directors Disqualification Act 1986 (as occurred in *Coulthard v Neville Russell*[43]).

(b)   Any person who receives assets of the company that form the subject-matter of the financial assistance and with knowledge of circumstances that render it unconscionable for the recipient to retain those assets may be liable as a constructive trustee to ensure such assets are restored to the company.

(c)   The parties to an infringing agreement may be liable for damages in the tort of conspiracy, although the company (as it is a victim) will not have the knowledge of its directors imputed to it in order to make it party to such a conspiracy: *Belmont Finance Corp Ltd v Williams Furniture Ltd (No 2)*.[44]

(d)   A loan made in contravention of ss 678–679 cannot properly be treated as an asset of the lending company; so, a balance sheet in which such a loan is shown as an asset of the company will fail to show a true and fair view of its financial affairs (*Coulthard v Neville Russell*[45]).

But where a contract for the sale and purchase of shares is entered into in conjunction with the issue, to the vendors and by (for the purposes of illustration) a public limited company in which they are selling the shares, of an unlawful security over that company's assets, the court may permit the vendors to enforce the sale contract on its own by severing from it the unlawful security, as in *Carney v Herbert*[46] (see also *Spink (Bournemouth) Ltd v Spink*;[47] *South Western Mineral Water Co Ltd v Ashmore*[48]). As Lord Brightman, delivering the judgment of the Privy Council stated:

> 'Subject to a caveat that it is undesirable, if not impossible, to lay down any rule which will cover all problems in this field, their Lordships venture to suggest that, as a general rule, where parties enter into a lawful contract of, for example, sale and purchase, and there is an ancillary provision which is illegal but exists for the exclusive benefit of the plaintiff, the court may and probably will, if the justice of the case so requires, and there is no public policy objection, permit the plaintiff if he so wishes to enforce the contract without the illegal provision.'

---

[40]   [1942] 1 All ER 224.
[41]   [1968] 2 All ER 1073.
[42]   [1963] 3 All ER 770.
[43]   [1998] BCC 359.
[44]   [1980] 1 All ER 393.
[45]   [1998] BCC 359.
[46]   [1985] 1 All ER 438.
[47]   [1936] 1 All ER 597.
[48]   [1967] 2 All ER 953.

The 'unconditional' exceptions to both of the general rules

11.31 Section 681 of the CA 2006 makes it clear that ss 678–679 do not prohibit:

(a) a distribution of a company's assets by way of dividend lawfully made or a distribution made in the course of the company's winding up;

(b) the allotment of bonus shares;

(c) a reduction of capital under Chapter 10 of the CA 2006 (that is, whether confirmed by order of the court or, in the case of a private limited company, by way of a solvency statement);

(d) a redemption or purchase of shares made in accordance with Chapters 3 and 4 of the CA 2006; although this exception only covers the actual payment whereby the redemption or purchase is completed, it is considered that if the company has to borrow money for the purpose of financing the redemption or purchase, any security which it has to give in connection with that borrowing should not constitute a giving of financial assistance capable of infringing the prohibition on the giving of financial assistance, on the grounds that it is implicit that the 'person' mentioned in those subsections refers to someone other than the company (the *obiter* comment of Arden LJ in *Chaston v SWP Group Ltd* to contrary effect was explained by the Government spokesperson in the Parliamentary debate on the Bill that became the CA 2006 as not being inconsistent with the Government's view that references to a 'person' did not include the company itself (Hansard SC Deb (M) 20 July 2006 c 857));

(e) anything done in pursuance of an order of the court under Part 26 of the CA 2006 (compromises and arrangements with creditors and members);

(f) anything done under an arrangement in pursuance of s 110 of the Insolvency Act 1986 (where a liquidator in a winding up accepts shares as consideration for the disposal of property by the company being wound up); or

(g) anything done under an arrangement made between a company and its creditors which is binding on the creditors by virtue of Part I of the Insolvency Act 1986.

These exceptions are 'unconditional' and apply to all private and public companies regardless of the assisting company's net asset position. The exceptions are largely self-explanatory. However, it should be made clear that, in relation to (a), the exception for a distribution of a company's assets by way of a dividend lawfully made is confined to dividends. It does not create an exception for other distributions of the company's property that do not involve a dividend, for example the intra-group transfer of assets.

11.32 However, while this list of permitted transactions in s 681 includes matters that are expressly regulated by other statutory provisions, it is curious that it does not address the payment of a lawful commission. This appears to be little more than an omission. Section 553 of the CA 2006 expressly makes it lawful, subject to various conditions, for a company to pay a commission to any person in consideration of his subscribing or agreeing to subscribe (whether absolutely or conditionally), or procuring or agreeing to procure subscriptions (whether absolute or conditional), for any shares in the company. Otherwise, a company is prohibited from applying any of its shares or capital money either directly or indirectly in payment of any such commission (CA 2006, s 552).

The 'conditional' exceptions to both of the general rules

11.33 Financial assistance is also permitted in other circumstances, even where the primary prohibition in ss 678–679 applies.

Subject to a qualification in the case of public companies, ss 678–679 of the CA 2006 also do not prohibit:

> '(a)   where the lending of money is part of the ordinary business of the company, the lending of money by the company in the ordinary course of the company's business …' (CA 2006, s 682(2)(a))

It has been held by the Privy Council, when construing substantially the same wording in the Companies Act of New South Wales, that this para (a) can only apply where the company's business includes that of general money-lending, a key feature of that type of business being that the borrower is not normally restricted by the lender in the use to which he applies the money – otherwise, para (d) below would be otiose (*Steen v Law*[49]).

11.34

> '(b)   the provision by the company, in good faith in the interests of the company or its holding company, of financial assistance for the purposes of an employees' share scheme;
>
> (c)   the provision of financial assistance by the company for the purposes of or in connection with anything done by the company (or another company in the same group) for the purpose of enabling or facilitating transactions in shares in the first-mentioned company or its holding company between, and involving the acquisition of beneficial ownership of those shares by–,
>
> (i)   *bona fide* employees or former employees of that company (or another company in the same group); or
>
> (ii)   spouses or civil partners, widows, widowers or surviving civil partners, or minor children or step-children of any such employees or former employees;
>
> (d)   the making by the company of loans to persons (other than directors) employed in good faith by the company with a view to enabling those

---

[49]   [1963] 3 All ER 770.

persons to acquire fully paid shares in the company or its holding company to be held by them by way of beneficial ownership.' (CA 2006, s 682(2))

11.35 For the purposes of para (c) above, a company is in the same group as another company if it is a holding company or subsidiary of that company, or a subsidiary of a holding company of that company (CA 2006, s 682(5)).

11.36 The current wording of para (b) of s 682(2) allows the company not only to give financial assistance in the form of a cash contribution to the trustees of an employees' share scheme, but also to give a guarantee in respect of any borrowing made by those trustees. In order for para (b) to be capable of applying, the financial assistance must be given for the purposes of an 'employees' share scheme', which is defined by s 1166 of the CA 2006 as:

'a scheme for encouraging or facilitating the holding of shares in or debentures of a company by or for the benefit of –

(a)   the bona fide employees or former employees of –
   (i)   the company,
   (ii)   any subsidiary of the company, or
   (iii) the company's holding company or any subsidiary of the company's holding company, or
(b)   the spouses, civil partners, surviving spouses, surviving civil partners, or minor children or step-children of such employees or former employees.'

11.37 Failure to bring an employee trust within this definition will result in s 682(2)(b) not applying to prevent financial assistance given to the trustees from breaching the general prohibition. In order for an employee trust to come within the s 1166 definition, requirements to be fulfilled include the following:

(a)   the trustees must be required by the terms of the trust to apply the trust assets in acquiring shares (or debentures) in the relevant company (normally the company which set up the trust), and the trustees' powers of investment must be restricted to acquiring shares in (or debentures of) that company and building up liquid funds in preparation for making such acquisitions;

(b)   the scope of the class of eligible beneficiaries must be restricted to those mentioned in s 1166; thus sub-contractors and non-executive directors must not fall within that class, nor must the employees of any company which is not a 'subsidiary' within the meaning of s 1159 of the CA 2006, such as a company in which the voting rights are held in equal shares by two companies, neither of which has the right to appoint or remove a majority of the board of directors. It may be noted that the class of potential beneficiaries of such assistance is wider than under s 682(2)(b) and (c).

11.38 As noted the excepted transactions identified in s 682, CA 2006 are 'conditional' exceptions to the general prohibitions. Where there is an excepted transaction in s 682, neither ss 678 nor 679 prohibit the giving of financial assistance where the company giving the financial assistance is a private company. However, where the company giving the assistance is a public company, the exceptions in s 682(2) of the CA 2006 only apply if the company has 'net assets' that are not reduced by the giving of the assistance or, to the extent that those assets are so reduced, the assistance is provided out of 'distributable profits' (CA 2006, s 682(1)). 'Net assets' here means the amount by which the aggregate of the company's assets exceeds the aggregate of its 'liabilities', taking the amount of both assets and liabilities to be as stated in the company's accounting records immediately before the financial assistance is given (this requirement to look at 'book value' instead of current actual value is the distinguishing feature between this definition of 'net assets' and the one given in s 677(2) of the CA 2006 – see **11.24**). 'Liabilities' here includes any amount retained as reasonably necessary for the purpose of providing for a liability the nature of which is clearly defined and that is either likely to be incurred or certain to be incurred but uncertain as to amount or as to the date on which it will arise (CA 2006, s 682(4)). 'Distributable profits' means those profits out of which the company could lawfully make a distribution equal in value to the financial assistance; and includes, in a case where the financial assistance consists of or includes, or is treated as arising in consequence of, the sale, transfer or other disposition of a non-cash asset, any profit that, if the company were to make a distribution of that character, would be available for that purpose under s 846 of the CA 2006 (distributions in kind) (CA 2006, s 683(1)).

Exception relating to a present or future acquisition

11.39 Sections 678 and 679 contain exceptions where the giving of financial assistance in circumstances where the assistance with the acquisition is not the sole purpose for which the assistance is given. Accordingly, neither s 678 nor s 679 prohibit a company, otherwise subject to those provisions, from giving financial assistance for the purpose of an acquisition of shares in it or its holding company if:

(a) the company's principal purpose in giving that assistance is not to give it for the purpose of any such acquisition, or

(b) the giving of the assistance for that purpose is only an incidental part of some larger purpose of the company; and

(c) the assistance is given in good faith in the interests of the company (CA 2006, ss 678(2) and 679(2)).

Exception relating to a past acquisition

11.40 Sections 678 and 679 also do not prohibit the giving of financial assistance in relation to a past acquisition if:

(a) the company's principal purpose in giving the assistance is not to 'reduce or discharge' any 'liability incurred' by a person for the purpose of the acquisition of shares in the company or its holding company, or

(b) the reduction or discharge of any such liability is only an incidental part of some larger purpose of the company; and

(c) the assistance is given in good faith in the interests of the company (CA 2006, ss 678(4) and 679(4)).

In (a) above, the words 'reduce or discharge' and 'liability incurred' have the same extended meanings given to them for the purposes of ss 678(3) and 679(3) of the CA 2006 (see **11.11**).

11.41 The following points emerge from the House of Lords' decision in *Brady v Brady*,[50] a case concerning s 153(2) of the CA 1985, which contained a general prohibition on the giving of financial assistance after the acquisition of shares.

1. In the *Brady* case itself, there was a scheme to place various companies into two groups in order that each of two warring factions of a family could end up with a separate business and go its own way. Part of the scheme involved the making of certain transfers of assets between one of the groups of companies to the other, in order to discharge loan stock which, as part of the consideration for the acquisition of another company's shares, had been issued previously by the company which was to receive the assets and for the purpose of equalising the values of the two groups of companies. The companies transferring the assets would become creditors in respect of the value of those assets. It was held that para (a) of what is now addressed by ss 678(3) and 679(3) was clearly inapplicable. It was also held that para (b) was inapplicable, the reasoning being expressed as follows:

    'My Lords, I confess that I have not found the concept of a "larger purpose" easy to grasp, but if the paragraph is to be given any meaning that does not in effect provide a blank cheque for avoiding the effective application of [the prohibition] in every case, the concept must be narrower than that for which the appellants contend. The matter can, perhaps, most easily be tested by reference to [what are now ss 678(2)(a)–(b) and 679(2)(a)–(b)], where the same formula is used. Here the words are "or the giving of the assistance for that purpose [i.e. the acquisition of shares] is ... an incidental part of some larger purpose of the company". The words "larger purpose" must here have the same meaning as the same words in [what are now ss 678(4)(a)–(b) and 679(4)(a)–(b)]. In applying [ss 678(2)(a)–(b) and 679(2)(a)–(b)] one has, therefore, to look for some larger purpose in the giving of financial assistance than the mere purpose of the acquisition of the shares and to ask whether the giving of assistance is a mere incident of that purpose. My

---

[50] [1998] 2 All ER 617.

Lords, "purpose" is, in some contexts, a word of wide content, but in construing it in the context of the fasciculus of sections regulating the provision of finance by a company in connection with the purchase of its own shares there has always to be borne in mind the mischief against which [the prohibition on financial assistance] is aimed. In particular, if the section is not, effectively, to be deprived of any useful application, it is important to distinguish between a purpose and the reason why a purpose is formed. The ultimate reason for forming the purpose of financing an acquisition may, and in most cases probably will, be more important to those making the decision than the immediate transaction itself. But "larger" is not the same thing as "more important" nor is "reason" the same as "purpose". If one postulates the case of a bidder for control of a public company financing his bid from the company's own funds, the obvious mischief at which the section is aimed, the immediate purpose which it is sought to achieve is that of completing the purchase and vesting control of the company in the bidder. The reasons why that course is considered desirable may be many and varied. The company may have fallen on hard times so that a change of management is considered necessary to avert disaster. It may merely be thought, and no doubt would be thought by the purchaser and the directors whom he nominates once he has control, that the business of the company will be more profitable under his management than it was heretofore. These may be excellent reasons but they cannot, in my judgment, constitute a "larger purpose" of which the provision of assistance is merely an incident. The purpose and the only purpose of the financial assistance is and remains that of enabling the shares to be acquired, and the financial or commercial advantages flowing from the acquisition, whilst they may form the reason for forming the purpose of providing assistance, are a by-product of it rather than an independent purpose of which the assistance can be considered to be an incident.' (*per* Lord Oliver at 633e)

'I do not think that a larger purpose can be found in the benefits considered to be likely to flow or the disadvantages considered to be likely to be avoided by the acquisition which it was the purpose of the assistance to facilitate. The acquisition was not a mere incident of the scheme devised to break the deadlock. It was the essence of the scheme itself and the object which the scheme set out to achieve.' (*per* Lord Oliver at 634c)

2.   With regard to the requirement now to be found in ss 678(4) and 679(4), it was held that the words 'in good faith in the interests of the company' form a single composite expression and postulate a requirement that those responsible for procuring the company to provide the assistance act in the genuine belief that it is being done in the company's interest (at 632b).

11.42 The outcome of the House of Lords' decision in *Brady v Brady*[51] was that even though the requirement that the assistance be given in good faith in the interests of the company was made out, the need for a recognisable larger purpose of the company to which purpose the financial assistance was incidental was not satisfied, and therefore the exemption could not apply. Nevertheless, given the terms of the legislation as it then stood, it was possible

---

[51]   [1998] 2 All ER 617.

to follow the 'whitewash' provisions then in force in ss 155–158, CA 1985 and thereby avoid the provision of unlawful financial assistance.

11.43   *Plaut v Steiner*[52] was a similar case to *Brady* in that it involved an action for specific performance of an agreement designed to divide up between two family factions a closely integrated business in which four companies were involved and which operated from two different addresses. Included in the terms of the agreement between the family members were provisions whereby two of the companies would, for no consideration, make certain payments, undertake certain liabilities, and give a charge over one of the properties to secure the same, all for the purpose of achieving equality of value between the two groups. Morritt J had no difficulty in finding that these terms would constitute the provision of financial assistance within what are now s 677(1)(a), (b) and (d), it being quite clear that neither side had considered the proposals from the point of view of the individual companies. He held that none of the possible exceptions to the general prohibition applied.

(a)   The financial assistance was plainly being given for the purpose of the acquisition of the shares, and that the giving of the financial assistance could not be seen as a merely incidental part of a larger purpose of effecting the division of the business.

(b)   Although this was not strictly necessary to the decision, he held that the requirement that any financial assistance be given in good faith in the interests of the company was also not applicable. One of the two companies was a trading company and would have become insolvent if it had given the financial assistance required by the agreement. The other company, which held a valuable property, would have had to discharge the trading company's share of the liabilities resulting from the giving of the financial assistance, and because the management deadlock affected the trading companies but not the property company, no reasonable board of directors of the property company could have properly concluded that it would be in the interests of that company to give the financial assistance.

The result was that the agreement infringed the prohibition and was unenforceable.

11.44   The full practical scope of ss 678(2)–(4) and 679(2)–(4) is therefore uncertain. In *Brady v Brady*,[53] it was suggested that the likely purpose for introducing the materially identical provisions of the CA 1985 was to dispel any doubts resulting from the query raised in *Belmont Finance Corp Ltd v Williams Furniture Ltd (No 2)*[54] as to whether a transaction entered into partly with a genuine view to the commercial interests of the company and partly with a view to putting a purchaser of shares in the company in funds to complete his purchase was in breach of s 54 of the CA 1948. Such a transaction would,

---

[52]   (1989) 5 BCC 352.
[53]   [1998] 2 All ER 617 at 632h.
[54]   [1980] 1 All ER 393.

however, only constitute the giving of financial assistance if the company has no net assets (see **11.24**), and in such a case it should satisfy para (a) of ss 678(4) or 679(4), as the purpose of giving the financial assistance would not be the *principal* purpose of the transaction; and the requirement that the assistance be given in good faith in the interests of the company would be satisfied if the transaction were in the commercial interests of the company.

11.45   A different situation to which ss 678(4) and 679(4) of the CA 2006 might apply is where a company's articles of association provide that shares must normally be transferred at a price which is determined by a valuation expert, whose fees for making the valuation are to be paid by the company. An illustration of this type of provision is at para (G) of the transfer clause set out at **9.7**. A payment of fees by the company in accordance with such a provision will normally be made after the transfer of the shares has taken place and will not 'reduce or discharge' any 'liability incurred' by a person for the purpose of the relevant share acquisition, and the payment should also clearly satisfy the requirement that it be given in good faith in the interests of the company (see **11.40**). In the absence of ss 678(4) and 679(4), such a payment could (depending on the facts) constitute the giving of financial assistance within s 677(1)(d) (see **11.24**).

Chapter 12

TAX: 'DISTRIBUTION' TREATMENT

12.1 This chapter looks at the ways in which, leaving aside the provisions originally introduced in the FA 1982 and now to be found in ss 1033–1048 of the Corporation Tax Act 2010 (CTA 2010), own share purchases, and redemptions of redeemable shares, may give rise to taxable 'distributions' for income and corporation tax purposes, and what the tax consequences of such distributions may be. These may be regarded as the 'normal' income and corporation tax consequences, in contrast to the consequences where the special rules for capital treatment in ss 1033–1048 apply (those sections are analysed in Chapter 13).

OWN SHARE PURCHASES

12.2 In cases where s 1033 of the CTA 2010 does not apply, the tax consequences of a company purchasing its own shares are determined as follows.

The proceeds of sale must be divided into two parts, a capital element and a distribution element.

(a) The capital element is the part (if any) which represents whatever amount or value was received by the company upon the issue of the shares in question; this part will be equal to nil if the shares are identified as having originally been issued as fully paid bonus shares. This part is always treated as capital for tax purposes (TCGA 1992, s 122). The value of this part may need to be agreed with HM Revenue & Customs.

(b) Once the capital element has been determined, the balance is the distribution element. This part will be treated as an income distribution for tax purposes (CTA 2010, ss 1000(1)B and 1115(4), (6)); see below for the tax treatment of this element.

For example, if the 1000 ordinary shares of £1 each which a company is purchasing for £5000 were originally issued by the company for cash at par, £1000 of the proceeds will be treated as capital for tax purposes in any event, and the remaining £4000 will be taxed as a distribution unless s 1033 applies.

12.3 This result follows from the complex statutory provisions which define the word 'distribution'. The starting point is s 1000 of the CTA 2010, which reads (in part) as follows:

'In the Corporation Tax Acts "distribution", in relation to any company, means anything falling within any of the following paragraphs.

A   Any dividend paid by the company, including a capital dividend;
B   Any other distribution out of assets of the company in respect of shares in the company, except however much (if any) of the distribution—
      (a)   represents repayment of capital on the shares, or
      (b)   is (when it is made) equal in amount or value to any new consideration received by the company for the distribution.

For the purposes of this paragraph it does not matter whether the distribution is in cash or not.'

12.4 Accordingly, the distribution element of the payment made by the company for the purchase of its own shares will comprise a 'distribution' unless, and to the extent that, new consideration is received by the company in respect of the payment.

12.5 One next has to consider what 'new consideration' the company has received. If the purchase price which the company pays for its shares does not exceed the current market value of those shares, the conclusion would be that, if s 1000(1)B could be construed on its own, the entire purchase price would fall outside the scope of a 'distribution', on the basis that the company 'receives' the shares in itself which it is buying and this could be regarded as consideration; even where a company chooses to cancel the acquired shares under s 729 of the CA 2006 (see **6.42** et seq), it is only once the own share purchase has been completed that shares will be cancelled so the company will receive and hold the shares for at least a short period of time.

However, s 1000(1)B has to be construed subject to s 1115(4)–(6) of the CTA 2010, which applies to an acquisition by a company of its own shares. These sub-sections could allow cancellation of share capital to be regarded as consideration, but only to the extent of the new consideration (if any) received by the company when those shares were first issued. Such new consideration has, however, already been taken into account in establishing the element that is repayment of capital and so is not taken into account again.

12.6 The last-mentioned consequences flow from the terms of s 1115(4)–(6) of the CTA 2010, which, where relevant, reads as follows:

'(4)   The general rule is that no consideration derived from the value of any share capital or security of a company, or from voting or other rights in a company, is to be treated for the purposes of this Part as new consideration.
(5)   The general rule in subsection (4) applies unless the consideration consists of—

(a)   ...
(b)   money received from the company as a payment which for the purposes of this Part constitutes a repayment of the share capital in question ... or
(c)   the giving up of the right to the share capital ... on its cancellation, extinguishment or acquisition by the company.

This is subject to subsection (6).

(6)   No amount is regarded as new consideration by virtue of subsection (5)(b) or (c) so far as it exceeds—
(a)   any new consideration received by the company for the issue of the share capital ... in question, or
(b)   in the case of share capital which constituted a qualifying distribution on issue, the nominal value of that share capital.'

SHARE EXCHANGES

12.7 If company A acquires the issued share capital in company B in exchange for an issue of shares in company A to the shareholders of company B, it is very desirable to record the actual value of the shares in company B which company A is receiving as consideration for an issue of its own shares.

If the value of company B is greater than the nominal value of the shares issued by company A, those shares will be issued at a premium, and the premium should be recorded in the register of members and also on the Form 88(2) submitted to Companies House, even if the directors intend to rely on s 641 of the CA 2006 for the purpose of not recognising that share premium in any share premium account. Although accounts which rely on s 641 are not thereby prevented from showing a 'true and fair' view of the company's share capital, the lack of any share premium account reflecting the premium for which the shares were issued may result in the accounts presenting a view of the share capital which is misleading in relation to any future own share purchase of those shares.

The income element of the proceeds of sale of such an own share purchase is determined by deducting the premium for which the shares were originally issued, even if the accounts fail to reflect the existence of that premium. The greater the premium, the greater the potential significance of this point.

REDEMPTIONS OF REDEEMABLE SHARES

12.8 In cases where s 1033 of the CTA 2010 does not apply, the normal tax consequences (see **12.10** for 'abnormal' consequences) of a company redeeming its own redeemable shares are that such part of the redemption money as exceeds the amount paid up on the shares is a taxable 'distribution', creating a liability to income tax for the shareholder who is an individual (CTA 2010, s 1000(1)B; see **12.3**).

This is on the basis that the redemption moneys can be treated as including a 'repayment of share capital' within the ordinary meaning of that expression; it is submitted that they can, on the ground that a key feature of a redeemable share is that the terms of its existence include a term that the company is or may become liable to redeem the share before the commencement of the company's winding up. Therefore, just as in a winding up there can be said to occur a 'repayment' of the capital originally subscribed for an irredeemable share (because it is a term of the existence of the share that this should happen if there is a surplus of assets over liabilities in the winding up), so too one can say that a 'repayment' of capital occurs when, in accordance with the terms of a redeemable share's existence, the company redeems it.

The 'repayment of capital' must be limited to whatever amount was originally paid to the company upon the issue of the share. This inherent limitation is re-stated (presumably, for the avoidance of doubt) by s 1024 of the CTA 2010; this provides that premiums paid on a redemption of share capital are not to be treated as repayments of capital, except and to the extent that the shares themselves were issued at a premium representing new consideration. Section 1024 thereby recognises that a repayment of capital may occur on a redemption of redeemable shares.

12.9   Looking at the rest of the wording of s 1000(1)B, it is considered that the company does not 'receive' anything when its redeemable shares are redeemed, as the act of redemption terminates the right of the shares to exist in accordance with the terms of that existence. Hence, the final words of s 1000(1)B cannot apply.

12.10   The 'abnormal' tax consequences, referred to at **12.8**, of a redemption of redeemable shares (in a case where s 1033 of the CTA 2010 does not apply) arise where the company has previously issued bonus shares and s 1026 of the CTA 2010 applies (see **12.12**). Where s 1026 applies, the redemption of the redeemable shares will not be treated as giving rise to any repayment of capital except to the extent that the amount which would ordinarily have been a repayment of capital exceeds the amount paid up on the previously issued bonus shares (to the extent that that amount has not given rise to similar deemed 'distributions' in the past).

BONUS ISSUES AND REDEEMABLE SHARES

12.11   An issue of bonus redeemable shares is itself a taxable distribution under s 1000(1)C of the CTA 2010, albeit not a 'qualifying distribution' (CTA 2010, s 1136(1)(a)).

12.12   Sections 1026–1027 of the CTA 2010 provides that where:

(a)   a company issues any share capital as paid up otherwise than by the receipt of new consideration (ie the company issues bonus shares), and

(b) any amount so paid up does not fall to be treated as a qualifying distribution,

then the general rule is that distributions afterwards made by the company in respect of shares representing that share capital are not to be treated as repayments of share capital (and thus outside the scope of being a distribution) for the purposes of s 1000 of the CTA 2010, except to the extent to which those distributions, together with any previous distributions that have been treated in the same way, exceed the amounts so paid up (then or previously) on such shares and not falling to be treated as qualifying distributions (CTA 2010, s 1027). This is an anti-avoidance measure, to prevent a company from returning cash to shareholders without an overall reduction in their shareholdings.

For these purposes, all shares of the same class are to be treated as representing the same share capital; and where shares are issued in respect of other shares, or are directly or indirectly converted into or exchanged for other shares, all such shares are also to be treated as representing the same share capital (CTA 2010, s 1026(4)).

Example

An individual holding 1,000 ordinary shares of £1 each in X Ltd receives 100 more of those shares as bonus shares. Subsequently, as part of a reduction of capital, this shareholder receives £300. The first £100 of that £300 will be denied by s 1026 and s 1027 the status of a 'repayment of share capital', and hence will be taxable as a distribution. The result would have been the same even if the bonus shares had been preference shares, issued in respect of his ordinary shares.

12.13 There are two exceptions to the general rule laid down by s 1026 of the CTA 2010.

(a) In the case of a company which is not a relevant company (s 739 of the CTA 2010; broadly, a relevant company is a non-close publicly listed company), s 1026 does not prevent a distribution from being a repayment of capital if that distribution is made:

   (i) more than 10 years after the bonus shares were issued, and
   (ii) in respect of share capital other than redeemable share capital (CTA 2010, s 1026(3)(b)).

(b) Where share capital is issued at a premium representing new consideration, and bonus shares are later issued by capitalising the share premium account, and later still a repayment of capital occurs, those bonus shares are to be treated as having been paid up by the receipt of new consideration to the extent that they have been paid up out of the share premium account (CTA 2010, s 1025).

Subsequent bonus issue

12.14 Section 1022 of the CTA 2010 applies where there is a bonus issue taking place after the completion of the own share purchase, such that the amount of the subsequent bonus issue is treated as a distribution for tax purposes, to the extent that the amount of that bonus issue does not exceed the amount of the capital element of the preceding share purchase (and after deducting the total amount of any previous bonus issue treated as a distribution by virtue of that same own share purchase). As with s 1026, this is intended as an anti-avoidance measure, to prevent companies from effectively returning cash to shareholders without an overall reduction in their shareholdings.

Similarly to s 1026 of the CTA 2010, there are two exceptions:

(1) Where the shares purchased consist of fully paid 'preference shares' and those shares existed as issued and fully paid preference shares, issued for new consideration not derived from ordinary shares, and throughout the period from their issue until the purchase those shares continued to be fully paid preference shares (s 1023(3)). For these purposes, the following definitions apply (CTA 2010, s 1023(4), (5)):

> '"preference shares" means shares:
>
> (a) which do not carry any right to dividends other than dividends at a rate per cent of the nominal value of the shares which is fixed, and
> (b) which carry rights in respect of dividends and capital which are comparable with those general for fixed-dividend shares listed in the official UK list;
>
> "ordinary shares" means shares other than "preference shares";
>
> "new consideration not derived from ordinary shares" means new consideration other than consideration:
>
> (a) consisting of the surrender, transfer or cancellation of ordinary shares of the company or any other company or consisting of the variation of rights in ordinary shares of the company or any other company, or
> (b) derived from a repayment of share capital paid in respect of ordinary shares of the company or of any other company.'

(2) Where, except in the case of a non-relevant company (see **12.8** above), the bonus shares:

(a) are not of redeemable share capital; and
(b) are issued more than ten years after the 'repayment of share capital' in question (CTA 2010, s 1023(1), (2)).

12.15 Where a company has implemented an own share purchase and later wishes to make a bonus issue, a way of avoiding the area of difficulty would be for a new holding company to be set up and for it to issue shares in itself in exchange for the shares in the original company. The new holding company should then (once the reserves of its subsidiary have been distributed up to it) be able to make a bonus issue without fear of s 1022 of the CTA 2010, as the holding company will never have engaged in any transaction which could be alleged to have constituted a 'repayment of capital'.

Clearance should, however, be sought as to whether this would be challenged under the "transaction in securities" legislation in Chapter 1 of Part 13 of ITA 2007 and Part 15 of the CTA 2010, as HMRC could issue a tax assessment to counter any tax advantage obtained by a shareholder as a result of the interposition of the holding company.

TAX CONSEQUENCES OF A DISTRIBUTION

Individuals

12.16   A recipient of the distribution who is an individual will be chargeable to income tax on it. For these purposes, the distribution carries with it a tax credit equal to one-ninth of the distribution, which must be grossed up by the amount of that tax credit. If the amount of the grossed up distribution, when added to the recipient's other income and after deducting his personal allowances, does not exceed the basic rate limit (£32,010 for 2013/14), he will not be liable to any further tax in respect of the distribution – the tax credit is available as an offset against tax otherwise payable, though can never itself be converted into a cash payment from the Treasury. But if and to the extent that the grossed up distribution, when considered as the top slice of the recipient's income, is above the basic rate limit but below the higher rate limit (£150,000 for 2013/14), he will be liable to income tax on it at the dividend higher rate (32.5%), but with the benefit of the tax credit – the net result being income tax at an effective rate of 25% of the actual distribution. If and to the extent that the grossed up distribution, when considered as the top slice of the recipient's income, is above the higher rate limit then he will be liable to income tax on it at the dividend additional rate (37.5% for 2013/14), also with the benefit of the tax credit, so that the net result is income tax at an effective rate of 30.56% (for 2013/14) of the actual distribution.

Example

An individual is treated as receiving a distribution of £4,900 out of the proceeds of an own share purchase in May 2013. His other income on its own is sufficient to make him liable to the higher rate of income tax but not the additional rate of income tax. His income tax liability in respect of the distribution of £4,900 is as follows:

Distribution	£4,900
Tax credit @ 1/9	£544

Taxable @ 32.5%	£5,444
Tax @ 32.5% =	£1,769
Less: tax credit	(£544)
Tax payable	£1,255

which also equals 25% of £4,900

Companies

12.25   Where the recipient of the distribution is a UK-resident company, that company's main potential tax liability on it will be to corporation tax on chargeable gains, subject to the availability of the substantial shareholdings exemption (see **18.4**). However, the distribution plus tax credit also fall within the definition of 'franked investment income' (CTA 2010, s 1126), the role of which these days is limited to the calculation of eligibility for 'small companies' relief (CTA 2010, s 32) and the calculation of so-called 'shadow ACT' under the Corporation Tax (Treatment of Unrelieved Surplus Advance Corporation Tax) Regulations 1999, SI 1999/1358. Either of these provisions is capable of causing the receipt of the distribution to affect the amount of corporation tax which the company eventually has to pay on its profits.

Trustees

12.18   The income element of the proceeds of an own share purchase is treated in the hands of trustees of discretionary trusts as income to which s 481 of the Income Tax Act 2007 (ITA 2007) applies (ITA 2007, s 482 – Type 1). The income element is grossed up with a non-payable tax credit of one-ninth and is chargeable to income tax at the dividend trust rate (37.5% for the year 2013/14.

Example

In May 2013, a company makes an own share purchase from trustees of a discretionary trust. The trustees sell for £9,000 shares which were originally issued by the company for £1,000. There therefore arises a taxable distribution of £8,000, carrying a tax credit of one-ninth (£888.89). The trustees are liable for tax as follows:

Distribution	£8,000.00
Tax credit @ 1/9	£888.89
Income taxable @ 37.5%	£8,888.89
On which tax @ 37.5% =	3,333.33
Less: tax credit	(£888.89)
Income tax payable	£2,444.44

representing 30.56% of the distribution element actually received by the trustees.

12.20 By way of exception to the above-stated general rule, this s 481 treatment does not apply:

(a)   if the trustees are trustees of a unit trust scheme;

(b)   to trustees of a charitable trust.

'Trustees' does not include personal representatives (ITA 2007, s 463).

12.28 It is considered that no charge to income tax can be levied on the life tenant of an interest in possession trust as a result of an own share purchase, as the shares sold by the trustees will almost always be treated as part of the capital of the trust fund, to which the life tenant has no entitlement as a matter of trust law.

Chapter 13

PURCHASES FOR THE BENEFIT OF THE TRADE

13.1 Section 1033 of the CTA 2010 seeks to provide two alternative exemptions from being treated as a taxable 'distribution' in favour of a payment made by a company for the purchase, redemption or repayment of any of its own shares (see Chapter 12). The first of these exemptions is considered in this chapter, the second in Chapter 14. Although the original enactment of this section was intended as a relied, s 1033 can in some cases be a potential trap for the unwary, possibly resulting in more tax being payable where it applies than where it does not apply.

13.2 Section 1033(1) of the CTA 2010 provides that references in the Corporation Tax Acts to taxable 'distributions' of a company do not include references to a payment made by a company on the redemption, repayment or purchase of its own shares if the company is an unquoted trading company, or the unquoted holding company of a trading group and one of two conditions (A, dealt with in this chapter, or B, dealt with in chapter 14) are fulfilled. For this purpose, the word 'payment' includes anything else that is (or would but for s 1033 be) a taxable 'distribution' (CTA 2010, s 1033(6)). There are limited exclusions to the conditions, discussed at **13.70**.

13.3 In ss 1033–1047, the word 'shares' includes stock, and an 'owner' of shares means the beneficial owner except where the shares are held on trusts (other than bare trusts), or are comprised in the estate of a deceased person, in which case the 'owners' of the shares are the trustees or the deceased's personal representatives (CTA 2010, s 1048(1)–(3)). The word 'tax' in s 1033 means 'income tax' or 'corporation tax' (CTA 2010, s 1119).

UNQUOTED COMPANY

13.4 The company must be an 'unquoted company', and either a 'trading company' or the 'holding company' of a 'trading group' (CTA 2010, s 1033(1)(a)).

13.5 An 'unquoted company' is defined to mean a company which is neither a quoted company nor a 51% subsidiary of a quoted company. A 'quoted company' means a company whose shares (or any class of whose shares) are listed in the official list of a stock exchange (CTA 2010, s 1048(1)); it does not include a company whose shares are merely dealt in on the Alternative

Investment Market (HMRC Corporation Tax Manual CTM17507). If a company with several classes of shares merely has one of them listed, the company will be a 'quoted company' in relation to all its classes of shares. The term '51% subsidiary' has its normal CTA 2010, s 1154 meaning.

13.6 A 'trading company' is defined to mean a company whose business consists wholly or mainly of the carrying on of a trade or trades. The trades of dealing in shares, securities, land or futures do not constitute 'trades' for these purposes (CTA 2010, s 1048(1)). HMRC appear to decide whether a business consists "wholly or mainly" of carrying on a trade by reference to whether the majority (over half) of the company's activities are trading activities. HMRC will take into account the totality of the activities of the business – the capital employed in the business, the income generated by the activities, the split of management time (HMRC Share Valuation Manual SVM111150, in the context of whether a business consists wholly or mainly trading activities for IHT purposes, but the principle remains the same). This view accords with the interpretation placed on the word 'mainly' in *FPH Finance Trust Ltd v IRC*,[1] where it was held to mean 'more than half' (per Viscount Maugham at 149, in the context of measuring a company's investment income), and the decision in *Farmer v IRC*,[2] where the Special Commissioner said it was '… necessary to stand back and consider in the round whether the business consisted mainly of making or holding investments' rather than trading activities. In one case, HMRC refused an application for clearance in relation to a company which had been carrying on a farming trade at a loss and which had farming assets of about £100,000 and cash of about £180,000 invested in building society deposits.

13.7 A 'trading group' is defined to mean a group the business of whose members, taken together, consists wholly or mainly of the carrying on of a trade or trades, and for this purpose 'group' means a company which has one or more 75% subsidiaries together with those subsidiaries. A 'holding company' means a company whose business (disregarding any trade carried on by it) consists wholly or mainly of the holding of shares or securities of one or more companies which are its 75% subsidiaries (CTA 2010, s 1048(1)). The term '75% subsidiary' has its normal CTA 2010, s 1154 meaning.

Condition A

Requirement for trade benefit

13.8 Condition A is that:

(a) the redemption, repayment or purchase is made wholly or mainly for the purpose of benefiting a trade carried on by the company or any of its 75% subsidiaries;

---

[1] (1944) 26 TC 131.
[2] (1999) SpC 216.

(b) the redemption, repayment or purchase does not form part of a scheme or arrangement the main purpose or one of the main purposes of which is:

    (i) to enable the owner of the shares to participate in the profits of the company without receiving a dividend; or

    (ii) the avoidance of tax; and

(c) the requirements set out in ss 1034–1043 (so far as applicable) are met.

13.9 In this Condition A, there are three separate, though closely allied, hurdles to be overcome together with the further requirements referred to in s 1033(2)(c). The purpose of the transaction must encompass:

(a) the benefit of a trade carried on by the company or by any of its 75% subsidiaries;

(b) a lack of intent by the owner of shares to participate in profits without receiving a dividend; and

(c) a lack of intent to avoid tax.

It seems that (b) and (c) overlap to a great extent, as it is difficult to see why anyone should wish to participate in the profits of a company without receiving a dividend unless he also intends to avoid tax. However, (c) seems to be wider than (b), as under (b) the person whose state of mind is relevant is the owner of the shares which the company is to buy, whereas under (c) it seems that the relevant states of mind include also those of the shareholders and directors whose votes bring about the passing of the necessary resolutions.

13.10 Nevertheless, if the company's history shows the accumulation of retained profits within the company, then HMRC are unlikely to agree that (b) is satisfied, and the payment would be treated as a distribution with a corresponding income tax charge and any entitlement to entrepreneur's relief lost.

13.11 However, if the circumstances of the case are such that there is tax which could be avoided, and yet there is no intent to avoid tax, the doing of the transaction for the benefit of the trade is only one of several conceivable alternative motives for the operation. Another alternative is that it is being done for the personal benefit of the person whose shares are being bought – e g if he were in urgent need of cash.

13.12 The requirement for a trade to be benefited (a) seems to be the most problematical of the three. It requires the taxpayer to prove something positive, whereas (b) and (c) require him to prove two negatives. The legislation does not elaborate on what is meant by benefiting a trade; but it is considered that this makes it necessary to show that the transaction is likely, in the short or long term, to improve the financial performance of the company as a trader.

13.13 Whether or not a purchase satisfies this trade benefit condition is a question of fact, to be determined by agreement with HMRC (or if necessary by an appeal to the Tax Tribunal). The relevant facts must be proved by evidence. The fulfilment of the trade benefit condition cannot be proved merely by the seller of the shares making a bald assertion to that effect (as was attempted by the taxpayer conducting his own case in *Moody v Tyler*,[3] whose appeal against the General Commissioners' findings was described by the judge as 'hopeless').

The relief is primarily intended to apply where shares are bought back from shareholders who want to retire or otherwise leave the business, or to deal with dissenting shareholder in a boardroom disputes, and buying out external investors (HMRC Statement of Practice 2/82, see **13.14** below). Where a shareholder sells all his shares back to the company, HMRC usually regard the purchase by the company as being for the benefit of the company's trade.

Nevertheless, the trade benefit of even a sale of an entire interest needs to be considered, particularly where the shareholders are retiring and own substantially all of the business. In *Allum and anor v Marsh*,[4] the taxpayers sold their entire interest in the company on retirement – all the shares of the company except one. To be able to fund the purchase (and repay the loans outstanding to the taxpayers), the company sold the property from which it traded. Without the loans, and the taxpayers' services, the company was unable to locate suitable alternative premises. As a result, the court held that the arrangements had not benefited the company's trade and so the company purchase of the shares was treated as a distribution.

13.14 If the trade benefit requirement were to be interpreted and applied by HMRC in a strict manner, relatively few share purchases might come within s 1033. However, experience indicates that HMRC apply this test less strictly than they might. An indication of HMRC's interpretation may be gleaned from paras 1–3 of their Statement of Practice No 2/82 (as amended):

> '1. The Company's sole or main purpose in making the payment must be to benefit a trade carried on by it or by its 75% subsidiary. The condition is not satisfied where, for example, the transaction is designed to serve the personal or wider commercial interests of the vending shareholder (although usually he will benefit from it) or where the intended benefit for the company is to some non-trading activity which it also carries on.

> 2. If there is a disagreement between the shareholders over the management of the company and that disagreement is having or is expected to have an adverse effect on the company's trade, then the purchase will be regarded as satisfying the trade benefit test provided the effect of the transaction is to remove the dissenting shareholder entirely. Similarly, if the purpose is to ensure that an unwilling shareholder who wishes to end his association with the company does not sell his

---

³　　[2000] STC 296.
⁴　　[2005] STC (SCD) 191.

shares to someone who might not be acceptable to the other shareholders, the purchase will normally be regarded as benefiting the company's trade.

Examples of unwilling shareholders are:

* an outside shareholder who has provided equity finance (whether or not with the expectation of redemption or sale to the company) and who now wishes to withdraw that finance;

* a controlling shareholder who is retiring as a director and wishes to make way for new management;

* personal representatives of a deceased shareholder, where they wish to realise the value of the shares;

* a legatee of a deceased shareholder, where he does not wish to hold shares in the company.

If the company is not buying all the shares owned by the seller or if although the seller is selling all his shares he is retaining some other connection with the company – for example, a directorship or an appointment as consultant – it would seem unlikely that the transaction could benefit the company's trade, so the trade benefit test will probably not be satisfied. However, there are exceptions; for example, where a company does not currently have the resources to buy out its retiring controlling shareholder completely but purchases as many of his shares as it can afford with the intention of buying the remainder where possible. In these circumstances, it may still be possible for the company to show that the main purpose is to benefit its trade. Also, the Board do not raise any objection if for sentimental reasons it is desired that a retiring director of a company should retain a small shareholding in it, not exceeding 5% of the issued share capital.'

Further requirements for Condition A (ss 1034–1043)

Requirements as to seller residence (s 1034)

13.15 The seller must be resident (and ordinarily resident, prior to the abolition of the ordinary residence concept in Finance Act 2013 anticipated at the time of writing) in the UK in the year of assessment in which the purchase is made. If the shares are held through a nominee, the nominee must also be so resident and ordinarily resident (CTA 2010, s 1034).

13.16 Where the sellers are trustees, their residence will be determined by the general trustee residence rules in s 475 of the ITA 2007. Trustees are considered resident and ordinary resident in the UK at any time when either:

(a) all the trustees are resident in the UK; or

(b) at least one trustee is resident in the UK and one is not UK resident, and the settlor was resident, ordinarily resident or domiciled in the UK when the settlement was made.

Before 6 April 2007, trustees were generally regarded as resident and ordinarily resident in the UK unless:

(a) the administration of the trust was carried on outside the UK; and

(b) the majority of the trustees were not UK resident or ordinarily resident.

A trustee who is not resident in the UK will be treated as resident for tax purposes at any time when he acts as trustee in the course of a business which he carries on in the UK through a branch, agency or permanent establishment (ITA 2007, s 475(6)).

13.17 When considering residence for buyback purposes, the residence (and ordinary residence, prior to abolition of the concept) of personal representatives is the same as that of the deceased immediately before his death (CTA 2010, s 1034(3)).

13.18 Apart from the provisions in the two immediately preceding paragraphs, the general law applies as to what constitutes residence (and ordinary residence, prior to abolition of the concept) (e g *Lysaght v IRC*;[5] *Miesegaes v IRC*[6]). In the case of a company, the references to 'ordinary' residence have always been disregarded (CTA 2010, s 1034(4)). A company incorporated within the UK is tax resident in the UK, under s 14 of the CTA 2009, unless this residence status is overridden by provisions in a tax treaty.

13.19 In ss 1034–1043 of the CTA 2010, the term 'seller' means the owner of the shares at the time the redemption, repayment or purchase is made (s 1033(5) of the CTA 2010).

13.20 It is thought that the reason for the exclusion of non-resident sellers from the scope of s 1033 is due partly to HMRC's fear that they would have difficulty in verifying the beneficial ownership of shares held by non-residents, and partly to the fact that a person who is not resident (or was not ordinarily resident) in the UK is not liable to capital gains tax (TCGA 1992, s 2(1)). If legislation did not exclude non-residents from the scope of s 1033, they would (assuming s 1033 would then apply) be liable to neither income tax nor capital gains tax in respect of the profit on the sale.

---

[5] (1928) 13 TC 511.
[6] (1957) 37 TC 493.

Requirement as to the period of ownership (s 1035)

13.21   The shares must have been owned by the seller throughout the period of five years ending with the date of the purchase (CTA 2010, s 1035(1)) (for the meaning of the word 'own', see **13.3**). The strictness of this 'five-year' condition is relaxed in the following four ways:

Spouses

13.22   If at any time during the five-year period the shares were transferred to the seller by a person who was then his spouse (or civil partner) living with him, the shares are treated as having been owned by the seller for any period of time during which they were in fact owned by his spouse (or civil partner), unless that person is alive at the date of the purchase but is no longer the seller's spouse (or civil partner) living with him (CTA 2010, s 1036). The ordinary case where this provision will apply will be where the seller and his spouse (or civil partner) have at all material times been living together.

13.23   Section 1011 of the ITA 2007 provides that married persons or civil partners are to be treated for income tax purposes as living together, unless they are separated:

(a)   under an order of a court of competent jurisdiction; or

(b)   by deed of separation; or

(c)   they are in fact separated in such circumstances that the separation is likely to be permanent.

Deceased persons

13.24   If the seller comes to own the shares by virtue either of being a personal representative of a deceased person or of being a beneficiary under a will or on an intestacy, the five-year minimum period of ownership is reduced to three, and any period of ownership by the deceased (and, where the seller is a beneficiary, by the personal representatives) is treated as a period of ownership by the seller (CTA 2010, s 1036(3)).

13.25   The two preceding relaxations are not cumulative, as they each only apply in relation to the seller. So if, for example, within the five-year period the seller receives a transfer of the shares from his wife, who in turn had inherited them (also within the five-year period), the five-year requirement imposed on him is not fulfilled.

First in, first out

13.26   Where the shares which are purchased by the company are of the same class and were acquired by the seller at different times, the seller is treated as having sold shares which he acquired earlier before those which he acquired later (ie first in, first out), and, if he has made any previous disposals of shares of that class, his earlier disposals are treated as having consisted of shares acquired later rather than of shares acquired earlier (ie last in, first out) (CTA 2010, s 1035(2)). This deemed manner of dealing with his shares is that which increases the chances of all the seller's shares falling within s 1033 of the CTA 2010.

Example

A shareholder acquires 600 shares in X Ltd in 2007 and a further 400 in 2008. In 2010, he sells 400 of his shares. In 2013, X Ltd purchases his remaining 600 shares from him. The five-year requirement is satisfied in respect of both purchases.

Company reorganisations

13.27   If for CGT purposes the shares which are purchased by the company fall to be treated as the same asset as other shares or securities acquired on a date earlier than that on which the shares being purchased were actually acquired, the five-year (or three-year) period is calculated by reference to the acquisition date of the original shares or securities, unless the shares being purchased were allotted for payment or comprised 'stock dividends' to which s 1049 of the CTA 2010 applied (CTA 2010, s 1035(3)).

The factual situations which may give rise to this relaxation include most instances of where there has been a 'reorganisation' of a company's share capital within the meaning of Chapter 2 of Part 4 of the TCGA 1992 (eg bonus issues, share exchanges). However, the relaxation will not apply where there has been a rights issue, as that would involve an allotment of shares for payment; in such a case, the relaxation described at **13.26** above will apply – ie the shares being purchased by the company will be identified first with the original holding of shares, and only any surplus will be identified with the shares acquired on the rights issue.

13.28   There is nothing to prevent the relaxation discussed in the immediately preceding paragraph from being cumulated with either of the relaxation discussed at **13.22** and **13.23** above. Thus, if the seller received a transfer of the shares from his wife (falling within **13.22** above) two years prior to the purchase by the company, and, two years before that, she had received the shares in a reorganisation in exchange for shares in another company which she had owned for 18 months, the five-year requirement imposed on the seller would be fulfilled.

13.29   It is noteworthy that a fresh five-year period starts to run in all the following circumstances.

(a) Where the shares are transferred by Company A to Company B, both of which are members of the same group (on any definition of that word). This is on the assumption that the transfer is occurring otherwise than on a share exchange (in which case the relaxation at (e) above would probably apply).

(b) Where a beneficiary under a trust becomes absolutely entitled to the shares as against the trustees. The distinction drawn by the legislation is between, on the one hand, bare trusts, and on the other hand, trusts which are not bare trusts. In the case of a bare trust, it is the beneficial owner who 'owns' the shares; and in the case of any other trust, it is the trustees who 'own' them (CTA 2010, s 1048(3)).

(c) Where shares become settled property, ie where they become subjected to trusts other than bare trusts, and the settlor transfers the shares to trustees who do not include himself. However, it is arguable that if the settlor (who has hitherto been the beneficial owner of the shares) merely declares himself the sole trustee of the shares on trusts which are not bare trusts, there will be no change in the 'ownership' of shares for the purposes of s 1033, notwithstanding the change of capacity which has occurred. Where the settlor becomes one of several trustees, it is arguable that there is a pro rata continuity of ownership.

Requirement that there be a substantial reduction of seller's shareholding (s 1037)

13.30 If immediately after the purchase the seller owns shares in the company, his interest as a shareholder must be 'substantially reduced' (CTA 2010, s 1037(1) – taking into account the holdings of associates). If a shareholder is bought out of the company completely, so that they have no shares left in the company, then this condition will obviously not need to be considered further.

13.31 There are two tests which must be satisfied if a reduction in a shareholding is to qualify as being 'substantial'. The first test has regard to the extent of the shareholding after the purchase, and the second has regard to the shareholder's entitlement to profits after the purchase.

The shareholding test

13.32 It is provided that the seller's interest as a shareholder is to be taken as substantially reduced if, and only if, the total nominal value of the shares owned by him immediately after the purchase, expressed as a fraction of the issued share capital of the company at that time, does not exceed 75% of the corresponding fraction immediately before the purchase (CTA 2010, s 1037(3)).

Example

The issued share capital in a company comprises 1,000 ordinary £1 shares. They are owned as to 600 by A, 300 by B and 100 by C. The company purchases 200 of A's shares.

Before the purchase A owns 60% of the shares. After the purchase he owns 400 out of 800 shares, or 50%. We compare 50% with 75% of 60%, which is 45%. As 50% is greater than 45%, A's shareholding has not been 'substantially' reduced.

13.33   It can be seen from the last example that it is not correct to suggest that a shareholder need merely sell at least 25% of his shareholding in order to satisfy the test. The exact minimum number of shares which he needs to sell varies according to the size of his holding as a percentage of the total and also according to whether or not the shares of any other shareholder are being purchased by the company at the same time. Certain formulae can be deduced from the legislation, and these are set out in the following two paragraphs.

Where only one person's shares are being bought

13.34   Where it is proposed that the company should purchase part of the shareholding of just one shareholder, the following formula gives the minimum number of shares which he must sell in order to satisfy the shareholding test:

$$m = \frac{nx}{4x - 3n}$$

where m = the number of shares he must sell,
n = the number of shares in his existing holding, and
x =   the total nominal value of the company's issued share capital.

It is assumed for this purpose that all the shares have the same par value. The answer should always be rounded up to the nearest whole number.

Example

The issued share capital in a company comprises 1,000 ordinary £1 shares. They are owned as to 600 by A, 300 by B and 100 by C. It is wished that the company purchase a sufficient number of the shares held by A with a view to his holding less than 50% of the remaining issued share capital. What is the minimum number of shares which he must sell?

$$n = 600. \quad x = 1,000$$

So:

$$m = \frac{600 \times 1,000}{4 \times 1,000 - 3 \times 600} = \frac{6,000}{22}$$

So:

$$m = 273$$

Double check: Before the purchase A owned 60% of the shares. After the sale A owns 327 out of 727 shares, or 44.97937%, which is less than 45% (ie 75% of 60%).

NB Although in this example the shareholding test is satisfied in relation to the purchase of Mr A's shares, the condition that he must not remain 'connected' with the company (**13.46**) is not.

13.35 Where the shareholder from whom shares are to be purchased by the company holds more than 40% of the shares, the following formula yields the minimum number of shares he must sell in order to satisfy both the shareholding test and also the requirement that he must not remain 'connected' with the company (see **13.46**):

$$m = \frac{10n - 3x}{7}$$

where m, n and x mean the same as in the previous formula (at **13.34**).

Example

Six hundred shares are owned by A, out of an issued share capital of 1,000 ordinary £1 shares. The minimum number of shares which A must sell in order to satisfy both tests is:

$$\frac{10 \times 600 - 3 \times 1,000}{7} = \frac{3,000}{7} = 428.57$$

which = 429 rounded up

Double check: 600 − 429 = 171. 1,000 − 429 = 571. 171/571 = 29.94746%.

Where more than one person's shares are being bought

13.36 Where it is proposed that the company should purchase part of the shareholdings of several shareholders, and each of those shareholders is to sell to the company the same proportion of his shares as the others, then the existing holdings of those shareholders can be aggregated and the minimum number of shares which they must respectively sell can be evaluated from the formula stated in the preceding paragraph, ie:

$$m = \frac{nx}{4x - 3n}$$

where m = the total number of shares they must sell,
n = the total number of shares in their existing holdings, and
x = the total nominal value of the company's issued share capital.

Again, it is assumed for this purpose that all the shares have the same par value. The answer for m should always be rounded up to the nearest whole number.

Example

A company has an issued share capital of 1,000 ordinary £1 shares held as follows:

Mr A	550	
Mr B	140	140
Mr C	70	
Mr D	100	100
Mr E	140	
		240

The company is to buy shares from Mr B and Mr D pro rata their shareholdings. What is the minimum number which the company must buy from each if the shareholding test is to be satisfied?

$$n = 240. \quad x = 1,000.$$

So:

$$m = \frac{240 \times 1,000}{4 \times 1,000 - 3 \times 240} = \frac{24,000}{328}$$

So: $m = 73.170732 = 74$, rounded up

As the purchases are to be pro rata, Mr B must sell:

$$\frac{140}{240} \times 74 = 43,166667 = 43$$

rounded to the nearest whole number.

Before the purchase, Mr B owns 14% of the shares. Afterwards, he owns 97 out of 926, or 10.475162%. This is less than 75% of 14% (which is 10.5%).

Mr D must sell:

$$\frac{100}{240} \times 74 = 30.833333 = 31$$

rounded to the nearest whole number.

Before the purchase, Mr D owns 10% of the shares. Afterwards, he owns 69 out of 926, or 7.4514039%. This is less than 75% of 10% (which is 7.5%).

However, where the purchases are not to be pro rata the existing shareholdings of the selling shareholders, the position is less straightforward. Basing ourselves on the facts of the last example, the following are the relevant formulae:

$$h = \frac{bx + 3bk}{4x - 3b} \text{ and } k = \frac{dx + 3dk}{4x - 3d}$$

where h = the number of shares B must or will sell,
k = the number of shares D must or will sell,
b = the number of shares in B's existing holding,
d = the number of shares in D's existing holding, and
x = the total nominal value of the company's issued share capital.

Thus, if in the last example Mr B wishes to sell not just 43 shares but 50, the minimum number which Mr D must sell is:

$$k = \frac{dx + 3dh}{4x - 3d} = \frac{100,000 + 3 \times 100 \times 50}{4,000 - 300}$$

Before the purchase, D owns 10% of the shares. Afterwards, he owns 68 out of 918, or 7.4074074%. This is less than 75% of 10% (which is 7.5%).

13.37 The following three general statements can be deduced from the shareholding test:

(a) Where the shares in a company are beneficially owned by just one person, he can never 'substantially' reduce his shareholding, as he will always own 100% of the company, regardless of the number of shares owned.

(b) Where the shares in a company are beneficially owned by several persons, and it is proposed that the company should purchase shares from all of them pro rata their existing shareholdings, they can never 'substantially' reduce their shareholdings as their relative shareholding percentages will be maintained.

(c)   Accordingly, a 'substantial' reduction in a person's shareholding can only occur where there will be an alteration in the shareholding percentages of the various shareholders.

The distributions test

13.38   The distributions test must also be satisfied if the reduction in the shareholding is to be treated as 'substantial'. This test is designed to prevent a reduction from being treated as 'substantial' where the shareholding test is satisfied but where the shareholder is nevertheless (by virtue of the different rights attaching to separate classes of share) entitled to more than 75% of the profits available for distribution to which he would have been entitled but for the purchase by the company.

13.39   It is provided that a seller's interest as a shareholder is not to be treated as substantially reduced where:

(a)   he would, if the company distributed all its profits available for distribution immediately after the purchase, be entitled to a share of those profits; and

(b)   that share, expressed as a fraction of the total of those profits, exceeds 75% of the corresponding fraction immediately before the purchase (CTA 2010, s 1038).

13.40   In determining for these purposes the division of profits among the persons entitled to them, a person entitled to a periodic distribution calculated by reference to fixed rates or amounts is regarded as being entitled to a distribution of the amount or maximum amount to which he would be entitled for a year (CTA 2010, s 1038(2)). For example, a holder of 7% non-participating £1 preference shares is treated as being entitled to a distribution of 7p per share.

13.41   The phrase 'profits available for distribution' has the same meaning as in s 830(2) of the CA 2006, with the addition of:

(a)   £100; and

(b)   in the case of a company from which any person is entitled to periodic distributions calculated by reference to fixed rates or amounts, a further amount equal to the amount or maximum amount to which he would be entitled for a year; and

(c)   where the aggregate of the sums payable by the company on the purchase and on any contemporaneous repayment, redemption or purchase of other shares in the company exceeds the amount of the profits available for distribution immediately before the purchase, an amount equal to the excess.

CTA 2010, S 1038(3)–(5)

13.42   The 'profits available for distribution' of a company are the company's 'accumulated, realised profits, so far as not previously utilised by distribution or capitalisation, less its accumulated, realised losses, so far as not previously written off in a reduction or reorganisation of capital duly made' (CA 2006, s 830(2)). Accordingly, where a company has, as a matter of company law, no profits available for distribution, the distributions test is applied to a notional profit, computed as described in the preceding paragraph. It is considered that where a company has an excess of losses over profits, the amount of the company's profits available for distribution (as a matter of company law) is zero, and not a negative amount – if it were a negative amount, the addition of £100 would in many cases still produce a negative result, with the consequence that no notional distribution of profits could be made. As a matter of company law, a company either has profits available for distribution, or it does not.

13.43   It is expressly provided that the word 'entitlement', where used in s 1038 in relation to profits, means beneficial entitlement, except in the case of trustees and personal representatives (CTA 2010, s 1038(6)).

Requirement that the shareholdings of associates be taken into account (s 1037(2))

13.44   If immediately after the purchase any 'associate' of the seller owns shares in the company, then the combined interests as shareholders of the seller and his associates must be 'substantially reduced'. Whether or not a 'substantial reduction' has occurred is determined as for s 1037, but with the difference that the seller is deemed to own the interests of his associates as well as his own (CTA 2010, s 1037(2)). This condition has effect subject to the exclusion at **13.69** et seq in favour of sales by associates.

13.45   The legislation sets out a definition of 'associate' for the purposes of Chapter 3 of Part 23 of CTA 2010, including ss 1033–1038. There are seven limbs to the definition (CTA 2010, s 1059–1061).

(a)   A husband and wife, or civil partners, living together are associates of one another (CTA 2010, s 1059(2)).

(b)   A person under the age of 18 is an associate of his parents, and his parents are his associates (CTA 2010, s 1059(3)).

(c)   A person 'connected' with a company is an associate of the company and
      of any company controlled by it, and the company and any company
      controlled by it are his associates (CTA 2010, s 1059(4)).

(d)   Where a person 'connected' with one company has control of another
      company, the second company is an associate of the first (CTA 2010,
      s 1059(5)).

(e)   Where one person is accustomed to act on the directions of another in
      relation to the affairs of a company, then in relation to that company the
      two persons are associates of one another (CTA 2010, s 1059(6)).

(f)   Where shares in a company are held by trustees of a settlement then in
      relation to that company, in their capacity as trustees, the trustees are
      associates of:

      (i)   any person who directly or indirectly provided property to the
             trustees or has made a reciprocal arrangement for another to do so,
             and
      (ii)   any person who is, by virtue of (a) or (b) above, an associate of a
             person within (i) above, and
      (iii) any person who is or may become beneficially entitled to a
             'significant interest' in the shares;
      and any such person is an associate of the trustees (CTA 2010, s 1060(1)).
      However, this paragraph (ie para (e)) does not apply to shares held on
      trusts which:

      (i)   relate exclusively to a registered pension scheme; or
      (ii)   are exclusively for the benefit of the employees, or the employees and
             directors, of the company or of companies in a 'group' to which the
             company belongs, or their dependants (and are not wholly or mainly
             for the benefit of directors or their relatives). Here, the word 'group'
             means a company which has one or more 51% subsidiaries, together
             with those subsidiaries (CTA 2010, s 1060(2)–(5)).
      Note that trustees will not be associated with a person in a personal
      capacity solely because they are associated with that person in their
      trustee capacity.

(g)   Where shares in a company are comprised in the estate of a deceased
      person, then in relation to that company the deceased's personal
      representatives are associates of any person who is or may become
      beneficially entitled to a 'significant interest' in the shares, and any such
      person is an associate of the personal representatives (CTA 2010,
      s 1061(1)).

For the purposes of (f) and (g), a person's interest is 'significant' if its value
exceeds 5% of the value of all the property held on the trusts or, as the case

may be, comprised in the estate concerned, excluding any property in which he is not and cannot become beneficially entitled (CTA 2010, s 1061(2)).

13.46 In order to appreciate the scope of limbs (c) and (d) above of the definition of 'associate', it is necessary to bear in mind the s 1062 definition of when a person is 'connected' with a company. This definition comes in two main parts: the first part lays down general principles and covers straightforward corporate financing structures. The second part is aimed at preventing the general principles laid down in the first part from being circumvented by complex corporate financing structures; and the legislators have chosen to do so by making cross-references to Chapter 6 of Part 5 of the CTA 2010. Accordingly, the first and main part of the definition is set out in **13.47**, whilst the second part is set out at length in Appendix H.

13.47 It is provided (CTA 2010, s 1062) that a person is connected with a company if:

(a) he has control of it (within the meaning of s 1124 of the CTA 2010) (CTA 2010, s 1062(7)); or

(b) he directly or indirectly possesses or is 'entitled to acquire' more than 30% of:

    (i) the issued ordinary share capital of the company; or
    (ii) the 'loan capital' and issued share capital of the company; or
    (iii) the voting power in the company (CTA 2010, s 1062(2)).

For this purpose:

(a) a person is assumed to have the rights or powers of his associates as well as his own (CTA 2010, s 1063(4));

(b) a person is treated as entitled to acquire anything which he is entitled to acquire at a future date or will at a future date be entitled to acquire (CTA 2010 1988, s 1063(3));

(c) the 'loan capital' of a company means any debt incurred by the company:

    (i) for any money borrowed or capital assets acquired by the company; or
    (ii) for any right to receive income created in favour of the company; or
    (iii) for consideration the value of which to the company was (at the time when the debt was incurred) substantially less than the amount of the debt (including any premium thereon) (CTA 2010, s 1063(1)).

However, where a person:

(a) acquired or became entitled to acquire loan capital of a company in the ordinary course of a business which includes the lending of money; and

(b) takes no part in the management or conduct of the company;

his interest in that loan capital is to be disregarded (CTA 2010, s 1062(3)). This exclusion will apply mainly in favour of banks which provide loans and overdrafts to companies.

13.48 One common factual situation in which this requirement to take into account shareholdings of associates may prevent s 1033 from applying is where an individual holding shares in a family trading company has created a family settlement and transferred part of his shareholding to the trustees. He and the trustees will be 'associates', so that his and their shareholdings will be aggregated for the purpose of determining whether, if the company purchases his shareholding, there has been a 'substantial reduction'. Similarly, where an individual shareholder is also a beneficiary in respect of only a part of some shares held by trustees, the entire shareholding of the trustees will be aggregated with his own (assuming always that he has a 'significant' interest in the shares held by the trustees (see **13.45**)).

13.49 Another factual situation in which this requirement may prevent s 1033 from applying is where the shareholder whose shares are being purchased by the company holds a 30% or greater shareholding in a second company which in turn holds shares in the company which is buying its own shares.

For example:

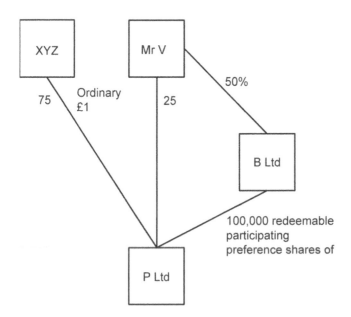

In the above shareholding structure, the substantial reduction test (as expanded by s 1037(2)) will not be satisfied if P Ltd merely purchases the 25 ordinary shares held by Mr V, as Mr V is connected with B Ltd and is therefore an associate of B Ltd. This means that B Ltd's holding of participating preference shares (which are 'ordinary share capital'; CTA 2010, s 1119) must be treated as belonging to Mr V in applying the substantial reduction test. If all the redeemable participating preference shares were to be redeemed on the same day as the purchase of the 25 ordinary shares from Mr V, then the substantial reduction test would be satisfied in relation to both the purchase and the redemption.

Requirement that there be a substantial reduction of interest in group (s 1039)

13.50 The object of this condition is to apply the 'substantial reduction' requirement (discussed above) to the situation where the purchasing company is immediately before the purchase a member of a 'group'. The term 'group' is defined elaborately (see **13.59**), but for the purposes of comprehending the approximate scope of the present condition, the word 'group' may be read to mean a company and its 51% subsidiaries. If either:

(a) immediately after the purchase the seller owns shares in one or more other members of the group (whether or not he then owns shares in the company making the purchase), or

(b) immediately after the purchase the seller owns shares in the company making the purchase and immediately before the purchase he owned shares in one or more other members of the group,

then the seller's interest as a shareholder in the group must be 'substantially reduced' (CTA 2010, s 1039(3)). Clearly, if the seller is not left with any shares in group companies after the purchase, this condition is satisfied. Also, this condition has effect subject to the exclusion at **13.69** et seq in favour of sales by associates.

13.51 The seller's interest as a shareholder in the group is ascertained by:

(a) expressing the total nominal value of the shares owned by him in each member of the group as a fraction of the issued share capital of each such company;

(b) adding together the fractions so obtained; and

(c) dividing the result by the number of companies in the group in which he owns shares immediately before or immediately after the purchase.

CTA 2010, S 1040(2)

13.52   The legislation applies two cumulative tests – a shareholding test and a distributions test – for the purpose of ascertaining whether or not the seller's interest as a shareholder in the group is 'substantially reduced'.

The shareholding test

13.53   The seller's interest as a shareholder in the group is 'substantially reduced' if and only if it does not exceed 75% of the corresponding interest immediately before the purchase (CTA 2010, s 1040(1)).

Example

In a group of four companies, the shareholdings (totalling in each case 100 ordinary £1 shares) are as follows:

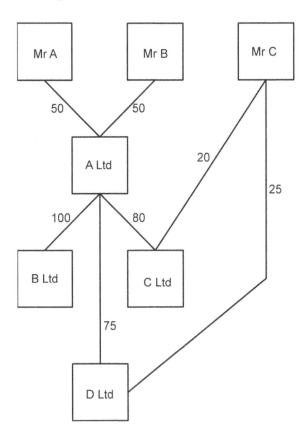

C Ltd buys from Mr C his 20 shares. Prior to the purchase Mr C's interest in the group is:

$$\left(\frac{20}{100} + \frac{25}{100} \right) \times \frac{1}{2} = 22.5\%$$

After the purchase his interest in the group is:

$$\frac{25}{100} \times \frac{1}{2} = 12.5\%$$

As 12.5% is less than 75% of 22.5% (ie 16.875%), Mr C's interest in the group has been substantially reduced.

13.54 In order to determine the minimum number of shares in group companies which a shareholder need sell in order to satisfy the test, the principles set out in **13.31** et seq apply in relation to shareholdings in a single company.

13.55 The following general statements can be deduced from the shareholding test.

(a) Where all the shares in companies in a group are beneficially owned (directly or through the medium of other shareholdings) by just one person, he can never 'substantially' reduce his interest as a shareholder in the group.

(b) Where the shares in companies in a group are beneficially owned by several persons, and it is proposed that a company in the group should purchase shares from all of them pro rata their existing shareholdings, they can never 'substantially' reduce their interests as shareholders in the group.

(c) Accordingly, a 'substantial' reduction in a person's interest as a shareholder in a group can only occur where there will be an alteration in the ratios in which the various shareholders hold shares in the group as a whole. Where the shareholding percentages are altered, however, note that the value-shifting anti-avoidance provisions in capital gains tax legislation (TCGA 1992, ss 29, 30) must also be considered.

(d) The particular structure of an individual's ownership of shares in more than one group company may give rise to an arbitrary result in applying the substantial reduction test. This is principally because the shareholding test pays no regard to the size of the companies concerned. Generally, the fragmentation of shareholdings between two or more group companies will make it less likely that the shareholder will satisfy the test.

The distributions test

13.56 The distributions test must also be satisfied if the reduction in the seller's interest as a shareholder in the group is to be treated as 'substantial'. This test is designed to prevent a reduction from being treated as 'substantial' where the shareholding test is satisfied but where the shareholder is nevertheless (eg by virtue of the different companies in the group having differing levels of profits available for distribution) entitled to more than 75% of the group's profits available for distribution to which he would have been entitled but for the purchase.

13.57 It is provided that the seller's interest as a shareholder in the group is not to be treated as substantially reduced where:

(a)   he would, if every member of the group distributed all its profits available for distribution immediately after the purchase (including any profits received by it on a distribution by another member), be entitled to a share of the profits of one or more of them; and

(b)   the new entitlement, being that share, or the aggregate of those shares, expressed as a fraction of the aggregate of the profits available for distribution of every member of the group which is:

(i)   a member of the group in which the seller owns shares immediately before or immediately after the purchase, or

(ii)   a 51% subsidiary of such a company,

exceeds 75% of the corresponding fraction immediately before the purchase (CTA 2010, s 1041(1)).

13.58   The determination for these purposes of the division of profits among the persons entitled to them, and the meaning of the phrase 'profits available for distribution', are the same as for the main substantial reduction test (see **13.38** et seq).

A 'group'

13.59   There is a special definition of the word 'group' for the purposes of ss 1033–1047. The general principle is that a 'group' means a company which has one or more 51% subsidiaries, but which is not itself a 51% subsidiary of any other company, together with those subsidiaries (CTA 2010, s 1047(1)). The term '51% subsidiary' has its ordinary CTA 2010, s 1154 meaning. However, to the general principle there exist the following two exceptions of an anti-avoidance nature.

Companies taking over part of purchasing company's business

13.60   Where, three years or less prior to the time of the purchase, an unquoted company begins to carry on, as the whole or a significant part of its business, business that was previously carried on by:

(a)   the company making the purchase, or

(b)   a company which is (apart from this paragraph) a member of a group to which the company making the purchase belongs,

the unquoted company in question, and any company of which it is a 51% subsidiary, are treated as being members of the same group as the company making the purchase (whether or not, apart from this paragraph, the company making the purchase is a member of a group) (CTA 2010, s 1047(2), (3)).

Example 1

The shares in A Ltd are owned in equal proportions by six individuals. In 2010, A Ltd sells for cash a small part of its business to B Ltd, a newly formed company also owned in equal proportions by the same six individuals. The purchased business comprises B Ltd's sole activity. In 2012, one of the shareholders in A Ltd sells his shares to the company, but retains his shares in B Ltd. Neither company is a 51% subsidiary of any other company, but s 1047(2) of the CTA 2010 requires them to be treated as members of the same 'group'. It can be seen that the need to look back three years prior to the share purchase in question for the purpose of confirming that two apparently independent companies are not members of the same 'group' constitutes a trap for the unwary.

Example 2

Mr V owns 10% of the shares in P Ltd, which has several 51% subsidiaries, including T Ltd. It is proposed that P Ltd should buy back Mr V's 10% shareholding, and that Mr V should use part of the proceeds to buy the shares in T Ltd from P Ltd. Mr V might consider either acquiring the T Ltd shares himself, or forming Newco Ltd to acquire the T Ltd shares and act as a holding company.

(a) If Mr V acquires the shares in T Ltd himself, there should be no risk of s 1047(2) of the CTA 2010 applying, unless:

   (i) T Ltd has, within the three years prior to the completion of Mr V's own share purchase, begun to carry on some business which was previously carried on by some other company which is a member of the group on that completion date; and

   (ii) at some time prior to the completion of Mr V's own share purchase, T Ltd ceased to be a 51% subsidiary of P Ltd (eg upon the coming into existence of an unconditional contract for the sale of the T Ltd shares),

   in which case T Ltd would be deemed by s 1047(2) to remain a member of the same group as P Ltd.

(b) If Mr V forms Newco Ltd to acquire the T Ltd shares and act as a holding company, care must be taken to ensure that s 1047(2) does not become applicable on the basis that Newco Ltd is the 'unquoted company' carrying on 'business' (ie the holding of T Ltd shares; see *American Leaf Blending Co Sdn Bhd v D-Gof IR*[7]) previously carried on by P Ltd. Here, it would be important to ensure that T Ltd remains a 51% subsidiary of P Ltd on the date when the own share purchase is completed and for an interval of time thereafter.

---

[7]   [1978] STC 561.

Where a former subsidiary is deemed still to be a subsidiary

13.61 A company which has ceased to be a 51% subsidiary of another company before the time of the purchase is treated as continuing to be such a subsidiary if at that time there exist arrangements under which it could again become such a subsidiary (CTA 2010, s 1047(4)).

The term 'arrangements' has been used frequently in anti-avoidance legislation, and its general meaning is extremely wide. *Scottish and Universal Newspapers Ltd v Fisher* the Special Commissioners found that:[8]

> '"arrangements" is a wide expression which will often mean something less than a legally binding contract. Perhaps the normal example will be a non-binding agreement made subject to contract. Such an agreement is likely to contain many terms which at that stage are not fully set out or which will require further negotiation ... even though arrangements need not be legally binding, they still must ... be something which can take effect.'

The court in *Scottish and Universal Newspapers* applied the dictum in *Pilkington Bros Ltd v IRC*[9] where the term was considered in the High Court:

> 'The material dictionary meanings of "arrangement" are: a structure or combination of things for a purpose; a disposition of measures for a particular purpose. Both these definitions require that the individual elements of an arrangement should be combined or disposed for a particular purpose, and I do not think that, unless there is a context to the contrary, that requirement is displaced by the use of the plural as opposed to the singular. All that that adds is the possibility that there may be more than one combination of things or more than one disposition of measures. But without a context it would, as it seems to me, be unnatural to read the plural as dispensing with the need for some unifying link between each of the combinations or dispositions. I therefore construe this provision in the expectation that it is intended to refer to things or measures which are combined or disposed for a particular purpose.'

This definition was then modified by the House of Lords, so that no unifying link was necessary between the various transactions before they constitute arrangements for the purposes of these provisions.

Requirement to tax account of the interests of associates in a group (s 1039(4))

13.62 Where, immediately before the purchase, the company making it is a member of a 'group' and an 'associate' of the seller owns shares in any member of the group, then the combined interests as shareholders in the group of the seller and his associates must be 'substantially reduced' (CTA 2010, s 1039(4)).

---

[8]   [1996] STC (SCD) 311.
[9]   [1981] STC 219 (reversed [1982] STC 103, HL).

13.63 This requirement has effect subject to the exclusion at **13.70** et seq in favour of sales by associates. The term 'group' is defined at **13.58** et seq, and the word 'associate' at **13.45** et seq. The question whether there has been a 'substantial' reduction in the combined interests as shareholders in the group of the seller and his associates is determined in the same way as the question whether a seller's interest as a shareholder in a group is substantially reduced, but on the assumption that the seller has the interests of his associates as well as his own (CTA 2010, s 1040(4)).

Requirement that the seller not remain 'connected' with the purchasing company (s 1042(1))

13.64 The seller must not immediately after the purchase be 'connected' with the company making the purchase or with any company which is a member of the same 'group' as that company (CTA 2010, s 1042(1)).

13.65 This requirement has effect subject to the exclusion at **13.70** et seq in favour of sales by associates. For the definition of the word 'connected', see **13.46**. The term 'group' is defined at **13.58** et seq. Thus, for example, a person who sells shares to the company and is left with more than 30% of the issued ordinary share capital will fail to satisfy this condition.

Requirement that there be no scheme or arrangement (s 1042(2))

13.66 The purchase must not be part of a scheme or arrangement which is designed or likely to result in the seller or any 'associate' of his having interests in any company such that, if he had those interests immediately after the purchase, any of the requirements as to the reduction of the seller's shareholding (in the company or group, taking into account the holdings of associates) in ss 1037 and 1039 could not be satisfied (CTA 2010, s 1042(2)). This condition has effect subject to the exclusion at **13.70** et seq in favour of sales by associates.

13.67 For these purposes, a transaction occurring within one year after the purchase is deemed to be part of a scheme or arrangement of which the purchase is also part (CTA 2010, s 1042(3)). This deeming provision appears to be conclusive, so as to render irrelevant any evidence suggesting that a transaction occurring within one year after the purchase is not part of a scheme or arrangement of which the purchase is also part. As regards transactions occurring later than one year after the purchase, there is nothing to prevent there being adduced evidence to the effect that the transaction forms part of a scheme or arrangement of which the purchase also forms part. The word 'associate' is defined at **13.46**.

Example

Mr X owns 10% of the issued share capital of XYZ Ltd. The company purchases his shares. There is an understanding between Mr X and the directors of the company to the effect that if Mrs X at any time in the future applies for any shares in the company at market value, shares comprising not more than a 10% holding will, upon payment in cash, be allotted to her at a premium reflecting their market value. It is arguable that this arrangement infringes the 'no scheme or arrangement' requirement, on the ground that it is likely to result in Mrs X having an interest in the company such that, if Mrs X held that interest immediately after the purchase, the requirement as to reduction in shareholding (including holdings of associates) would not be satisfied. The very existence of such an arrangement is sufficient to infringe the requirement that there not be a scheme or arrangement in place. Proving the existence of the arrangement is facilitated by the one-year deeming provision. Thus, if ten months after the purchase Mrs X were allotted an 8% holding of shares in the company, the deeming provision would cause this requirement to be infringed as regards the purchase by the company of Mr X's shares.

13.68 If an arrangement is entered into whereby, following an own share purchase, the company is to receive a loan from the seller of the shares, the loan may result in him being 'connected' with the company within one year after the purchase – he could be so 'connected' by possessing more than 30% of the loan capital and issued share capital of the company (see **13.46** for the meaning of 'connected'). This could easily occur where the shares have a high market value and the issued share capital is relatively small.

In these circumstances, HMRC have indicated (in Tax Bulletin 21) that 'there is no reason why' the shareholder should not 'lend part of the consideration back to the company immediately afterwards' and that 'it is acceptable for the company to avoid [the shareholder's interest exceeding 30% after the loan] by making a bonus issue before the own share purchase takes place, thus increasing its issued share capital'. HMRC provide the following example:

'Norman owns 3,000 out of the 10,000 issued £1 shares of a company.

It is agreed that the company will buy the shares for £50,000, which is their market value, and that Norman will then lend the company £25,000.

But this would mean that Norman held loan capital of £25,000 out of the company's combined share and loan capital of £32,000, so he would be connected with the company, and both parties are agreed that they would prefer the transaction to come within [s 1033 of the CTA 2010].

So before making the purchase the company makes a bonus issue of 9 shares for each one held.

Norman then sells back his 30,000 shares for £50,000 and lends the company £25,000. He now holds loan capital of £25,000 out of the company's combined share and loan capital of £95,000, and since this is less than 30% of the whole he is not connected with the company.'

Whilst it is helpful to know that HMRC would not seek to attack such an arrangement, within their example (and their related commentary) there lurks a hidden danger, namely that if, before the purchase takes place, a binding agreement is entered into that the seller will lend back to the company all or part of the proceeds of sale, there is a very real risk of such an agreement creating a breach of s 691(2) of the CA 2006. Section 691(2) requires that payment of the purchase price must occur upon completion of the purchase; and in this context the word 'payment' means actual payment and not merely the giving of some loan note or other acknowledgement of indebtedness. Failure to comply with that requirement would render the purchase void. If, however, there is merely a non-binding arrangement or expectation that the seller will lend back to the company all or part of the proceeds of sale, and the company actually pays the full amount of the consideration to the seller, who subsequently lends all or part of it back to the company, that should not invalidate the transaction.

13.69   Any person 'connected' with the company who knows of any scheme or arrangement infringing this requirement in relation to a payment for share capital which is otherwise being treated as fulfilling the conditions of s 1033 of the CTA 2010 is under an obligation to give a notice in writing to the inspector containing particulars of the scheme or arrangement. He must serve this notice within 60 days after he first knows of both the payment and the scheme or arrangement (CTA 2010, s 1046(3)). Failure to give the notice makes him liable to penalties under s 98 of the TMA 1970 (see **15.6**).

Relaxation of requirements (s 1043)

13.70   This exclusion has effect where the 'associate' of a seller sells shares to the company in order to enable that seller to comply with the requirements in s 1037(2) or s 1039(4) – ie where, but for the associate selling some of his own shares, the seller's interest in the company or group would not be 'substantially reduced'.

13.71   Where requirements which are applicable are not satisfied in relation to the associate's sale of shares to the company, but he proposed or agreed to the purchase in order to enable the seller (of whom he is an associate) to comply with the requirements in s 1037(2) or s 1039(4), then the applicable requirements are deemed to be satisfied in relation to the associate's sale to the extent that his sale enables the seller to comply with the requirements in s 1037(2) or s 1039(4) (CTA 2010, s 1043). If the associate sells more shares than is necessary to enable the seller to comply with the requirements in s 1037(2) or s 1039(4), this exclusion does not apply in relation to the excess.

Example

Mr E and Mr F are brothers. Mr E owns ten out of the 100 shares in Y Ltd. Mr F owns all the shares in Z Ltd which in turn owns 25 of the shares in Y Ltd. Mr F has granted to Mr E an option to purchase 35% of the shares in Z Ltd. It is proposed that Y Ltd should buy from Mr E his 10% holding. However, it is then noticed that Z Ltd is an 'associate' of Mr E by virtue of Mr E being 'connected' with Z Ltd (as a result of the option). The requirement to take into account the holdings of associates is therefore relevant and, as the following workings show, would mean that the substantial reduction requirement would not be fulfilled by the proposed transaction.

Taking into account Z Ltd's 25% holding in Y Ltd, Mr E notionally holds 35% of the shares in Y Ltd prior to the purchase. After the purchase he would notionally hold:

$$\frac{25}{90} = 27.777778\%,$$

which is greater than 75% of 35% (26.25%).

For the purpose of enabling the payment for Mr E's shares in Y Ltd to fall within s 1033 of the CTA 2010, Z Ltd is willing to sell to Y Ltd part of its 25% holding. In order to ascertain the minimum number of shares necessary for this purpose, the formula presented at **13.34** above can be used:

$$m = \frac{nx}{4x - 3n}$$

where m = the number of shares which Mr E and Z Ltd together must sell, n = the total number of shares in the existing holdings of Mr E and Z Ltd, and x = the total nominal value of Y Ltd's issued share capital.

The answer should be rounded up to the nearest whole number.

Accordingly,

$$m = \frac{35 \times 100}{4 \times 100 - 3 \times 35} = 11.864407$$

As ten of these shares are to come from Mr E, the remaining two will come from Z Ltd.

Looking at the transaction from the point of view of Z Ltd selling two out of its 25 shares, the requirement to substantially reduce the shareholding would not be satisfied, as prior to the sale Z Ltd owns 25% of the shares, and afterwards it would own 23 out of 88 shares, ie 26.14%, which is of course greater than 75% of 25% (ie 18.75%). The mere fact that the requirement to take account of associates' holdings will no longer apply in relation to Z Ltd does not bring the purchase within s 1033 if the requirement that the shareholding be substantially reduced is not also satisfied. However, by virtue of the exclusion in s 1043 of the CTA 2010, the substantial reduction requirement is treated as satisfied in relation to Z Ltd in these circumstances.

On the other hand, if Z Ltd wished to sell more than the minimum number of two shares, the exclusion would not apply in relation to the excess; so the excess shares would not be covered by s 1033.

In practice, sales by companies are relevant primarily where they assist by relaxing requirements for individual sellers. A company selling shares as part of the purchase of own shares by another company is likely to find that, where the sale gives rise to a distribution, the proceeds are exempt from corporation tax as an exempt distribution (provided that it falls into one of the exempt classes) or, where the sale is treated as a capital disposal, that it may be covered by the substantial shareholding exemption.

13.72   The question that the last sentence of the preceding paragraph raises is, what is the likely effect of a share purchase falling partly within s 1033 and partly outside it?

13.73   Where s 1033 applies, its effect is to exclude a payment by a company for the purchase of its own shares from the scope of the definition in the Corporation Tax Acts of the word 'distribution'. Where a payment falls partly within s 1033 and partly outside it, it is arguable that the part falling inside is the one which would otherwise constitute a distribution, and the part falling outside is the part which would partly constitute a distribution and partly not.

13.74   An alternative view is that the exemption conferred by s 1033 should be conferred in respect of the shares being purchased on a pro rata basis. On this view, only the element of distribution attributable to the two shares would be within s 1033, with the result that the full amount of the distribution attributable to the shares outside s 1033 would be a taxable distribution.

Chapter 14

PAYMENTS TO ASSIST IN DISCHARGING A LIABILITY TO INHERITANCE TAX

14.1 The alternative condition that can be satisfied to ensure that a payment by a company on the redemption, repayment or purchase of any of its own shares is not treated as a distribution is conferred by s 1033(3) of the CTA 2010. This provides that references in the Corporation Tax Acts to distributions of a company do not include references to a payment made by a company on the redemption, repayment or purchase of its own shares if two requirements are fulfilled. For this purpose, the word 'payment' includes anything else that is (or would but for the rest of s 1033 be) a distribution (CTA 2010, s 1033(6)).

14.2 The company must also meet the initial requirement that it be an unquoted company, and either a trading company or the holding company of a trading group (CTA 2010, s 1033(1)(a)). For the definitions of these terms, see **13.4–13.6**.

CONDITION B

Requirement that the purchase be to discharge an inheritance tax liability (s 1033(3)(a))

14.3 The whole or substantially the whole of the payment (apart from any sum applied in paying CGT charged on the redemption, repayment or purchase) must be applied by the person to whom it is made in discharging a liability of his for inheritance tax (IHT) charged on a death, and be so applied within the period of two years after the death. The liability to IHT must be that of the vendor of the shares, and not that of someone else (e.g. his spouse). In the original version of their Statement of Practice No 2/1982 HMRC stated that they interpret the words 'substantially the whole' to mean 'almost all'.

14.4 Where personal representatives acquire shares on death there will be an uplift in the CGT base value of the shares to their market value at the date of death. If the personal representatives subsequently sell the shares to the company, they will be liable to CGT on any amount by which the sale proceeds exceed the market value at the date of death (or, in the case of a shareholding which confers 'control' within the meaning of s 450 of the CTA 2010, they will be liable to CGT on any amount by which the market value at the date of purchase exceeds the market value at the date of death (TCGA 1992, ss 17(1),

286). Any CGT attributable to the sale may be paid by the personal representatives out of the proceeds of sale without jeopardising their chances of obtaining relief under s 1033.

14.5   The question whether or not a person is liable for IHT charged on a death is governed mainly by s 200 of the Inheritance Tax Act (IHTA) 1984. The persons liable in respect of property comprised in the free estate of the deceased are his personal representatives. Where property was comprised in a settlement immediately before the death, the trustees are accountable, and liability may also attach to a person in whom property is vested at any time after the death or who has an interest in possession in it, or for whose benefit any of the property or income from it is applied. The other applicable provision governing liability for IHT on a death is s 209 of the IHTA 1984, which imposes liability on a person who, being entitled in Scotland to do so, claims legitim in respect of a deceased person's estate.

14.6   Although the person to whom the sale proceeds of the shares are payable must be the person liable to discharge the IHT, that tax need not, however, be directly attributable to those shares, nor is it necessary for the shares themselves to have passed on the death; a beneficiary under a will might wish to sell shares he owned in order to pay IHT arising on other property he has inherited.

Requirement that IHT could not be otherwise discharged without hardship (s 1033(4))

14.7   Section 1033(3) does not apply to a payment to the extent that the liability for IHT could without undue hardship have been discharged otherwise than through the redemption, repayment or purchase of shares in the company or another unquoted trading company, or unquoted holding company of a trading group.

14.8   It seems clear from the wording of this condition that the burden of proof lies on HMRC to show that the liability for IHT could have been discharged without undue hardship. What constitutes 'undue hardship' must depend on the circumstances of every case – the term allows HMRC a certain amount of flexibility and allows the taxpayer to increase his chances of success through persuasive argument. Tactically, however, the burden of proof will be on the taxpayer where he submits an application for clearance.

14.9   The use of the words 'to the extent that' means that a claim for relief under s 1033(3) may be denied in part as well as in whole. The uncertainty that is inherent in the 'hardship' condition renders it nearly always essential to submit an application for clearance prior to a proposed share purchase to which it is hoped that s 1033(3) may apply.

14.10   Where the shares gave the deceased control of the unquoted company immediately prior to his death, one factor which has to be considered in deciding whether the company should purchase the deceased's shares is that if such a purchase is made and relief under s 1033(3) is claimed, the ability to pay IHT by interest-free instalments over eight years will be lost, because the grant of relief under s 1033(3) requires the IHT to be paid within two years of the death. This factor may also arise where the deceased's shareholding did not give him control (see s 228 of the IHTA 1984). A second factor to be considered is that the ability to pay IHT by instalments is likely to weaken any claim that the IHT cannot be paid without undue hardship.

14.11   There is a further possible difficulty in claiming relief under s 1033(3) where the deceased had a controlling interest immediately prior to his death. This is that HMRC take the view that, if the company has sufficient surplus funds with which to discharge the IHT liability, there can be no hardship because the liability could be met by dividend payments from the company. This view was made publicly known in the following House of Lords written answer on 17 March 1988 (Hansard, vol 494, col 1349):

> 'Viscount Mackintosh of Halifax asked whether, given their stated aim of creating a climate where family companies can flourish, it is their intention that clearance under [CTA 2001, s 1033(3)] will in all cases be refused on the death of a controlling shareholder where sufficient dividends can be voted by the executors to enable the inheritance tax liability to be met by instalments on the basis that hardship would not arise as the executors control the Company and thus control the flow of dividends.
>
> Lord Brabazon of Tara: I understand that there have been very few cases of the kind in question. However, where the company has surplus funds sufficient to discharge the inheritance tax liability, HMRC take the view that there would be no hardship since the liability could be met by dividend payments from the company.'

14.12   In summary, the 'hardship' condition means that the cases where s 1033(3) of the CTA 2010 applies are likely to be few in number and readily identifiable as being extreme cases.

Chapter 15

SECTION 219: RETURNS, CLEARANCES AND POWERS OF INFORMATION

15.1 The returns, clearances and powers of information discussed in this chapter relate solely to situations where a company is treating a purchase, redemption or repayment of any of its shares as one to which s 1033 of the CTA 2010 applies.

RETURNS

15.2 A company which treats a payment made by it as one to which s 1033 of the CTA 2010 applies is under a duty to make a return to an officer of HMRC giving particulars of the payment and of the circumstances by reason of which s 1033 is regarded as applying to it. The return must be submitted within 60 days after the making of the payment (CTA 2010, s 1046(1), (2)). Failure to make the return renders the company liable to penalties under s 98 of the Taxes Management Act 1970 (TMA 1970).

15.3 In their Tax Bulletin 21, HMRC state that if clearance was requested, the officer will have received a copy of the letter of clearance (or refusal), so all that is needed is a short letter detailing any changes from the arrangements advised to HMRC and reporting the date of the transaction. If clearance was not requested, the officer will need to know the date of the purchase, the name of the vendor, the number of shares and the amount of the consideration, and the grounds on which it was considered that the 'trade benefit' test was satisfied.

15.4 A person 'connected' with a company who knows of any scheme or arrangement in relation to a payment for share capital which is otherwise being treated by the company as falling within s 1033 of the CTA 2010 by virtue of fulfilling Condition A, is under an obligation to give a notice to an officer of HMRC containing particulars of the scheme or arrangement (CTA 2010, s 1046(3)). He must give the notice within 60 days after he first knows of both the payment and the scheme or arrangement (s 1046(4)). Failure to give the notice makes him liable to penalties under s 98 of the TMA 1970. See **13.66** for the details of the requirement that there be no scheme or arrangement ie s 1042(2) of the CTA 2010, and **13.46** for the meaning of 'connected'.

INFORMATION

15.5 The recipient of a payment treated by a company as one to which s 1033 of the CTA 2010 applies, and any person on whose behalf such a payment is received, may be required by an officer of HMRC to state whether the payment received by him or on his behalf is received on behalf of any person other than himself and, if so, the name and address of that person (CTA 2010, s 1046(5)–(7), prior to 1 April 2012; Finance Act 2011, para 14, Part 2, Sch 23 from 1 April 2012). Failure to comply may make the recipient liable to penalties under s 98 of the TMA 1970.

PENALTIES

15.6 For failure to give any of the returns described above or to comply with any such requests for information, the penalties which may be imposed under s 98 of the TMA 1970 are as follows:

(a) an initial penalty of up to £300;

(b) if the failure continues after the initial penalty has been imposed, a further penalty of up to £60 for each day on which the failure continues after the day on which the initial penalty was imposed.

However, no such penalty at all can be imposed at any time after the failure has been remedied in respect of a failure to provide a declaration or information under s 1046(5) or (7) (see **15.4**). By contrast, where the failure consists of a failure either by the company to make a return under s 1046(1) of the CTA 2010 (see **15.2**) or by a connected person to give, under s 1046(3) of the CTA 2010, particulars of a scheme or arrangement (see **15.3**), an initial penalty of £300 (but not the daily rate penalty of £60) can be imposed even after the failure has been remedied (TMA 1970, s 98(3), (4)).

If a person gives any information or makes any such declaration fraudulently or negligently, he is liable to a penalty of up to £3,000 (TMA 1970, s 98(2)).

THE CLEARANCE PROCEDURE

15.7 A company may in writing apply to the Commissioners asking them whether they are satisfied that s 1033 of the CTA 2010 will apply to a proposed redemption, repayment or purchase by the company of its own shares. The company may also ask whether the Board are satisfied that s 1033 will not apply.

15.8 The application can only be made prior to the share purchase in question. Upon receipt of the application, the Commissioners must notify their decision to the applicant within 30 days unless, within that 30-day period, they request the applicant to furnish further particulars for the purpose of enabling the Commissioners to make their decision (CTA 2010, s 1045(5)).

15.9 If a request for further particulars is not complied with within 30 days or such longer period as the Commissioners may allow, the Commissioners need not proceed further on the application (s 1045(4)).

15.10 Upon receipt of requested further particulars, the Board must notify their decision to the applicant within 30 days unless, within that 30-day period, they request the applicant to furnish yet more particulars (s 1045(5)). In Tax Bulletin 21, HMRC state that they try to give a response well within the statutory deadline of 30 days, but in some cases that response has to take the form of a request for further information. 'It is therefore advisable to allow a reasonable time for a decision to be reached and not to leave the application until the last moment.'

15.11 A precedent for an application is set out in Appendix I. HMRC's guidance notes (from SP 2/82) on how to submit an application for clearance are set out in Appendix J.

15.12 If the Board notify the company that they are satisfied that s 1033 will apply to the proposed transaction, then, subject to **15.11**, the transaction is treated as one to which s 1033 does apply (CTA 2010, s 1042(2)).

15.13 Conversely, if the Board notify the company that they are satisfied that s 1033 will not apply to the proposed transaction, then, subject to **15.11**, the transaction is treated as one to which s 1033 does not apply (s 1042(3)). This provision appears to be designed to enable a company to receive confirmation that a proposed payment will not be prevented by s 1033 from being a distribution. It is believed that the Board state that they are satisfied that s 1033 will not apply only when expressly invited to do so (i.e. in response to an application for 'negative' clearance).

15.14 The negative clearance procedure enables any shareholder, who is proposing to sell shares to the company in which the shares are held, to achieve some measure of certainty if he would prefer to receive any income element of his proceeds of sale taxable as a distribution instead of as capital. The main reasons why the selling shareholder might prefer to receive the income element as a distribution are described in Chapter 19.

15.15 It is noteworthy that in such circumstances the selling shareholder must persuade the purchasing company not to contend that s 1033 applies, as an application for clearance may only be submitted by the purchasing company. In practice, cases often arise where the treatment of the income element as a distribution is regarded as sufficiently certain without the need for any negative clearance application to be submitted (eg where the shareholder has held his shares for less than five years).

15.16   If the particulars furnished by the company do not fully and accurately disclose all facts and circumstances material for the decision of the Board, any resulting notification by the Board is void (CTA 2010, s 1046(5)). An application for clearance under s 1044 should be as detailed as the constraints of relevance and prolixity allow.

15.17   The requirements that there be a trade benefit and that there be no relevant scheme or arrangement are the two conditions which create the greatest uncertainty as to whether or not s 1033 applies. The application should desirably include relevant detail of the history of the company and of the background to the situation which has arisen rendering the share purchase desirable or expedient. It should also give details of the associates of the individual vendor and of his dealings with them – both his past dealings and also any dealings contemplated in the future, particularly dealings likely to occur within one year after the share purchase. The breadth of the words 'scheme or arrangement' must be borne in mind when drafting the application. The application should seek to deny to HMRC all opportunity of later revoking a successful application on the ground that they were not fully and accurately told everything that it was material for them to know. A specimen application is set out in Appendix I.

15.18   It is not strictly necessary for an application for clearance under s 1044 to be submitted, for if a transaction to which s 1033 might apply is entered into, there is nothing to prevent a taxpayer (eg a vendor of shares to the company) from contending that s 1033 applies to it notwithstanding the absence of a clearance application. That being said, it is considered that, viewed as a practical matter, it is highly desirable for an application for clearance to be made if the circumstances are such that one or more of the parties consider that it would be advantageous for s 1033 to apply (ie where any income element would be taxed as capital).

15.19   Clearance applications under s 1044 are handled at the same address as applications under s 701 of the ITA 2007 and s 748 of the CTA 2010. Where clearance is being sought under s 701/748 as well as under s 1044, a single letter should be sent, showing clearly at the top what clearances are being applied for; this should result in both clearances being dealt with together.

Chapter 16

TAXES ON INCOME: OTHER CONSEQUENCES OF PURCHASES AND REDEMPTIONS

SECTION 695 OF THE ITA 2007/SECTION 743 OF THE CTA 2010: TRANSACTIONS IN SECURITIES

16.1 A notice pursuant to s 695 of the ITA 2007 (income tax) or s 743 of the CTA 2010 (corporation tax) may, if certain conditions are fulfilled, be served on the taxpayer by an officer of HMRC to counteract a specified tax advantage with regard to a transaction. Such counteraction may often take the form of an assessment to income tax on an individual who has obtained the tax advantage.

Note that the General Anti-Abuse Rule (GAAR) which is, at the time of writing, expected to be introduced in the UK is not discussed in this book as the GAAR will not be specific to such transactions in securities.

16.2 An own share purchase is a 'transaction in securities' (CTA 2010, s 751; ITA 2007, s 684), as the identity of the purchaser is irrelevant for this purpose. So too, probably, is a redemption of redeemable shares. The first condition for s 695/743 to apply will therefore be fulfilled.

16.3 The second condition is that a 'tax advantage' must be obtained or obtainable in consequence of the transaction in securities. If, but for s 1033, the purchase price for the shares would contain an element of 'distribution', there is likely to be a 'tax advantage'.

An income tax advantage (ITA 2007, s 687) is obtained if:

(a) the amount of any income tax which would be payable by the person in respect of the relevant consideration if it constituted a qualifying distribution exceeds the amount of any capital gains tax payable in respect of it; or

(b) income tax would be payable by the person in respect of the relevant consideration if it constituted a qualifying distribution and no capital gains tax is payable in respect of it.

A corporation tax advantage (CTA 2010, s 732) means:

(a)   a relief from corporation tax or increased relief from corporation tax,

(b)   a repayment of corporation tax or increased repayment of corporation tax,

(c)   the avoidance or reduction of a charge to corporation tax or an assessment to corporation tax, or

(d)   the avoidance of a possible assessment to corporation tax.

16.4 The third condition for s 695/743 to apply is that one of the circumstances in s 685 of the ITA 2007 (income tax) or s 733(2) of the CTA 2010 (corporation tax) must be present.

16.5 If one of the relevant circumstances applies then, in determining then whether or not s 695/743 counteraction procedure may be invoked, the 'bona fide commercial' defence (s 684(2)/s 734) will be relevant. Section 695 does not apply if the taxpayer shows that the transaction or transactions did not have as their main object, or one of their main objects, to enable tax advantages to be obtained. Section 734 does not apply where the transaction or transactions are effected for genuine commercial reasons and obtaining a corporation tax advantage is not the main object or one of the main objects of the transaction.

16.6 Section 695/743 is also precluded from applying if (under s 701 of the ITA 2007 or section 748 of the CTA 2010) a clearance from HMRC is obtained to that effect.

16.7 Whenever, therefore, the three conditions for liability under s 695/743 are present in an own share purchase transaction, or where redeemable shares are being redeemed, consideration should be given to submitting an application for clearance under s 701/748 as well as under s 1044. If clearance is obtained to the effect that s 1033 applies (so that the trade benefit test is regarded as satisfied (see **13.7**)), it is more than likely that the bona fide commercial defence to s 695/743 will also be satisfied. Submitting a clearance under s 701/748 should remove any doubts.

16.8 HMRC state that where applications are to be submitted under s 701, s 748 and s 1044, a single application may be made under both provisions, enclosing a copy of the application and its enclosures (see Appendix I).

ENTERPRISE INVESTMENT SCHEME AND SEED ENTERPRISE INVESTMENT SCHEME

16.9 Some relief from income tax is conferred in certain cases where an individual subscribes for eligible shares in a qualifying company under the Enterprise Investment Scheme (ITA 2007, Part 5) or the Seed Enterprise Investment Scheme (ITA 2007, Part 5A, introduced with effect from April

2012). The effect of s 213 (EIS) or s 257FE (SEIS) of the ITA 2007 is that the relief given to an individual in respect of an investment in a new qualifying company can be wholly or partly withdrawn if, inter alia, the company were, within the period of five (EIS) or three (SEIS) years after the issue of the shares, to purchase or redeem any of its shares either from the individual in question or from any other shareholder.

ENTERPRISE MANAGEMENT INCENTIVE SHARE OPTION SCHEMES

16.10   Share options may be granted to selected employees in certain favoured sectors of business; these options, so-called EMI or Enterprise Management Incentives options (under Chapter 9 of Part 7 of the ITEPA 2003), are considerably more flexible as regards their workings and potential benefits to employees than the provisions governing HMRC-approved share option schemes under Chapters 6-8 of Part 7 of the ITEPA 2003. However, the HMRC-approved schemes are capable of applying to companies of all sizes in all business sectors. In addition, share options can be granted without any of the potential tax advantages under EMI – or Revenue-approved options.

16.11   Whatever type of share option is to be granted, where the shares are shares in an unquoted company, it may well be desirable for the company to have power to purchase its own shares; it would then be able to purchase shares acquired by an employee pursuant to the scheme in the event of the employee leaving the company. In the absence of this power, the need for the other shareholders to purchase the shares themselves might become a source of inconvenience or dissension. Where the individual who ceases to be an employee leaves as a result of dismissal or resignation following a disagreement with colleagues, and it is a term of his departure that the company purchases his shares, the purchase would seem likely to fulfil the requirement of being for the purpose of benefiting the trade. Where he simply resigns or retires from his employment without this having been precipitated by a dispute, it may be less easy to show that the own share purchase is for the benefit of the company's trade. However, the view of HMRC is understood to be that, in general, a company ought to be able to demonstrate the fulfilment of that test in such circumstances.

16.12   Conversely, it would seem more difficult to argue that an own share purchase is for the benefit of the company's trade where the employee who sells the shares remains in employment thereafter. It is arguable that it is for the benefit of an unquoted company's trade for it to create an internal market in its own shares with a view to enabling its employees to sell easily the shares which they have acquired pursuant to a share option scheme, as the ability to convert the shares into cash may make the share scheme more attractive and therefore act as a greater incentive to the employees. However, it is understood that such an argument has not, in the past, been favoured by HMRC. The opposite, and perhaps more convincing, argument is that the company's trade is more likely to be benefited if its employees remain shareholders with a stake in the long-term prosperity of the company. In practice, therefore, it is considered most unlikely that HMRC would ever give clearance in respect of an own share purchase where the vendor-employee is to continue in employment, and the main object of the purchase is to place cash in his hands in the form of capital and not income.

LEGAL EXPENSES

16.13   Legal (or other) expenditure incurred by a trading company on the redemption, repayment or purchase of its own shares is considered by HMRC to be capital expenditure, 'on the grounds that the costs are capital expenditure in respect of the company's share capital, or within Section [53 of the CTA 2009]. The expenditure is also likely to fail the wholly and exclusively test under Section [54 of the CTA 2009].' (HMRC Manual CTM17600).

DEMERGERS

16.14   Where a company purchases or redeems any of its own shares within five years after the occurrence of an 'exempt distribution' in which it was 'concerned' (within the meaning of s 1090(1) of the CTA 2010), the sale proceeds or redemption moneys are unlikely to constitute a 'chargeable payment' within the meaning of s 1088 of the CTA 2010. This is on the twin grounds that:

(a)   a payment which is a 'distribution' cannot be a 'chargeable payment' (CTA 2010, s 1088(5)); and

(b)   a payment which is not a 'distribution' can only be a 'chargeable payment' if, inter alia, it is made otherwise than for genuine commercial reasons or forms part of a scheme or arrangement the main purpose or one of the main purposes of which is the avoidance of tax (including stamp duty) (CTA 2010, s 1088(4)). A payment of that nature would almost certainly not be prevented by s 1033 of the CTA 2010 from being treated as a 'distribution'.

Accordingly, it appears that the only situation in which the sale proceeds or redemption moneys might constitute a chargeable payment is where the shares (not being bonus shares) are purchased or redeemed for a sum which is equal or near to the price for which they were originally issued, and a tax avoidance purpose is present. If the chargeable payment were made within five years after the making of the exempt distribution, the payment would be treated as miscellaneous income and would carry the other tax consequences described in s 928 of ITA 2007 (income tax) or s 1086 of the CTA 2010 (corporation tax).

INCOME TAX LOSS RELIEF

16.15   Where a company purchases its own shares from an individual who was the original subscriber of those shares, and he is now selling the shares to the company for less than what he subscribed for them, the allowable loss for capital gains purposes arising upon his sale to the company may in certain circumstances be offset against his income for income tax purposes; those circumstances are defined in Chapter 6 of Part 4 of the ITA 2007.

VOID OWN SHARE PURCHASES

16.16   If a limited company purports to do an own share purchase but fails to observe some legal requirement thereof, with the result that the purported purchase is both unlawful and void, the relevant shareholder will remain the owner of the shares in question. If any payment purporting to be the purchase price was made by the company and is held by the shareholder as a constructive trustee for the company, the company may become liable to tax under s 1033 of the CTA 2010 unless the shareholder refunds the payment before the end of the company's accounting period.

Chapter 17

OTHER FISCAL CONSEQUENCES

PURCHASES AND REDEMPTIONS

Capital gains tax

17.1   Where a company purchases or redeems its own shares, the person selling his shares or having them redeemed (the 'disponor') will make a disposal of his shares for CGT purposes. This will be material where the disponor is resident and/or ordinarily resident in the UK. Where s 1033 of the CTA 2010 applies, the entire proceeds of sale will come into the CGT computation. On the other hand, where s 1033 does not apply, the tax treatment of a disponor who is an individual has always been clear: s 37 of the TCGA 1992 will operate to exclude from the CGT computation any part of the consideration which is treated as a 'distribution' within the charge to income tax.

Corporate shareholder

17.2   Prior to July 2009, where the disponor was a UK-resident company and s 1033 did not apply, the 'distribution' element was included in the consideration of the disposal of the shares when calculating the corporation tax due on any gain, given that the distribution would otherwise not be chargeable, as a distribution received by a UK company was generally not subject to corporation tax. This was confirmed by the decision of the Court of Appeal in *Vojak v Strand Futures and Options Ltd.*[1] The Court, considering s 208 of the Taxes Act 1988, later s 1285 of the CTA 2009, held that a disponor who was a UK-resident company was within the charge to corporation tax on any capital gain arising in respect of a disposal by that company of shares to the company in which the shares are held.

17.3   The corporation tax rules in respect of distributions received changed in the Finance Act 2009 so that distributions received are subject to corporation tax unless they fall into one of the exemptions: s 1285 of the CTA 2009 has been repealed accordingly. Where the distribution is not exempt on receipt by the corporate shareholder, that element will be excluded under s 37 of the TCGA 1992 in the computation of the corporation tax on the gain as it will already have been taken into account for the purposes of calculating profits (even where an exemption applies).

---

[1]   [2003] EWCA Civ 1457, [2004] STC 64.

17.4   For a disposal of a shareholding of more than 10% of the company, which has been held for more than 12 months at the date of disposal, the capital element of a disposal is likely to fall within the substantial shareholdings exemption such that the disponor company suffers no corporation tax on the gain.

Example

17.5   In December 2009, a shareholder subscribed £100,000 for 100,000 shares in X Ltd. In October 2012, X Ltd purchases these 100,000 shares from that same shareholder for £1 million. Section 1033 cannot apply, because the shareholder has held the shares for less than five years (see **13.21**). The vendor-shareholder's capital gains position is as follows, according to whether he is a company or an individual, assuming that the "distribution" element is considered to be within one of the exempt classes:

Vendor	Individual		Company
	£		£
Proceeds	1,000,000		1,000,000
Less:			
Acquisition cost	100,000		100,000
Indexation (say 7%)	N/A		7,000
Taxable as income, subject to any reliefs	900,000		Nil (exempt)
Taxable as a gain, subject to any reliefs	Nil		Nil

17.6   Apart from the indexation allowance available to the company, both the company and the individual are chargeable to tax in the same amount, but under different taxing provisions.

Previous purchase from a third party

17.7   Where the vendor purchased the shares from a third party (as opposed to subscribing for them from the company) and s 1033 does not apply to the own share purchase, the capital gains consequences are as follows:

(a) the vendor will be treated as receiving a distribution equal to the amount (if any) by which his sale proceeds exceed the amount originally subscribed for the shares;

(b) if the vendor is an individual, he may either make a CGT loss equal to the amount by which the price he paid for the shares exceeded the amount originally subscribed for them, or make a chargeable gain if his purchase price was less than that amount.

(c) if the vendor is a UK-resident company, it will be in the same position as if it had subscribed for the shares at the same price as it in fact bought them.

Example

17.8 In 2009, a shareholder paid £40,000 for 100,000 shares in Y Ltd for which £100,000 had been originally subscribed. In October 2012, he sold these shares to Y Ltd itself for £120,000. Section 1033 cannot apply, because the shareholder has held the shares for less than five years (see **13.21**). The vendor-shareholder's capital gains position is as follows, according to whether he is a company or an individual, and assuming that the "distribution" element is within one of the exempt classes.

Vendor	Individual		Company
	£		£
Proceeds	120,000		120,000
Less:			
Acquisition cost	40,000		40,000
Indexation (say 6%)	N/A		2,400
Taxable as income	20,000		Nil (exempt)
Gain within the charge to CGT	60,000		
Gain within the charge to corporation tax on gains			Nil

The purchasing company's position

17.9 A company's acquisition of any of its own shares by way of purchase is deemed not to be the acquisition of an asset, for the purposes of IHT and of all taxes on income and capital gains (FA 2003, s 195(2); SI 2003/3077). Instead, the company's issued share capital is to be treated as if it had been reduced by the nominal value of the shares acquired, and the purchased shares are treated as having been immediately cancelled; any subsequent cancellation by the company of any of those shares is to be disregarded (and, accordingly, is not the disposal of an asset and does not give rise to an allowable loss for capital gains purposes (FA 2003, s 195(4))).

17.10 As the acquisition of own shares is deemed not to be the acquisition of an asset, it follows that the restriction on losses on a disposal to a connected person under s 18 of the TCGA 1992 does not apply as there is no acquisition and disposal, as required by s 18(1). Similarly, the provisions of s 171 of the TCGA 1992 in respect of intra-group transfers of assets will not apply.

The level of the purchase price

17.11 It is normally desirable from both the tax and commercial viewpoints that the vendor shareholder should receive for his shares a consideration approximating to their market value. Otherwise, it may be alleged that there is an element of gift or bounty in the transaction, with possible adverse IHT consequences, or with the possible consequence that a 'settlement' within the meaning of s 620 of the ITTOIA 2005 has been created.

17.12 In particular, where a controlling shareholder, or one of several shareholders who together have control, votes in favour of a share purchase which involves the purchase by the company of his own shares, care should be taken that a 'value-shift' does not occur under s 29(2) of the TCGA 1992. However, because a company's acquisition of any of its own shares by way of purchase is deemed not to be the acquisition of an asset (see **17.10**), a controlling shareholder cannot be deemed by ss 17 and 18 of the TCGA 1992 to sell his shares at market value – as s 18 can only apply where there is an acquisition of an asset and not just a disposal.

17.13 By contrast, a redemption of redeemable shares should involve no element of bounty, assuming that the shares are redeemed in accordance with their terms of redemption and that those terms conferred no bounty. If the terms of redemption did confer bounty, the bulk of any value-shift might well occur as at the date of issue of the shares or at any subsequent date when those terms are bounteously varied.

Borrowing to fund the buy-back

17.14 Where a company borrows to fund a buy-back, HMRC have confirmed (HMRC Corporate Finance Manual CFM38180) that the unallowable purpose provisions of the loan relationships rules under s 441 of the CTA 2009 will not be applied to deny the deduction for tax purposes provided that the arrangements are not structured to provide a tax advantage, and/or the amount borrowed is at arm's length. The manual refers to borrowing by a UK plc rather than to all companies but this appears to be an out-of-date reference to company law rather than to a specific intention to restrict the confirmation to public limited companies only.

The timing of the disposal

17.15 The timing of the shareholder's disposal for CGT purposes is governed by the normal rules in s 28 of the TCGA 1992, ie he will be deemed to dispose of the shares at the time when the contract is made (or, in the case of a conditional contract, when it becomes unconditional) and not upon the subsequent completion of the purchase. This point could be of significance where there is an interval between contract and completion and this interval straddles 5 April.

Example

A company with an accounting date of 31 March signs, on 26 March, an unconditional contract for the purchase of 1,000 of its own shares, with completion to take place 35 days later (in accordance with the requirements of s 723(1)(a) of the CA 2006, this purchase being financed out of capital).

The shareholder who is selling is treated by s 28 of the TCGA 1992 as disposing of the shares for CGT purposes on 26 March, even though he is not entitled to receive his money until 30 April. For tax purposes, the company is treated as having reduced its share capital by those 1,000 shares on 26 March. However, the company's accounts to 31 March should still show its issued share capital as including those 1,000 shares, although with a note giving information about the uncompleted purchase contract.

Stamp duty on own share purchases

17.16 A purchase of own shares by a company is subject to ad valorem stamp duty at the rate of 0.5% of the purchase price (FA 1999, Sch 13, para 3), unless within the low value exemption (see **18.18**) or the shares are held on an overseas branch register (by virtue of s 133 of the Companies Act 2006).

17.17 The Form SH03 must be stamped before being delivered to the Registrar of Companies (FA 1986, s 66; see **6.41**). This return is to be treated for all purposes of the Stamp Act 1891 as if it were an instrument transferring the shares on sale to the company in pursuance of the contract (or contracts) of purchase concerned (FA 1986, s 66(2)). Duty is charged at the rate of 0.5% of the purchase price (FA 1999, Sch 13, para 3).

17.18   Where the consideration is £1,000 or less, the exemption for low value transactions (FA 1999, Sch 13, para 1(3A)) means that the form SH03 does not need to be stamped before being submitted to Companies House, provided that the form is certified to confirm that the transaction is not part of a larger transaction, the consideration for which is more than £1,000. The standard Form SH03 which is available from Companies House has a section to be completed to make this certification.

There are criminal sanctions for failure to deliver the Form SH03 (see **6.41**).

17.19   Where a company acquires any shares in itself, whether by way of purchase under s 690 of the CA 2006 or otherwise, any instrument by which the shares are transferred to the company is exempt from stamp duty (FA 1999, Sch 13, para 1(4)). There is no need for such an instrument to be adjudicated in order for the exemption to apply.

17.20   The abolition of stamp duty on transfers of shares has been in statute for some time, but held in abeyance to take effect only from a date to be appointed by the Treasury by statutory instrument. The abolition of stamp duty on shares was originally thought to be necessary with the introduction of the TAURUS paperless securities settlement system. However, TAURUS was abandoned and so the abolition was indefinitely postponed. The CREST paperless settlement system was developed instead, removing the need for physical share certificates. However, despite the fact that a similar system to TAURUS was developed and implemented, there is no indication that the Government will implement the abolition of stamp duty on shares anytime soon.

Stamp Duty Reserve Tax

17.21   In the ordinary course of events a purchase by a company of its own shares will not generally result in any charge to stamp duty reserve tax (SDRT).

17.22   SDRT is a tax on transactions, not on documents, and has its own charging and administrative provisions, set out in Part IV of the FA 1986 and the Stamp Duty Reserve Tax Regulations 1986, SI 1986/1711 (SDRT Regulations 1986)). The principal situation which may give rise to a charge to SDRT is (FA 1986, s 87(1):

> ' . . . where a person (A) agrees with another person (B) to transfer chargeable securities (whether or not to B) for consideration in money or money's worth.'

'Chargeable securities' include shares (FA 1986, s 99(3)).

17.23   A charge to SDRT arises on the date when the agreement is made, or, if the agreement is conditional, on the day on which the condition is satisfied (FA 1986, s 87(2), (3)).

17.24 SDRT is charged at the rate of 0.5% of the amount or value of the consideration (FA 1986, s 87(6)) and becomes due and payable on the last day of the month following that in which the charge arose (SDRT Regulations 1986, reg 2).

17.25 The liability to pay the tax falls on B (as defined in the Regulations, see **17.22**), though certain agents acting for A or B (as defined in the Regulations) may also be accountable for the tax (SDRT Regulations 1986, reg 2).

17.26 Any charge to SDRT is cancelled retroactively if, before the expiry of six years beginning with the day on which the charge arose, the following two conditions are satisfied:

(a) an instrument is (or instruments are) executed in pursuance of the agreement and the instrument transfers (or the instruments between them transfer) to B or his nominee all the chargeable securities to which the agreement relates;

(b) the instrument (or each instrument) transferring the chargeable securities to which the agreement relates is duly stamped in accordance with the enactments relating to stamp duty or is not chargeable with stamp duty or otherwise required to be stamped under those enactments (FA 1986, s 92(1)–(3); Stamp Duty and Stamp Duty Land Tax (Consequential Amendment of Enactments) Regulations 2003, SI 2003/2868, reg 4).

17.27 A agreement under which a company purchases its own shares will be an agreement to transfer chargeable securities to the company for consideration in money or money's worth. That is because it is an agreement to purchase and sell shares, which inherently requires to be completed by means of a transfer.

17.28 As a result, a purchase of own shares will give rise to a charge to SDRT which can only be retroactively cancelled if the two conditions described above are satisfied. The form SH03 which the company must submit to the Registrar of Companies is subject to ad valorem stamp duty (FA 1986, s 66), provided that the consideration is for more than £1,000.

17.29 The form SH03 is treated as an instrument transferring the shares on sale to the company 'for all purposes of the Stamp Act 1891' (s 66(2) of the FA 1986) – which does not include the SDRT legislation in Part IV of the FA 1986. However, s 92(1C) specifically provides for the SDRT charge to be cancelled where a duly stamped form SH03 has been delivered to the Registrar of Companies within six years of the agreement for the buyback being made (or becoming unconditional, if the contract is conditional).

Stamp duty: redeemable shares

17.30 In the case of a redemption of redeemable shares, it is considered that no liability to ad valorem stamp duty will arise, on the ground that there is no 'sale' and therefore no 'conveyance or transfer on sale'. The process of redemption terminates the existence of a redeemable share according to the very terms of that existence; accordingly, no transfer or sale of the share is taking place. The position is directly analogous to that of the redemption of a debenture.

17.31 It is considered that a redemption of redeemable shares can never give rise to any charge to SDRT, on the ground that the redemption will not comprise an agreement to transfer chargeable securities to the company.

PAYMENT FOR AN OPTION, VARIATION OR RELEASE

17.32 The exemptions conferred by s 1033 of the CTA 2010 apply to a 'payment made by a company on the redemption, repayment or purchase of its own shares'. They do not apply to any payment made by a company for the grant of an option to purchase its own shares, nor for the release of any of the company's obligations under a contract to purchase its own shares or for the grant of an option over them. Such a payment will normally be treated in its entirety as a 'distribution', on the ground that it is a payment made 'in respect of shares' for the purposes of s 100(1)B of the CTA 2010. The same will apply to a payment made by a company for a variation of an existing contract to purchase its own shares or granting an option over them, except perhaps where the variation is followed quickly by the completion of the share purchase and the purchase money takes into account the variation.

SHARE VALUATIONS

17.33 It is possible that the existence in the articles of association of an unquoted company of a clause permitting it to purchase its own shares may have some effect on the values of minority shareholdings in the company. However, in practice it seems that HMRC's Shares and Assets Valuation specialists may not take this point:

> ' . . . the material question in arriving at the statutory open market value of a shareholding is whether, as a matter of general policy, the company would be prepared to buy back the shares of any shareholder and not only the holdings of, say, certain individuals who may be members of a family which effectively controls the company.'

The buy-back facility is one factor, amongst many others, to be taken into account in ascertaining the statutory open market value of a shareholding. It should not be given undue weight and should not be introduced into negotiations by [Shares and Asset Valuation].' (Previously in the Shares Valuation Manual, para 35070 – this has not been re-written to the new Shares and Assets Valuation Manual, but there is no material that contradicts this in the new manual.)

GIFTS AND BEQUESTS OF SHARES TO THE COMPANY

17.34 Plainly, s 1033 of the CTA 2010 is of no application to a gift or bequest to a company of shares in that company, as the company is not supplying any consideration for the shares. Upon completion of the gift, the company will become a member of itself. The transaction comprising the gift, and the state of affairs that subsequently ensues, appear to have the following fiscal consequences.

(a) An inter vivos gift of the shares will constitute a disposal of those shares for CGT purposes, but no gain will arise on that disposal if and to the extent that an election for hold-over relief is available and made pursuant to s 165 of the TCGA 1992. Where the gift is testamentary, there will be no disposal of the shares on death, but there will instead be an up-lift in the base value of the shares to their market value at the date of death (TCGA 1992, s 62).

(b) There will be no liability to ad valorem stamp duty, whether the gift of the shares operates inter vivos or is testamentary. Nor can there be any charge to SDRT, which can only apply to an agreement to transfer chargeable securities for consideration in money or money's worth (FA 1986, s 87(1)).

(c) The gift will constitute a transfer of value for IHT purposes, the consequences depending on the donor's circumstances and on the timing of the gift.

(d) Any later sale of the shares by the company will be a disposal for CGT purposes, which may attract a liability to corporation tax on chargeable gains. The same would apply where the company owns the shares immediately before its winding up.

THE COMPANY AS TRUSTEE OF ITS OWN SHARES

17.35 Where a company holds shares in itself in the capacity of a trustee, it seems that the tax consequences will be no different from what they would be if the trustees did not include or comprise the company.

Chapter 18

STRATEGY

TAXATION

A UK-resident individual

18.1 The lower rate of capital gains tax (up 28%) compared with income tax on distributions (up to an effective 30.56% for 2013/14) will generally mean that a UK-resident individual with sufficient income or gains to incur the additional rate of tax would generally prefer capital treatment, although the distinction is now less important than in earlier years for those on the additional rate. In particular, if entrepreneurs' relief is capable of applying to the gain, part or all of the gain on the disposal of the shares can be subject to capital gains tax at an effective rate of 10%. However, because the rules for eligibility to entrepreneurs' relief differ to the requirements of s 1033 of the CTA 2010, it does not follow that entrepreneurs' relief will always be available wherever capital treatment under s 1033 applies. Generally, the particular facts of any given situation need to be considered in order to determine whether an individual will be better off by having his proceeds of sale taxed either entirely as an item of capital or partly as an income distribution. The position is affected by the following factors:

(a) whether he can make immediate use of any capital loss arising as a result of the income element of the sale proceeds being treated as an income distribution;

(b) whether, if the proceeds of sale are taxable entirely as capital, the nature of the company's activities, coupled with the length of his period of ownership and personal circumstances, are such as to make available a entrepreneurs' relief;

(c) whether, for the tax year in which the sale is taking place, he has available to him all or part of his annual exemption for capital gains tax purposes;

(d) whether he is able to prevent a capital gain from giving rise to any significant charge to tax by offsetting it against any allowable losses or any other relief he may have available.

18.2 In the following example, in June 2004 the individual subscribed £10,000 for the shares which, in September 2013, he sells to the company, which has always been a trading company. The sale price is £60,000. If the individual has other income which already takes him above the additional rate limit and has already used up his CGT annual exemption but has not used any of his lifetime limit for entrepreneurs' relief, the following is the contrast between the distribution element being taxed as an income distribution and being taxed as a capital receipt.

Distribution treatment

Income element	£50,000.00		
Tax credit at one-ninth	£5,555.55		
Grossed up income	£55,555.55		
Income tax on which at 37.5% =		£20,833.33	
Less: tax credit		£(5,555.55)	
Additional rate tax payable		£15,277.78	£15,277.78
CGT computation: Proceeds of sale	£60,000.00		
Less: acquisition cost		£(10,000.00)	
Less: taxable as income (TCGA 1992, s 37)		£(50,000.00)	
		£(60,000.00)	
Result: no gain, no loss for CGT		£Nil	£Nil

Capital treatment

Proceeds of sale	£60,000	
Less: acquisition cost	£(10,000)	
Gain	£50,000	
Entrepreneurs' relief applies, therefore taxed at 10%		£5,000

Difference between distribution and capital treatment: £10,277.78.

18.3 Thus, entrepreneurs' relief can reduce the rate of capital gains tax to just 10%, and produce a better result than the effective income tax rate of 30.56% on an income distribution, even without the individual's CGT annual exemption.

18.4 Where the individual vendor was not the original subscriber for the shares, but instead purchased the shares for more than what they were subscribed for, that fact also may move the balance of advantage towards capital treatment. If distribution treatment applies, one ignores what the purchaser of the shares paid for them; instead, the taxable distribution is calculated by reference to the price at which the shares were originally issued (to whomever, and however long ago that was).

18.5 Conversely, under capital treatment, the CGT computation is based on what the current vendor previously paid for the shares, or on any other figure which the CGT legislation requires to be treated as his acquisition cost (eg market value, if the shares were not acquired under a bargain at arm's length). If, on the facts of the previous example, the shares being sold to the company for £60,000 in September 2013 had been purchased in June 2004 by the individual for £30,000 (having been issued originally for £10,000), the contrast would be as follows:

Distribution treatment

Additional rate tax payable (as before)		£15,277.78	£15,277.78
CGT computation: Proceeds of sale	£60,000.00		
Less: acquisition cost		£(30,000.00)	
Less: taxable as income (TCGA 1992, s 37)		£(50,000.00)	
		£(80,000.00)	
Result: capital loss		£(20,000.00)	

Capital treatment

Proceeds of sale	£60,000	
Less: acquisition cost	£(30,000)	

Gain	£30,000	
Entrepreneurs' relief applies, therefore taxed at 10%		£3,000

Difference between distribution and capital treatment (ignoring any benefit of the capital loss): £12,277.78.

If, under income treatment, the capital loss could be taken advantage of in the same year of assessment, this could produce a tax saving of 50% × £20,000 = £10,000, wiping out almost two-thirds of the £15,277.78 of income tax payable.

18.6   If the size of the payment from the company and the individual's other income are such that his income does not exceed the basic rate limit, there can be no harm in his receiving a distribution, as his liability to tax at the dividend ordinary rate in respect of the distribution will be fully offset against the tax credit carried by that distribution. Such an individual could, however, be harmed by receiving the income element of the sale proceeds as capital for tax purposes; because once his gain exceeds the amount of that part of his annual exemption which is otherwise available, he will be chargeable to CGT notwithstanding that the amount of the gain is such that, if it were taxable as income, it would not cross the basic rate limit.

A UK-resident company

18.7   A UK-resident vendor company may well be indifferent as to whether the income element of the proceeds of sale is received by it as a distribution or as capital: a distribution will usually fall within one of the exempt classes so that no corporation tax is payable on the receipt of the distribution. If the distribution is not within one of the exempt classes will the element of the consideration representing a distribution be excluded in the computation of the gain, as it will have been taken into account for the purposes of computing income. In either case, provided the amount bought back qualifies for substantial shareholdings exemption, no corporation tax will be due on the receipt.

18.8   However, the receipt of a distribution will constitute franked investment income in the hands of the vendor company, and this is capable of adversely affecting the company's entitlement to be taxed at the small companies rate (CTA 2010, s 32).

Conflicting interests

18.9   Where for some reason several vendors are selling at the same time and under similar circumstances, it may be in the interests of one vendor that the transaction should be treated as a 'capital' transaction, whilst another might prefer the payment to reach him as a distribution. Where prima facie all the various conditions in ss 1034–1047 of the CTA 2010 for s 1033 to apply appear to be satisfied in respect of both categories of vendor, one solution to the potential conflict of interests is for each vendor who wishes to ensure that the income element of his sale proceeds is treated as a distribution to transfer his shares to a non-resident nominee before the contract for the sale of his shares to the company is entered into (assuming that the Articles of Association of the company contain no insurmountable impediment to him doing so); he will then automatically fail to satisfy the residence requirement (see **13.13**).

18.10   A reasonable interval of time should be allowed to elapse between the transfer to the nominee and the signing of the purchase contract, so as to minimise the chances of the principle in *Furniss v Dawson*[1] being argued by HMRC – although such argument might demonstrate the presence of a tax avoidance motive, with the result that s 1033 would be prevented from applying by its own terms (see **13.7**).

18.11   This stratagem could be applied in relation to any purchase from a single vendor, as an alternative to trying to obtain a clearance from HMRC to the effect that s 1033 does not apply to the sale proceeds in question (see **15.9**).

18.12   Another way of deliberately preventing s 1033 of the CTA 2010 from applying to the sale proceeds would be to arrange for the vendor and the company to grant cross-options to each other and for these to be exercised on numerous separate occasions in such a way that the vendor's shareholdings in the company are not 'substantially reduced' until the last occasion when such an option is exercised; s 1037 of the CTA 2010 will thereby not be fulfilled (see **13.29**). HMRC have been known to take the view that such a fragmented disposal of a shareholding constituted a scheme having as one of its main purposes the avoidance of tax, with the desired consequence that s 1033 did not apply even to the exercise of the option over the final installment of the shares.

Securing 'capital' treatment

18.13   Where a vendor wishes to have 'capital' treatment for the sale proceeds of his shares and it appears unlikely that the purchase can be made to satisfy the necessary conditions in order for s 1033 of the CTA 2010 to apply, consideration should be given to the feasibility of selling the shares not to the company itself but to a third party. Such a third party might be a corporate investor, or a dealer in securities, or the trustees of an employee trust. The purchaser should have his own commercial or investment motives for acquiring the shares, and there should be no pre-ordained plan that the buyer should then sell the shares to the company. Under this approach, the sale proceeds ought to be taxable as capital and not as income in the vendor's hands, assuming there is no problem under s 695 of the ITA 2007 or s 748 of the CTA 2010.

---

[1]   [1984] STC 153.

18.14   If 'capital' treatment appears unattainable, a possible means of avoiding dividend higher or additional rate income tax for a vendor who is an individual and who is not otherwise liable to higher or additional rate tax is for his sale contract to provide for his shares to be sold to the company in two or possibly three instalments, each instalment falling in a different tax year. Assuming that the sale proceeds are to be drawn by the company from its distributable profits, there is no reason in company law why a single own share purchase contract should not provide for there to be different completion dates for different parcels of shares. There should be little problem in implementing this arrangement pursuant to an option contract where it is wished to spread the sales of the shares over just two years of assessment with the first sale taking place in March and the second after 5 April. This clearly will not assist with dissenting shareholders, but where the sale is amicable, appropriate arrangements should be able to be made, taking care that the vendor's beneficial ownership in the shares is not transferred prematurely.

Clearances

18.15   As a general rule, if reliance is to be placed on s 1033 applying, an application for clearance should be submitted to the Commissioners beforehand, pursuant to s 1044 of the CTA 2010 (see **15.7**).

COMMERCIAL STRATEGY

Redeemable shares

18.16   In any case where shares are to be issued to an investor in circumstances where it is likely that, after a number of years, the company may wish to 'buy him out', there should be considered the relative advantages and disadvantages of issuing him with redeemable shares or with ordinary irredeemable shares which the company will have the power to purchase.

18.17   The main advantage of issuing redeemable shares is that their redemption will not attract ad valorem stamp duty, whereas a purchase of irredeemable shares will (see **17.13** et seq). Conversely, a possible disadvantage of issuing redeemable shares is that the company may be restricted in its ability to make a bonus issue of further redeemable shares in respect of the original redeemable shares, as a bonus issue of redeemable shares is treated as a 'distribution' for income tax purposes (CTA 2010, s 1000(1)C). Indeed, following the redemption of the redeemable shares, the company is unlikely to be able to issue any bonus shares without giving rise to a taxable 'distribution' (see **12.20** and **16.10**).

Gifts of shares to the company

18.18   An arithmetical difficulty over shareholding percentages may be resolved by making a gift of shares in a company to the company itself. For example, the shareholders of a company comprise a father and his three sons. The father owns 40 shares and each son owns 20. The father, in his will, wishes to leave his 40 shares to his three sons in equal proportions. A simple way of resolving the arithmetical difficulty would be for the father to leave all 40 of his shares to the company; alternatively, he could leave just one share to the company and 13 to each son.

Numbering of shares

18.19 It is highly desirable, and sometimes actually necessary (as in **7.9**), to be able to identify exactly which shares are being purchased or redeemed and what consideration was received by the company for their issue. For this purpose, it is desirable for companies to continue numbering their shares, notwithstanding that, if all the shares of the class are fully paid up and rank pari passu for all purposes, there is no legal obligation to number them (CA 2006, s 543).

18.20 Where it is impossible or highly impractical to ascertain the original issue price of the shares being purchased or redeemed, it is possible for tax purposes to calculate an average issue price for the shares being purchased and to determine the 'distribution' element of the purchase price on the assumption that the shares being purchased are drawn from one or more pools of 'averaged' shares. Each (if more than one) pool should consist only of those shares whose exact issue price cannot be ascertained; there may need to be a separate pool for each group of shares whose date of issue can be identified by a process of eliminating any other such groups. HMRC are likely to accept any reasonable basis of calculation (Corporation Tax Manual, CTM17510). There is no statutory authority for this averaging process, which is simply a measure of last resort.

18.21 It is difficult to see how it could be justifiably applied for the purposes of s 687 and 692 of the CA 2006; thus, where shares are to be purchased or redeemed, it is only possible to finance more than the nominal value of those shares out of the proceeds of a new issue of shares if one can identify precisely the original issue price of the shares which are to be purchased or redeemed.

Reduction of capital

18.22 A reduction of capital may be better than an own share purchase where the company wishes to repay the nominal value of some of its issued shares and has sufficient cash with which to make the repayment, because there is no ad valorem stamp duty to pay on a reduction of capital.

Avoiding a winding up

18.23 An own share purchase, sourced out of capital, can be very useful where:

(a)   the company has ceased to conduct the trade or other activities which justified its existence;

(b)   the company has paid off all its creditors and is left with a pool of cash as its sole asset;

(c)   the amount of that cash (after distributing as much of it by way of dividend as is legally possible) is equal to or less than the amount of the consideration received by the company in return for the original issue of the shares, but is still a significant amount; and

(d)   the members wish legally to recover as much as possible of the company's cash and then to get rid of the company.

One way of achieving this objective would be for the company to go into members' voluntary liquidation. However, as no person may act as a liquidator of a company unless he is a qualified insolvency practitioner (Insolvency Act 1986, s 389) and the procedure for carrying out an own share purchase out of capital is likely to be simpler and less costly than the procedure for a winding up, an own share purchase may well prove to be preferable to a winding up. Once the own share purchase has been completed (using up the whole of the company's cash, and with the company purchasing all but one of its issued shares), the company will be in a position to apply to be struck off the register of companies under CA 2006, s 1003.

Appendix A

NOTICE OF GENERAL MEETING

_____ LIMITED

NOTICE OF MEETING

NOTICE IS HEREBY GIVEN that a GENERAL MEETING of the above-named Company will be held at _____ on _____ 201__ at _____am/pm for the purpose of considering and (if thought fit) passing the following resolution as a Special Resolution:

THAT the terms of the proposed contract, whereby the Company may become entitled and obliged to purchase [*from Mr* _____] _____ of its own [*Ordinary*] shares of [*£1*] each, and of which a copy is produced to the Meeting and initialled for the purpose of identification by the Chairman of the Directors, be and are hereby approved, and any director of the Company be and is hereby authorised to enter into the contract on behalf of the Company and to fulfil all obligations of the Company thereunder.

DATED the _____ day of _____ 201__

By Order of the Board

_____ Director

NOTE:

1. A copy of the draft contract is attached to this notice of meeting.

2. A member of the company entitled to attend and vote at the above-mentioned meeting is entitled to appoint another person as his proxy to attend, speak and vote at the meeting. A proxy need not be a member of the company, but must attend the meeting. A form of proxy and accompanying guidance notes are enclosed with this notice of meeting.

Appendix B

PRECEDENT FOR A WRITTEN RESOLUTION

THE COMPANIES ACT 2006   Company No_____

_____ LIMITED

WRITTEN RESOLUTION TO APPROVE AN OWN SHARE PURCHASE CONTRACT

We, the undersigned, being all the members of the above-named private company ('the Company') other than the member[s] holding shares to which the following resolution relates, hereby agree that the following resolution shall have effect as a written resolution of the Company in accordance with Chapter 2 of Part 13 of the Companies Act 2006, and we each hereby acknowledge receipt of a copy of the proposed contract to which the following resolution relates:

> THAT the terms of the proposed contract, whereby the Company may become entitled and obliged to purchase [*from Mr* _____] _____ of its own [*Ordinary*] shares of [*£1*] each, and of which a copy has been supplied to each member of the Company, be and are hereby approved, and any director of the Company be and is hereby authorised to enter into the contract on behalf of the Company and to fulfil all obligations of the Company thereunder.

_____   _____

(*name*)   (*name*)

Date: _____ 201_   Date: _____ 201_

_____   _____

(*name*)   (*name*)

Date: _____ 201_   Date: _____ 201_

Appendix C

EXTRACTS FROM THE FINANCIAL SERVICES AUTHORITY'S *LISTING RULES*[1]

February 2013

This chapter sets out the principal rules which apply to a company wishing to purchase its own listed securities, whether as a market purchase or an off-market purchase within the meaning of ss 694 and 701 of the Companies Act 2006 respectively. It also sets out the rules which apply to a company that (following a purchase of its own securities) holds a proportion of its own shares as treasury shares and wishes to sell, transfer or cancel such shares. The requirements mainly relate to the notification of purchases by a company of its own securities and dealings in treasury shares. The information required in annual accounts concerning the purchase of own securities and dealings in treasury shares is also reproduced below. Provisions having the status of "Guidance" are set out in italic type.

Chapter 12   Dealing in own securities and treasury shares: premium listing

12.1 Application

Application

12.1.1   This chapter applies to a company that has a premium listing of equity shares.

12.1.2   This chapter contains rules applicable to a listed company that:

(1)   purchases its own equity shares; or

(2)   purchases its own securities other than equity shares; or

(3)   sells or transfers treasury shares; or

(4)   purchases or redeems its own securities during a prohibited period; or

(5)   purchases its own securities from a related party.

---

[1]   Extracts from the UKLA *Listing Rules* reproduced by kind permission of the Financial Services Authority. Note that further reproduction of these extracts for inclusion in other documents requires express permission. From the 1st April, the Financial Conduct Authority.

Exceptions

12.1.3 LR 12.2 to LR 12.5 do not apply to a transaction entered into:

(1) in the ordinary course of business by a securities dealing business; or

(2) on behalf of third parties either by the company or any member of its group;

if the listed company has established and maintains effective Chinese walls between those responsible for any decision relating to the transaction and those in possession of inside information relating to the listed company.

12.2 Prohibition on purchase of own securities

12.2.1 A listed company must not purchase or redeem (or make any early redemptions of) its own securities and must ensure that no purchases in its securities are effected on its behalf or by any member of its group during a prohibited period unless:

(1) prior to the commencement of the prohibited period, the company has put in place a buy-back programme in which the dates and quantities of securities to be traded during the relevant period are fixed and have been disclosed in a notification made in accordance with LR 12.4.4 R; or

(2) prior to the commencement of the prohibited period, the company has put in place a buy-back programme managed by an independent third party which makes its trading decisions in relation to the company's securities independently of, and uninfluenced by, the company; or

(3) the company is purchasing or redeeming securities other than shares or securities whose price or value would be likely to be significantly affected by the publication of the information giving rise to the prohibited period; or

(4) the company is redeeming securities (other than equity shares) which, at the time of issue, set out:

(a) the date of redemption;
(b) the number of securities to be redeemed or the formula used to determine that number; and
(c) the redemption price or the formula used to determine the price.

12.3 Purchase from a related party

12.3.1 Where a purchase by a listed company of its own equity securities or preference shares is to be made from a related party, whether directly or through intermediaries, LR 11 (Related party transactions) must be complied with unless:

(1) a tender offer is made to all holders of the class of securities; or

(2) in the case of a market purchase pursuant to a general authority granted by shareholders, it is made without prior understanding, arrangement or agreement between the listed company and any related party.

12.4 Purchase of own equity shares

Purchases of less than 15%

12.4.1 Unless a tender offer is made to all holders of the class, purchases by a listed company of less than 15% of any class of its equity shares (excluding treasury shares) pursuant to a general authority granted by shareholders, may only be made if the price to be paid is not more than the higher of:

(1) 5% above the average market value of the company's equity shares for the 5 business days prior to the day the purchase is made; and

(2) that stipulated by Article 5(1) of the Buy-back and Stabilisation Regulation.

Purchases of 15% or more

12.4.2 Purchases by a listed company of 15% or more of any class of its equity shares (excluding treasury shares) must be by way of a tender offer to all shareholders of that class.

12.4.A Purchases of 15% or more of any class of its own equity shares may be made by a listed company, other than by way of a tender offer, provided that the full terms of the share buy-back have been specifically approved by the shareholders.

12.4.3 Where a series of purchases are made pursuant to a general authority granted by shareholders, which in aggregate amount to 15% or more of the number of equity shares of the relevant class in issue immediately following the shareholders meeting at which the general authority to purchase was granted, a tender offer need only be made in respect of any purchase that takes the aggregate to or above that level. Purchases that have been specifically approved by shareholders are not to be taken into account in determining whether the 15% level has been reached.

Notification prior to purchase

12.4.4

(1) Any decision by the board to submit to shareholders a proposal for the listed company to be authorised to purchase its own equity shares must be notified to a RIS as soon as possible.

(2) A notification required by paragraph (1) must set out whether the proposal relates to:

 (a) specific purchases and if so, the names of the persons from whom the purchases are to be made; or

 (b) a general authorisation to make purchases.

(3) The requirement set out in paragraph (1) does not apply to a decision by the board to submit to shareholders a proposal to renew an existing authority to purchase own equity shares.

12.4.5 A listed company must notify a RIS as soon as possible of the outcome of the shareholders' meeting to decide the proposal described in LR 12.4.4 R.

Notification of purchases

12.4.6 Any purchase of a listed company's own equity shares by or on behalf of the company or any other member of its group must be notified to a RIS as soon as possible, and in any event by no later than 7:30 a.m. on the business day following the calendar day on which the purchase occurred. The notification must include:

(1) the date of purchase;

(2) the number of equity shares purchased;

(3) the purchase price for each of the highest and lowest price paid, where relevant;

(4) the number of equity shares purchased for cancellation and the number of equity shares purchased to be held as treasury shares; and

(5) where equity shares were purchased to be held as treasury shares, a statement of:

 (a) the total number of treasury shares of each class held by the company following the purchase and non-cancellation of such equity shares; and

(b) the number of equity shares of each class that the company has in issue less the total number of treasury shares of each class held by the company following the purchase and non-cancellation of such equity shares.

Consent of other classes

12.4.7 Unless LR 12.4.8 R applies, a company with listed securities convertible into, or exchangeable for, or carrying a right to subscribe for equity shares of the class proposed to be purchased must (prior to entering into any agreement to purchase such shares):

(1) convene a separate meeting of the holders of those securities; and

(2) obtain their approval for the proposed purchase of equity shares by a special resolution.

12.4.8 LR 12.4.7 R does not apply if the trust deed or terms of issue of the relevant securities authorise the listed company to purchase its own equity shares.

12.4.9 A circular convening a meeting required by LR 12.4.7 R must include (in addition to the information in LR 13 (Contents of circulars)):

(1) a statement of the effect on the conversion expectations of holders in terms of attributable assets and earnings, on the basis that the company exercises the authority to purchase its equity shares in full at the maximum price allowed (where the price is to be determined by reference to a future market price the calculation must be made on the basis of market prices prevailing immediately prior to the publication of the circular and that basis must be disclosed); and

(2) any adjustments to the rights of the holders which the company may propose (in such a case, the information required under paragraph (1) must be restated on the revised basis).

Other similar transactions

12.4.10 *A listed company intending to enter into a transaction that would have an effect on the company similar to that of a purchase of own equity shares should consult with the FSA to discuss the application of LR 12.4.*

12.5 Purchase of own securities other than equity shares

12.5.1 Except where the purchases will consist of individual transactions made in accordance with the terms of issue of the relevant securities, where a listed company intends to purchase any of its securities convertible into its equity shares with a premium listing it must:

(1)   ensure that no dealings in the relevant securities are carried out by or on behalf of the company or any member of its group until the proposal has either been notified to a RIS or abandoned; and

(2)   notify a RIS of its decision to purchase.

Notification of purchases, early redemptions and cancellations

12.5.2   Any purchases, early redemptions or cancellations of a company's own securities convertible into equity shares with a premium listing, by or on behalf of the company or any other member of its group must be notified to a RIS when an aggregate of 10% of the initial amount of the relevant class of securities has been purchased, redeemed or cancelled, and for each 5% in aggregate of the initial amount of that class acquired thereafter.

12.5.3   The notification required by LR 12.5.2 R must be made as soon as possible and in any event no later than 7:30 a.m. on the business day following the calendar day on which the relevant threshold is reached or exceeded. The notification must state:

(1)   the amount of securities acquired, redeemed or cancelled since the last notification; and

(2)   whether or not the securities are to be cancelled and the number of that class of securities that remain outstanding.

12.5.4   [deleted]

Period between purchase and notification

12.5.5   In circumstances where the purchase is not being made pursuant to a tender offer and the purchase causes a relevant threshold in LR 12.5.2 R to be reached or exceeded, no further purchases may be undertaken until after a notification has been made in accordance with LR 12.5.2 R to LR 12.5.4 R.

Convertible securities

12.5.6   [deleted]

Warrants and options

12.5.7   Where, within a period of 12 months, a listed company purchases warrants or options over its own equity shares which, on exercise, convey the entitlement to equity shares representing 15% or more of the company's existing issued shares (excluding treasury shares), the company must send to its shareholders a circular containing the following information:

(1)   a statement of the directors' intentions regarding future purchases of the company's warrants and options;

(2)   the number and terms of the warrants or options acquired and to be acquired and the method of acquisition;

(3)   where warrants or options have been, or are to be, acquired from specific parties, a statement of the names of those parties and all material terms of the acquisition; and

(4)   details of the prices to be paid.

12.6 Treasury shares

Prohibition on sales or transfers of treasury shares

12.6.1   Subject to LR 12.6.2 R, sales for cash, or transfers for the purposes of, or pursuant to, an employees' share scheme, of treasury shares must not be made during a prohibited period.

Exemptions

12.6.2   LR 12.6.1 R does not apply to the following sales or transfers by a listed company of treasury shares:

(1)   transfers of treasury shares in connection with the operation of an employees' share scheme where the transfer facilitates dealings that do not fall within the provisions of the Model Code; or

(2)   sales or transfers by the company of treasury shares (other than equity shares) of a class whose price or value would not be likely to be significantly affected by the publication of the information giving rise to the prohibited period.

Notification of capitalisation issues and of sales, transfers and cancellations of treasury shares

12.6.3   If by virtue of its holding treasury shares, a listed company is allotted shares as part of a capitalisation issue, the company must notify a RIS as soon as possible and in any event by no later than 7:30 a.m. on the business day following the calendar day on which allotment occurred of the following information:

(1)   the date of the allotment;

(2)   the number of shares allotted;

(3) a statement as to what number of shares allotted have been cancelled and what number is being held as treasury shares; and

(4) where shares allotted are being held as treasury shares, a statement of:

    (a) the total number of treasury shares of each class held by the company following the allotment; and

    (b) the number of shares of each class that the company has in issue less the total number of treasury shares of each class held by the company following the allotment.

12.6.4 Any sale for cash, transfer for the purposes of or pursuant to an employees' share scheme or cancellation of treasury shares that represent over 0.5% of the listed company's share capital must be notified to a RIS as soon as possible and in any event by no later than 7:30 a.m. on the business day following the calendar day on which the sale, transfer or cancellation occurred. The notification must include:

(1) the date of the sale, transfer or cancellation;

(2) the number of shares sold, transferred or cancelled;

(3) the sale or transfer price for each of the highest and lowest prices paid, where relevant; and

(4) a statement of:

    (a) the total number of treasury shares of each class held by the company following the sale, transfer or cancellation; and

    (b) the number of shares of each class that the company has in issue less the total number of treasury shares of each class held by the company following the sale, transfer or cancellation.

Chapter 13 Contents of circulars: Premium listing

13.1 Preliminary

Application

13.1.1 This chapter applies to a company that has a premium listing.

Listed company to ensure circulars comply with chapter

13.1.2 A listed company must ensure that circulars it issues to holders of its listed equity shares comply with the requirements of this chapter.

When circulars about purchase of own equity shares need approval

13.2.3

(1) A circular relating to a resolution to give a listed company authority to purchase its own equity shares must be approved by the FSA under LR 13.2.1 R if:

    (a) the purchase by the company of its own equity shares is to be made from a related party (whether directly or through intermediaries); or

    (b) the exercise in full of the authority sought would result in the purchase of 25% or more of the company's issued equity shares (excluding treasury shares).

(2) A circular referred to in paragraph (1)(a) does not need to be approved if:

    (a) a tender is made to all holders of the class of securities on the same terms; or

    (b) for a market purchase under a general authority granted by shareholders, it is made without prior understanding, arrangement or agreement between the company and any related party.

13.7 Purchase of own equity shares

13.7.1

(1) A circular relating to a resolution proposing to give the company authority to purchase its own equity securities must also include:

    (a) if the authority sought is a general one, a statement of the directors' intentions about using the authority;

    (b) if known, the method by which the company intends to acquire its equity shares and the number to be acquired in that way;

    (c) a statement of whether the company intends to cancel the equity shares or hold them in treasury;

    (d) if the authority sought related to a proposal to purchase from specific parties, a statement of the names of the persons from whom equity shares are to be acquired together with all material terms of the proposal;

    (e) details about the price, or the maximum and minimum price, to be paid;

    (f) the total number of warrants and options to subscribe for equity shares that are outstanding at the latest practicable date before the circular is published and both the proportion of issued share capital (excluding treasury shares) that they represent at that time and will represent if the full authority to buyback shares (existing and being sought) is used; and

(g) where LR 12.4.2A R applies, an explanation of the potential impact of the proposed share buy-back, including whether control of the listed company may be concentrated following the proposed transaction.

(2) If the exercise in full of the authority sought would result in the purchase of 25% or more of the company's issued equity shares (excluding treasury shares) the circular must also include the following information referred to in the PD Regulation:

(a) Annex 1 item 4 – Risk factors;
(b) Annex 1 item 12 – Trend information;
(c) Annex 1 item 17.2 – Director's interests in shares;
(d) Annex 1 item 18.1 – Major interests in shares;
(e) Annex 1 item 20.9 – Significant changes;
(f) Annex 3 item 3.1 – Working capital (this must be based on the assumption that the authority sought will be used in full at the maximum price allowed and this assumption must be stated). This information is not required to be included in a circular issued by a closed-ended investment fund.

Pro forma financial information

13.7.2 *LR 13.3.3 R sets out requirements for pro forma information in a circular relating to the purchase by the company of 25% or more of the company's issued equity shares (excluding treasury shares).*

Annual Report and Accounts

Paragraph 9.86 of the *Listing Rules* (as at February 2013) requires the following items to be included in the annual report and accounts:

Additional information

9.8.6 In the case of a listed company incorporated in the United Kingdom, the following additional items must be included in its annual financial report:

  …

(4) a statement setting out:

(a) details of any shareholders authority for the purchase, by the listed company of its own shares that is still valid at the end of the period under review;
(b) in the case of purchases made otherwise than through the market or by tender to all shareholders, the names of sellers of such shares purchased, or proposed to be purchased, by the listed company during the period under review;

(c)   in the case of any purchases made otherwise than through the market or by tender or partial offer to all shareholders, or options or contracts to make such purchases, entered into since the end of the period covered by the report, information equivalent to that required under Part 2 of Schedule 7 to the Large & Medium Sized Companies and Groups (Accounts and Reports) Regulations 2008 (SI 2008/410) (Disclosure required by company acquiring its own shares etc); and

(d)   in the case of sales of treasury shares for cash made otherwise than through the market, or in connection with an employees' share scheme, or otherwise than pursuant to an opportunity which (so far as was practicable) was made available to all holders of the listed company's securities (or to all holders of a relevant class of its securities) on the same terms, particulars of the names of purchasers of such shares sold, or proposed to be sold, by the company during the period under review.

Appendix D

THE ASSOCIATION OF BRITISH INSURERS' RECOMMENDATIONS

Investment Committee Own Share Purchases

1 THE AUTHORITY FOR GENERAL SHAREHOLDER APPROVAL

The Committee has not published formal guidelines on this subject but the Secretariat has been asked to request companies:

(a) To provide that such powers can only be implemented by special resolution and not simply an ordinary resolution as is implied by Section 701 of the Companies Act 2006.

(b) To provide that the authority to purchase shares is renewable annually.

(c) To undertake in the document that the authority to purchase its own shares will only be exercised if so to do would result in an increase in earnings per share and is in the best interests of shareholders generally. In the case of property companies and investment trusts the undertaking would refer to an increase in asset value per share for the remaining shareholders.

2 OTHER CLASSES OF SHARE CAPITAL

Where the company has Preference share capital, class meeting consent should be obtained from the Preference shareholders and regard will be had to the resultant effect on their capital and dividend covers.

3 THE AMOUNT

Assuming the company is trading normally, authority to purchase up to 5% of the Ordinary share capital is unlikely to cause concern but regard will obviously be had to the effect on gearing etc, where larger amounts of capital are involved. Some institutional investors have indicated a reluctance to accept own share purchase powers over share capital in excess of 10% of the Issued Ordinary share capital.

4 THE PRICE

The Listing Rules requirements for purchases below the 15% level are for the price not to exceed 5% above the average middle market quotation over 5 business days before the purchase. The Committee regards this as an appropriate level, members having questioned other proposed bases, such as fixed prices, and companies have created problems for themselves by going beyond the basic requirements of the Listing Rules.

Enquiries to: Michael McKersie

dated 25 January 1990
(amended 30 November 2009)

Appendix E

PRECEDENTS FOR PAYMENTS OUT OF CAPITAL

Written resolution

THE COMPANIES ACT 2006   Company No_____

_____ LIMITED

WRITTEN RESOLUTIONS TO APPROVE AN OWN SHARE PUR-
CHASE CONTRACT AND TO APPROVE THE MAKING OF A PAY-
MENT OUT OF CAPITAL

Circulation Date: _____

We, the undersigned, being all the members of the above-named private
company ('the Company') other than the member[s] holding shares to which
the following resolutions relate, hereby irrevocably agree that, pursuant to
Chapter 2 of Part 13 of the Companies Act 2006, the two following resolutions
shall have effect as written resolutions of the Company and we each hereby
acknowledge receipt of a copy of the proposed contract to which the resolution
numbered '1' below relates and also a copy of the directors' statement and
auditors' report which are required by section 718 of the Companies Act 2006
in connection with the resolution numbered '2' below:

1   THAT the terms of the proposed contract, whereby the Company may
     become entitled and obliged to purchase from Mr _____ _____ of
     its own [Ordinary] shares of [£1] each, and of which a copy has been
     supplied to each member of the Company, be and are hereby approved,
     and any director of the Company be and is hereby authorised to enter
     into the contract on behalf of the Company and to fulfil all obligations of
     the Company thereunder.

2   THAT there be and is hereby approved the proposed payment of £_____
     out of 'capital' (within the meaning of section 716 of the Companies
     Act 2006) to be made in pursuance of the proposed agreement under
     which the Company may become entitled and obliged to purchase
     _____ of its own [Ordinary] shares of [£1] each and the terms of which
     are being approved by the written resolution numbered '1' above.

_____   _____

(*name*)   (*name*)

Date: _____ 201_   Date: _____ 201_

Auditors' report under section 714

The Directors

_____ Limited

[*date*]

Dear Sirs,

_____ Limited ('the Company')

We refer to the directors' statement dated _____ 201_ and made by you pursuant to section 714 of the Companies Act 2006 relating to a proposed payment of £_____ in respect of the total price for the purchase by the Company of certain of its own shares.

We declare that:

(a) we have inquired into the Company's state of affairs;

(b) the amount specified in your aforementioned statement as that which it is proposed to pay by way of the permissible capital payment is in our view properly determined in accordance with sections 710 to 712 of the Companies Act 2006; and

(c) we are not aware of anything to indicate that the opinion expressed by you in your statement is unreasonable in all the circumstances.

Yours faithfully,

Form of notice for publication in *The London Gazette* and in a national newspaper

_____ LIMITED

Notice is hereby given pursuant to section 719 of the Companies Act 2006 that on the _____201_ the above-named company approved a payment of £_____ out of capital for the purpose of purchasing _____ of its own shares; that the directors' statement and the auditors' report required by section 714 of the Companies Act 2006 are available for inspection at the Company's registered office (_____); and that any creditor of the Company may at any time within the 5 weeks immediately following the afore-mentioned date apply to the court under section 721 of the Companies Act 2006 for an order prohibiting the payment.

_____, Director.

Appendix F

UITF ABSTRACT 37[1]

Purchases and sales of own shares
(Issued 28 October 2003)

The issue

1. Companies legislation allows certain companies to purchase their own shares and hold them in treasury without cancelling them. A company that holds treasury shares is subsequently allowed to sell them. Companies legislation also allows certain subsidiaries to purchase, hold or sell shares in their holding companies. The issue is how an entity should account for purchases and sales of own shares.

2. This Abstract does not apply to an entity's own shares held by an ESOP trust (the accounting for which is specified in UITF Abstract 13 'Accounting for ESOP Trusts'). The recognition of the costs of awards to employees that take the form of shares or rights to shares is dealt with in UITF Abstract 17 'Employee share schemes'.

3. The Statement of Principles for Financial Reporting (Chapter 4) addresses the treatment of increases or decreases in an entity's ownership interest that result from transactions with owners in their capacity as owners. Such transactions are referred to as 'contributions from owners' and 'distributions to owners'; these elements of financial statements do not give rise to gains or losses. Distributions to owners include the payment of dividends and the return of capital. The Statement gives the purchase by a company of its own shares as an example of a return of capital, which is reflected in financial statements by reducing the amount of ownership interest. Ownership interest is defined as a residual interest, ie the amount that results from deducting all of an entity's liabilities from all of its assets.

4. An entity's purchase of its own shares gives rise to a reduction in the entity's ownership interest, not an asset. This principle is reflected in FRS 4 'Capital Instruments' (paragraph 39), which states 'Where shares are repurchased or redeemed, shareholders' funds should be reduced by the value of the consideration given'. Transactions in own shares do not give rise to gains or losses in the issuing entity's profit and loss account or statement of total

recognised gains and losses. The same applies to the consolidated financial statements of the issuing entity where shares in that entity are purchased or sold by a subsidiary.

5.   FRS 4 'Capital Instruments' requires shares to be classified as equity shares or non-equity shares. Whether a transaction in own shares relates to equity or non-equity shares, there is no effect on reported profit as it is a transaction affecting only shareholders' interests. Any difference between the carrying amount of shareholders' funds attributable to non-equity shares and the consideration paid for their purchase is reported as an appropriation of profits in the same manner as FRS 4 requires for finance costs in respect of non-equity shares.

UITF Consensus Pronouncements

6.   The requirements of this Abstract are consistent with International Financial Reporting Standards (IFRSs). SIC-16 'Share Capital – Reacquired Own Equity Instruments (Treasury Shares)' requires treasury shares to be presented in the balance sheet as a deduction from equity, not as assets. The acquisition and resale of treasury shares are presented as changes in equity and do not give rise to gains or losses. The basis for the treatment in IFRSs is that the acquisition and subsequent re-sale by an entity of its own equity instruments represents a transfer between those holders of equity instruments who have given up their equity interest and those who continue to hold an equity interest.

UITF Consensus

7.   The UITF reached a consensus that:

(a)   Consideration paid for an entity's own shares should be deducted in arriving at shareholders' funds.

(b)   No gain or loss should be recognised in the profit and loss account or statement of total recognised gains and losses on the purchase, sale or cancellation of an entity's own shares.

(c)   Consideration paid or received for the purchase or sale of an entity's own shares should be shown as separate amounts in the reconciliation of movements in shareholders' funds.

(d)   The amounts of reductions to shareholders' funds for an entity's own shares held, and the number of own shares held, should be disclosed separately.

8.   Where shares in a holding company are purchased, held or sold by a subsidiary, the requirements in paragraph 7 apply in the holding company's consolidated financial statements.

Date from which effective

9.   The accounting treatment required by this consensus should be adopted in financial statements relating to accounting periods ending on or after 23 December 2003.

Appendix G

COMPANIES FORMS

Form SH02

In accordance with
Section 619, 621 & 689
of the Companies Act
2006.

SH02

Notice of consolidation, sub-division, redemption of
shares or re-conversion of stock into shares

✓ What this form is for
You may use this form to give notice
of consolidation, sub-division,
redemption of shares or
re-conversion of stock into shares.

✗ What this form is NOT for
You cannot use this form to give
notice of a conversion of shares into
stock.

For further information, please
refer to our guidance at
www.companieshouse.gov.uk

1　Company details

Company number	
Company name in full	

→ Filling in this form
Please complete in typescript or in
bold black capitals.

All fields are mandatory unless
specified or indicated by *

2　Date of resolution

Date of resolution　d d　m m　y y y y

3　Consolidation

Please show the amendments to each class of share.

Class of shares (E.g. Ordinary/Preference etc.)	Previous share structure		New share structure	
	Number of issued shares	Nominal value of each share	Number of issued shares	Nominal value of each share

---

4　Sub-division

Please show the amendments to each class of share.

Class of shares (E.g. Ordinary/Preference etc.)	Previous share structure		New share structure	
	Number of issued shares	Nominal value of each share	Number of issued shares	Nominal value of each share

---

5　Redemption

Please show the class number and nominal value of shares that have been redeemed.
Only redeemable shares can be redeemed.

Class of shares (E.g. Ordinary/Preference etc.)	Number of issued shares	Nominal value of each share

---

BIS | Department for Business
Innovation & Skills

CHFP000
05/10 Version 4.0

SH02
Notice of consolidation, sub-division, redemption of shares or re-conversion of stock into shares

6 Re-conversion

Please show the class number and nominal value of shares following re-conversion from stock.

| Value of stock | New share structure | | |
	Class of shares (E.g. Ordinary/Preference etc.)	Number of issued shares	Nominal value of each share

Statment of capital

Section 7 (also **Section 8** and **Section 9** if appropriate) should reflect the company's issued capital following the changes made in this form.

7 Statement of capital (Share capital in pound sterling (£))

Please complete the table below to show each share classes held in pound sterling.
If all your issued capital is in sterling, only complete **Section 7** and then go to **Section 10**.

Class of shares (E.g. Ordinary/Preference etc.)	Amount paid up on each share ❶	Amount (if any) unpaid on each share ❶	Number of shares ❷	Aggregate nominal value ❸
				£
				£
				£
				£
			Totals	£

8 Statement of capital (Share capital in other currencies)

Please complete the table below to show any class of shares held in other currencies.
Please complete a separate table for each currency.

Currency

Class of shares (E.g. Ordinary / Preference etc.)	Amount paid up on each share❶	Amount (if any) unpaid on each share ❶	Number of shares ❷	Aggregate nominal value
			Totals	

Currency

Class of shares (E.g. Ordinary/Preference etc.)	Amount paid up on each share ❶	Amount (if any) unpaid on each share ❶	Number of shares ❷	Aggregate nominal value
			Totals	

❶ Including both the nominal value and any share premium.

❷ Total number of issued shares in this class.

❸ Number of shares issued multiplied by nominal value of each share.

Continuation pages
Please use a Statement of Capital continuation page if necessary.

CHFP000
05/10 Version 4.0

SH02
Notice of consolidation, sub-division, redemption of shares or re-conversion of stock into shares

9   **Statement of capital** (Totals)

	Please give the total number of shares and total aggregate nominal value of issued share capital.	❶ **Total aggregate nominal value** Please list total aggregate values in different currencies separately. For example: £100 + €100 + $10 etc.
Total number of shares		
Total aggregate nominal value ❶		

10   **Statement of capital** (Prescribed particulars of rights attached to shares) ❷

	Please give the prescribed particulars of rights attached to shares for each class of share shown in the statement of capital share tables in **Section 7** and **Section 8**.	❷ **Prescribed particulars of rights attached to shares** The particulars are:
Class of share		a. particulars of any voting rights, including rights that arise only in certain circumstances;
Prescribed particulars		b. particulars of any rights, as respects dividends, to participate in a distribution;
		c. particulars of any rights, as respects capital, to participate in a distribution (including on winding up); and
		d. whether the shares are to be redeemed or are liable to be redeemed at the option of the company or the shareholder and any terms or conditions relating to redemption of these shares.
		A separate table must be used for each class of share.
Class of share		Please use a Statement of capital continuation page if necessary.
Prescribed particulars		
Class of share		
Prescribed particulars		

SH02

Notice of consolidation, sub-division, redemption of shares or re-conversion of stock into shares

Class of share	
Prescribed particulars	

❶ Prescribed particulars of rights attached to shares

The particulars are:

a. particulars of any voting rights, including rights that arise only in certain circumstances;

b. particulars of any rights, as respects dividends, to participate in a distribution;

c. particulars of any rights, as respects capital, to participate in a distribution (including on winding up); and

d. whether the shares are to be redeemed or are liable to be redeemed at the option of the company or the shareholder and any terms or conditions relating to redemption of these shares.

Class of share	
Prescribed particulars	

A separate table must be used for each class of share.

Please use a Statement of capital continuation page if necessary.

11 Signature

I am signing this form on behalf of the company.

Signature	Signature **X**

X

This form may be signed by:
Director ❷, Secretary, Person authorised ❸, Administrator , Administrative Receiver, Receiver, Receiver manager, CIC manager.

❷ Societas Europaea
If the form is being filed on behalf of a Societas Europaea (SE) please delete 'director' and insert details of which organ of the SE the person signing has membership.

❸ Person authorised
Under either section 270 or 274 of the Companies Act 2006.

SH02

Notice of consolidation, sub-division, redemption of shares or re-conversion
of stock into shares

👤 Presenter information

You do not have to give any contact information, but if
you do it will help Companies House if there is a query
on the form. The contact information you give will be
visible to searchers of the public record.

Contact name

Company name

Address

Post town

County/Region

Postcode

Country

DX

Telephone

✓ Checklist

We may return forms completed incorrectly or
with information missing.

**Please make sure you have remembered the
following:**

- ☐ The company name and number match the
  information held on the public Register.
- ☐ You have entered the date of resolution in
  Section 2.
- ☐ Where applicable, you have completed Section 3, 4,
  5 or 6.
- ☐ You have completed the statement of capital.
- ☐ You have signed the form.

❗ Important information

**Please note that all information on this form will
appear on the public record.**

✉ Where to send

**You may return this form to any Companies House
address, however for expediency we advise you to
return it to the appropriate address below:**

For companies registered in England and Wales:
The Registrar of Companies, Companies House,
Crown Way, Cardiff, Wales, CF14 3UZ.
DX 33050 Cardiff.

For companies registered in Scotland:
The Registrar of Companies, Companies House,
Fourth floor, Edinburgh Quay 2,
139 Fountainbridge, Edinburgh, Scotland, EH3 9FF.
DX ED235 Edinburgh 1
or LP - 4 Edinburgh 2 (Legal Post).

For companies registered in Northern Ireland:
The Registrar of Companies, Companies House,
Second Floor, The Linenhall, 32-38 Linenhall Street,
Belfast, Northern Ireland, BT2 8BG.
DX 481 N.R. Belfast 1.

ℹ Further information

For further information, please see the guidance notes
on the website at www.companieshouse.gov.uk or
email enquiries@companieshouse.gov.uk

This form is available in an
alternative format. Please visit the
forms page on the website at
www.companieshouse.gov.uk

Form SH03

In accordance with
Section 707 of the
Companies Act 2006

SH03
Return of purchase of own shares

✓ **What this form is for**	✗ **What this form is NOT for**	For further information, please
You may use this form to give notice of a purchase by a limited company of its own shares.	You cannot use this form to give notice of a purchase by an unlimited company of its own shares.	refer to our guidance at www.companieshouse.gov.uk

1 **Company details**

Company number		→ **Filling in this form**
		Please complete in typescript or in bold black capitals.
Company name in full		All fields are mandatory unless specified or indicated by *

2 **Shares purchased for cancellation**

The section below should be completed by public limited companies (PLC) only.

Class of shares (E.g. Ordinary/Preference etc.)	Number of shares purchased	Nominal value of each share	Date that the shares were delivered to the company	Are these qualifying shares? ❶	Maximum price paid for each share	Minimum price paid for each share
			/ /	☐ Yes		
			/ /	☐ Yes		
			/ /	☐ Yes		
			/ /	☐ Yes		
			/ /	☐ Yes		

	Please show the aggregate amount paid on shares purchased for cancellation.	❶ **Qualifying shares**
Total aggregate amount		Qualifying shares are shares eligible to be placed into treasury.

For HM Revenue and Customs Stamp Office only

BIS | Department for Business Innovation & Skills

CHFP000
05/10 Version 4.0

SH03

Return of purchase of own shares

3   **Shares purchased into treasury** (PLCs only)

Please complete the table below if you are purchasing into treasury.
This section is to be completed by PLCs only.

Class of shares (E.g. Ordinary/Preference etc.)	Number of shares purchased	Nominal value of each share	Date that the shares were delivered to the company	Maximum price paid for each share	Minimum price paid for each share
			/ /		
			/ /		
			/ /		
			/ /		
			/ /		

Please show the aggregate amount paid by the company on shares purchased into treasury.

Total aggregate amount

4   **Stamp Duty**

Stamp Duty of 0.5% is payable for purchases where the amount or value of the consideration is over £1,000.
Please show the amount of Stamp Duty paid on shares purchased.

Stamp Duty ❶

£

Before this form is sent to Companies House it must be 'stamped' by HM Revenue and Customs Stamp Office to confirm that the appropriate amount of Stamp Duty has been paid.

After this form has been 'stamped' and returned to you by HM Revenue and Customs it must then be sent to Companies House.

No Stamp Duty payable

If Stamp Duty is **not payable** on shares purchased, please confirm the statement below by ticking the box:

☐   I/We certify that the transaction effected by this instrument does not form part of a larger transaction or series of transactions in respect of which the amount or value of the consideration exceeds £1,000.

If you have no stamp duty payable, please return this form directly to Companies House.

❶ **Stamp Duty**
The aggregate amount should be rounded up to the nearest multiple of £5.

Amount payable
Cheques for the Stamp Duty must be made payable to 'HM Revenue & Customs Taxes' and crossed 'Not Transferable'.

Stamp office address
Please send the form to:
HMRC Stamp Office.
9th Floor, City Centre House,
30 Union Street,
Birmingham. B2 4AR.

Further information
If you require further information on Stamp Duty. Please contact HM Revenue & Customs on:
0845 6030135 or visit their website:
www.hmrc.gov.uk

5   **Signature**

I am signing this form on behalf of the company.

Signature

Signature

X   **X**

Date

d	d		m	m		y	y	y	y	

This form may be signed by:
Director❷, Secretary, Person authorised❸, Administrator, Receiver, Receiver manager, CIC manager.

❷ **Societas Europaea**
If the form is being filed on behalf of a Societas Europaea (SE) please delete 'director' and insert details of which organ of the SE the person signing has membership.

❸ **Person authorised**
Under either section 270 or 274 of the Companies Act 2006.

CHFP000
05/10 Version 4.0

SH03
Return of purchase of own shares

👤 Presenter information

You do not have to give any contact information, but if you do it will help Companies House if there is a query on the form. The contact information you give will be visible to searchers of the public record.

Contact name

Company name

Address

Post town

County/Region

Postcode

Country

DX

Telephone

✔ Checklist

We may return forms completed incorrectly or with information missing.

Please make sure you have remembered the following:
- ☐ The company name and number match the information held on the public Register.
- ☐ You have completed Section 2 and/or Section 3 as appropriate.
- ☐ In Section 4, you have either had the form stamped by HMRC or ticked the certification section to
- ☐ indicate that no duty is payable.
- ☐ You have signed the form.

❗ Important information

Please note that all information on this form will appear on the public record.

✉ Where to send

You may return this form to any Companies House address, however for expediency we advise you to return it to the appropriate address below:

For companies registered in England and Wales:
The Registrar of Companies, Companies House, Crown Way, Cardiff, Wales, CF14 3UZ.
DX 33050 Cardiff.

For companies registered in Scotland:
The Registrar of Companies, Companies House, Fourth floor, Edinburgh Quay 2,
139 Fountainbridge, Edinburgh, Scotland, EH3 9FF.
DX ED235 Edinburgh 1
or LP - 4 Edinburgh 2 (Legal Post).

For companies registered in Northern Ireland:
The Registrar of Companies, Companies House, Second Floor, The Linenhall, 32-38 Linenhall Street Belfast, Northern Ireland, BT2 8BG.
DX 481 N.R. Belfast 1.

Stamp Duty
If Stamp Duty is to be paid, please first send this form to: HMRC Stamp Office, 9th Floor, City Centre House, 30 Union Street, Birmingham, B2 4AR.

ℹ Further information

For further information, please see the guidance notes on the website at www.companieshouse.gov.uk or email enquiries@companieshouse.gov.uk

This form is available in an alternative format. Please visit the forms page on the website at www.companieshouse.gov.uk

This form has been provided free of charge by Companies House.

CHFP000
05/10 Version 4.0

Form SH04

In accordance with
Section 728 of the
Companies Act 2006.

SH04

Notice of sale or transfer of treasury shares by a public limited company (PLC)

✓ **What this form is for**	✗ **What this form is NOT for**	For further information, please
You may use this form to give notice of a sale or transfer of treasury shares for a public limited company.	You cannot use this form to give notice of a cancellation of treasury shares in a public limited company. To do this, please use SH05.	refer to our guidance at www.companieshouse.gov.uk

---

1 **Company details**

Company number		→ **Filling in this form**
Company name in full		Please complete in typescript or in bold black capitals
		All fields are mandatory unless specified or indicated by *

---

2 **Treasury shares sold or transferred** ❶

Class of shares (E.g. Ordinary/Preference etc.)	Number of shares sold or transferred	Nominal value of each share	Date(s) shares were sold or transferred
			/ /
			/ /
			/ /
			/ /
			/ /
			/ /
			/ /
			/ /
			/ /
			/ /

❶ **Treasury shares sold or transferred**
Shares may only be transferred (as opposed to sold) from treasury for the purposes of, or in accordance with, an employees' share scheme.

---

3 **Signature**

I am signing this form on behalf of the company.

Signature	Signature ✗	✗

This form may be signed by:
Director ❷, Secretary, Person authorised ❸, Administrator, Administrative receiver, Receiver, Receiver manager, CIC manager.

❷ **Societas Europaea**
If the form is being filed on behalf of a Societas Europaea (SE), please delete 'director' and insert details of which organ of the SE the person signing has membership.

❸ **Person authorised**
Under either section 270 or 274 of the Companies Act 2006.

BIS | Department for Business Innovation & Skills

CHFP000
05/10 Version 4.0

SH04

Notice of sale or transfer of treasury shares by a public limited company (PLC)

Presenter information

You do not have to give any contact information, but if you do it will help Companies House if there is a query on the form. The contact information you give will be visible to searchers of the public record.

Contact name

Company name

Address

Post town

County/Region

Postcode

Country

DX

Telephone

Checklist

We may return forms completed incorrectly or with information missing.

Please make sure you have remembered the following:
- ☐ The company name and number match the information held on the public Register.
- ☐ You have entered the correct information in section 2.
- ☐ You have signed the form.

Important information

Please note that all information on this form will appear on the public record.

Where to send

You may return this form to any Companies House address, however for expediency we advise you to return it to the appropriate address below:

For companies registered in England and Wales:
The Registrar of Companies, Companies House, Crown Way, Cardiff, Wales, CF14 3UZ.
DX 33050 Cardiff.

For companies registered in Scotland:
The Registrar of Companies, Companies House, Fourth floor, Edinburgh Quay 2, 139 Fountainbridge, Edinburgh, Scotland, EH3 9FF.
DX ED235 Edinburgh 1
or LP - 4 Edinburgh 2 (Legal Post).

For companies registered in Northern Ireland:
The Registrar of Companies, Companies House, Second Floor, The Linenhall, 32-38 Linenhall Street, Belfast, Northern Ireland, BT2 8BG.
DX 481 N.R. Belfast 1.

Further information

For further information, please see the guidance notes on the website at www.companieshouse.gov.uk or email enquiries@companieshouse.gov.uk

This form is available in an alternative format. Please visit the forms page on the website at www.companieshouse.gov.uk

CHFP000
05/10 Version 4.0

This form has been provided free of charge by Companies House.

Form SH05

In accordance with
Section 730 of the
Companies Act 2006.

SH05

Notice of cancellation of treasury shares by a public limited company (PLC)

✓ **What this form is for**	✗ **What this form is NOT for**	For further information, please
You may use this form to give notice of a cancellation of treasury shares in a public limited company.	You cannot use this form to give notice of a sale or transfer of treasury shares for a public limited company. To do this, please use form SH04.	refer to our guidance at www.companieshouse.gov.uk

---

1   **Company details**

Company number	
Company name in full	

→ **Filling in this form**
Please complete in typescript or in bold black capitals.

All fields are mandatory unless specified or indicated by *

2   **Treasury shares cancelled**

Class of shares (E.g. Ordinary/Preference etc.)	Number of shares cancelled	Nominal value of each share	Date(s) shares were cancelled
			/ /
			/ /
			/ /
			/ /
			/ /
			/ /
			/ /
			/ /
			/ /
			/ /
			/ /
			/ /
			/ /
			/ /
			/ /
			/ /
			/ /
			/ /
			/ /
			/ /

SH05

Notice of cancellation of treasury shares by a public limited company (PLC)

3   **Statement of Capital   (Share capital in Pound Sterling (£))**

Please complete the table below to show each class of shares held in pound sterling.
If all your issued capital is in sterling, only complete **Section 3** and then go to **Section 6**.

Class of shares (E.g. Ordinary/Preference etc.)	Amount paid up on each share ❶	Amount (if any) unpaid on each share ❶	Number of shares ❷	Aggregate nominal value ❸
				£
				£
				£
				£
			Totals	£

4   **Statement of capital (Share capital in other currencies)**

Please complete the table below to show any class of shares held in other currencies.
Please complete a separate table for each currency.

Currency

Class of shares (E.g. Ordinary/Preference etc.)	Amount paid up on each share ❶	Amount (if any) unpaid on each share ❶	Number of shares ❷	Aggregate nominal value ❸
			Totals	

Currency

Class of shares (E.g. Ordinary/Preference etc.)	Amount paid up on each share ❶	Amount (if any) unpaid on each share ❶	Number of shares ❷	Aggregate nominal value ❸
			Totals	

5   **Statement of capital (Totals)**

	Please give the total number of shares and total aggregate nominal value of issued share capital.	**Total aggregate nominal value** Please list total aggregate values in different currencies separately. For example: £100 + 100 + $10 etc.
Total number of shares		
Total aggregate nominal value		

❶ Including both the nominal value and any share premium.

❷ Total number of issued shares in this class.

❸ Number of shares issued multiplied by nominal value of each share.

Continuation Pages
Please use a Statement of Capital continuation page if necessary.

CHFP000
05/10 Version 4.0

SH05
Notice of cancellation of treasury shares by a public limited company (PLC)

6   **Statement of capital** (Prescribed particulars of rights attached to shares)

Please give the prescribed particulars of rights attached to shares for each class of share shown in the statement of capital share tables in sections 3 and 4.	**❶ Prescribed particulars of rights attached to shares** The particulars are: a. particulars of any voting rights, including rights that arise only in certain circumstances; b. particulars of any rights, as respects dividends, to participate in a distribution; c. particulars of any rights, as respects capital, to participate in a distribution (including on winding up); and d. whether the shares are to be redeemed or are liable to be redeemed at the option of the company or the shareholder and any terms or conditions relating to redemption of these shares. A separate table must be used for each class of share. Please use the next page or a 'Statement of Capital (Prescribed particulars of rights attached to shares)' continuation page if necessary.
Class of share	
Prescribed particulars ❶	
Class of share	
Prescribed particulars ❶	
Class of share	
Prescribed particulars ❶	

7   **Signature**

I am signing this form on behalf of the company.	**❷ Societas Europaea** If the form is being filed on behalf of a Societas Europaea (SE), please delete 'director' and insert details of which organ of the SE the person signing has membership. **❸ Person authorised** Under either Section 270 or 274 of the Companies Act 2006.
Signature	Signature X X
	This form may be signed by: Director ❷, Secretary, Person authorised ❸, Administrator, Administrative receiver, Receiver, Receiver manager, CIC manager.

SH05

Notice of cancellation of treasury shares by a public limited company (PLC)

Presenter information

You do not have to give any contact information, but if you do it will help Companies House if there is a query on the form. The contact information you give will be visible to searchers of the public record.

Contact name

Company name

Address

Post town

County/Region

Postcode

Country

DX

Telephone

Checklist

We may return forms completed incorrectly or with information missing.

Please make sure you have remembered the following:
- ☐ The company name and number match the information held on the public Register.
- ☐ You have correctly completed section 2.
  You have completed the relevant sections of the
- ☐ Statement of Capital.
- ☐ You have signed the form.

Important information

Please note that all information on this form will appear on the public record.

Where to send

You may return this form to any Companies House address, however for expediency we advise you to return it to the appropriate address below:

For companies registered in England and Wales:
The Registrar of Companies, Companies House, Crown Way, Cardiff, Wales, CF14 3UZ.
DX 33050 Cardiff.

For companies registered in Scotland:
The Registrar of Companies, Companies House, Fourth floor, Edinburgh Quay 2,
139 Fountainbridge, Edinburgh, Scotland, EH3 9FF.
DX ED235 Edinburgh 1
or LP - 4 Edinburgh 2 (Legal Post).

For companies registered in Northern Ireland:
The Registrar of Companies, Companies House, Second Floor, The Linenhall, 32-38 Linenhall Street, Belfast, Northern Ireland, BT2 8BG.
DX 481 N.R. Belfast 1.

Further information

For further information, please see the guidance notes on the website at www.companieshouse.gov.uk or email enquiries@companieshouse.gov.uk

This form is available in an alternative format. Please visit the forms page on the website at www.companieshouse.gov.uk

CHFP000
05/10 Version 4.0

Appendix H

A PERSON 'CONNECTED' WITH A COMPANY

For the first and main part of this definition, see **13.47**. The provisions which are set out here lay down alternative tests to those at **13.47** for determining whether a person is 'connected' with a company.

H.1   Section 1062 of the CTA 2010 provides that a person is connected with a company if he directly or indirectly possesses or is entitled to acquire such rights as would, in the event of the winding up of the company or in any other circumstances, entitle him to receive more than 30% of the assets of the company which would then be available for distribution to 'equity holders' of the company. Sections 158-164 and 166-167 of the CTA 2010 are invoked (with adaptations) to determine what is meant by 'equity holder' and the percentage of assets of the company to which a person would be entitled.

H.2   An 'equity holder' of a company is any person who:

(a)   holds 'ordinary shares' in the company; or

(b)   is a 'loan creditor' of the company in respect of a loan which is not a 'normal commercial loan',

and the reference in s 1062 to assets available for distribution to a company's equity holders does not include a reference to any assets available for distribution to any equity holder otherwise than as an equity holder (CTA 2010, s 167(1)).

H.3   'Ordinary shares' means all shares other than 'restricted preference shares' (CTA 2010, s 160).

H.4   'Restricted preference shares' means shares which:

(a)   are issued for a consideration which is or includes 'new consideration'; and

(b)   do not carry any right either to conversion into shares or securities of any other description except:

(i)   shares which:

        (A) satisfy the requirements of paras (a) above and (c) and (d) below, and

        (B) do not carry any rights either to conversion into shares or securities of any other description except shares or securities in the company's 'quoted parent company', or to the acquisition of any additional shares or securities; or

  (ii)   securities representing a loan of or including new consideration and:

        (A) which satisfies the requirements of paras (b) and (c) of the definition of 'normal commercial loan' (see H.6); and

        (B) does not carry any rights either to conversion into shares or securities of any other description except shares or securities in the company's 'quoted parent company', or to the acquisition of any additional shares or securities; or

  (iii) shares or securities in the company's 'quoted parent company',

or to the acquisition of any additional shares or securities; and

(c)   do not carry any right to dividends other than dividends which:

    (i)   are of a fixed amount or at a fixed rate per cent. of the nominal value of the shares; and

    (ii) represent no more than a reasonable commercial return on the 'new consideration' received by the company in respect of the issue of the shares; and

(d)   on repayment do not carry any rights to an amount exceeding that 'new consideration' except in so far as those rights are reasonably comparable with those general for fixed dividend shares listed on a recognised stock exchange (CTA 2010, ss 160–164).

H.5   A 'loan creditor' means a creditor in respect of any debt incurred by the company:

(a)   for any money borrowed or capital assets acquired by the company; or

(b)   for any right to receive income created in favour of the company; or

(c)   for consideration the value of which to the company was (at the time when the debt was incurred) substantially less than the amount of the debt (including any premium thereon),

or in respect of any redeemable loan capital issued by the company (CTA 2010, s 158(2)). For these purposes, there is no exclusion in favour of bankers making loans in the ordinary course of their business.

H.6   'Normal commercial loan' means a loan of or including 'new consideration' and:

(a) which does not carry any right either to conversion into shares or securities of any other description except:

    (i) shares which:

        (A) satisfy the requirements of paras (a), (c) and (d) of the definition of 'restricted preference shares' (see H.4); and

        (B) do not carry any rights either to conversion into shares or securities of any other description except shares or securities in the company's 'quoted parent company', or to the acquisition of any additional shares or securities; or

    (ii) securities representing a loan of or including new consideration; and:

        (A) which satisfies the requirements of paras (b) and (c) below; and

        (B) does not carry any rights either to conversion into shares or securities of any other description except shares or securities in the company's 'quoted parent company', or to the acquisition of any additional shares or securities; or

    (iii) shares or securities in the company's 'quoted parent company', or to the acquisition of any additional shares or securities; and

(b) which does not entitle the loan creditor to any amount by way of interest which depends to any extent on the results of the company's business or any part of it or on the value of the company's assets or which exceeds a reasonable commercial return on the new consideration lent; however, this does not apply to a loan which provides for the rate of interest to be reduced if the company's business improves or if any of the company's assets increases in value, nor to a loan which is made for the purpose of facilitating the acquisition of land, none of which is acquired with a view to resale at a profit, and where the loan and the payment to the lender of any amount due in connection with it is secured on the land; and

(c) in respect of which the loan creditor is entitled, on repayment, to an amount which either does not exceed the new consideration lent or is reasonably comparable with the amount generally repayable (in relation to an equal amount of new consideration) under the terms of issue of securities listed on a recognised stock exchange (CTA 2010, ss162-164).

H.7 'New consideration' means consideration not provided directly or indirectly out of the assets of the company, and in particular does not include amounts retained by the company by way of capitalising a distribution. An exception applies where share capital has been issued at a premium representing new consideration: any part of that premium afterwards applied in paying up share capital is treated as new consideration also for that share capital, unless and to the extent that the premium has been taken into account under s 1025(2) of the CTA 2010, so as to enable a distribution to be treated as a repayment of share capital. The scope of the expression 'new consideration' is further restricted by reference to s 1115(4)-(6) of the CTA 2010, which is set out at **12.5** (CTA 2010, s 1115).

H.8   For the above purposes, a company ('the parent company') is another company's 'quoted parent company' if and only if:

(a)   the other company is a 75% subsidiary of the parent company;

(b)   the parent company is not a 75% subsidiary of any company; and

(c)   the ordinary share capital of the parent company (including, if its ordinary share capital is divided into two or more classes, the shares of each class) are quoted on a recognised stock exchange or dealt in on the Unlisted Securities Market (CTA 2010, s 164(3)).

In determining for the purposes of (a) above who are the equity holders of the other company (the need to do so resulting from the use of the defined expression '75% subsidiary'), it is to be assumed that the parent company is the other company's quoted parent company for the purposes of s 164(1)(b), (2)(c) or s 160(4)(c) or s 162(2)(c) of CTA 2010 (s 164(7)).

H.9   Notwithstanding anything in H.2–H.6 above, but subject to a qualification in favour of banks (H.10 below), where:

(a)   any person has, directly or indirectly, provided new consideration for any shares or securities in the company; and

(b)   that person, or any person 'connected' with him, uses for the purpose of his trade assets which belong to the company and in respect of which there is made to the company any capital allowance, being either an annual investment allowance, a first-year allowance, or writing-down allowance in respect of machinery or plant, or an allowance in respect of research and development under Chapter 3 of Part 6 of the Capital Allowances Act 1990,

then that person, and no other, is treated for the purposes of s 158 as being an equity holder in respect of those shares or securities and as being beneficially entitled to any distribution of assets attributable to those shares or securities (CTA 2010, s 159(2)). In para (b) the word 'connected' is given the appropriate ordinary s 1122 or s 1124 of the CTA 2010 meaning (CTA 2010, s 157(1)–(3)).

H.10   In any case where H.9 above applies in relation to a bank in such circumstances that:

(a)   the only new consideration provided by the bank as mentioned in sub-para (a) of H.9 is provided in the normal course of its banking business by way of a 'normal commercial loan'; and (b)　the cost to the company concerned of the assets falling within para (b) of H.9 which are used as mentioned in that paragraph by the bank or a person connected with the bank is less than the amount of that new consideration,

references in H.9 above, other than the reference in para (a) thereof, to shares or securities in the company are to be construed as a reference to so much only of the loan referred to in para (i) above as is equal to the cost referred to in para (ii) above (CTA 2010, s 157(4)).

H.11 For the purposes of s 1062(4), (and subject to an exception at H.13) the percentage to which an equity holder would be entitled beneficially of any assets of a company available for distribution to its equity holders in any circumstances (including a winding up) means the percentage to which the equity holder would be so entitled if the company were to be wound up and on that winding up the assets available for distribution to its equity holders (i.e. after deducting any liabilities to other persons) were equal to:

(a)　the excess, if any, of the total amount of the assets of the company, as shown in the balance sheet relating to its affairs at the end of the relevant accounting period, over the total amount of those of its liabilities as so shown which are not liabilities to equity holders as such; or

(b)　if there is no such excess or if the company's balance sheet is prepared to a date other than the end of the relevant accounting period, £100;

hereinafter referred to as 'the notional winding up' (CTA 2010, s 166(1)–(4)).

H.12 If, on 'the notional winding up', an equity holder would be entitled as such to an amount of assets of any description which, apart from this paragraph, would not be treated as a distribution of assets, it shall nevertheless be treated (subject to H.13 below) as an amount to which the equity holder is entitled on the distribution of assets on the notional winding up (CTA 2010, s 166(5)).

H.13 If an amount (called 'the returned amount') which corresponds to the whole or any part of the new consideration provided by an equity holder of a company for any shares or securities in respect of which he is an equity holder is applied by the company, directly or indirectly, in the making of a loan to, or in the acquisition of any shares or securities in, the equity holder or any person 'connected' with him, then:

(a)　the total amount referred to in para (a) of H.11 above is reduced by a sum equal to the returned amount; and

(b)　the amount of assets to which the equity holder is beneficially entitled on the notional winding up is reduced by a sum equal to the returned amount (CTA 2010, s 166(7).

The word 'connected' here is given the appropriate ordinary s 1122 or s 1124 ICTA 1988 meaning (CTA 2010, s 1176).

Appendix I

SPECIMEN LETTER OF APPLICATION FOR CLEARANCE UNDER CTA 2010, S 1044

As an alternative to being sent by post, clearance applications may be sent by e-mail to: reconstructions@gtnet.gov.uk or by fax to 020 7438 4409.

In this regard, HMRC state that:

* Only one single application is necessary by one method only: email, fax or letter.

* 'For emailed applications please show clearly whether you want an emailed reply otherwise we will send it by post.'

Where the application concerns a market sensitive transaction, it should addressed to the Team Leader, Clearance and Counter-Action Team, Anti-Avoidance Group at the address below.

Specimen letter

Clearance and Counter-Action Team
Anti-Avoidance Group
22 Kingsway
London
WC2B 6NR

1 January 2011

Dear Sirs,

Clearances under sections 1044(2) and 748 of the CTA 2010 and section 701 of the ITA 2007

Re: Weird & Wonderful Ltd

We act for Weird & Wonderful Ltd ('WWL'). We are hereby submitting applications for clearance under sections 1044 and 748 of the Corporation Tax Act 2010 and section 701 of the Income Tax Act 2007 in relation to certain proposed purchases by WWL of its own shares. It is considered that these purchases will, if implemented, fall within section 1033(1) of the CTA 2010 by virtue of Condition A.

The tax affairs of WWL are dealt with by HM Inspector of Taxes _____ District under reference _____.

WWL is both an 'unquoted company' and a 'trading company' within the meanings conferred upon those expressions by section 1048(1) of the CTA 2010, and is not a member of any 'group' within the meaning of section 1047 of the CTA 2010.

The current issued share capital of WWL and its shareholders is as follows:

	Ordinary shares of £1 each
Mr W	1,060
Mrs W	1,040
Mr W Junior	400
Mr Y	2,000
Mrs Y	500

Mr W Junior is the son of Mr W and is over 18 years of age. Mrs W is the wife of Mr W, and Mrs Y is the wife of Mr Y.

WWL carries on the business of importing and selling novelties and toys, mainly from the Far East. Much of WWL's sales are achieved by mail order. It began trading in 2001, having been set up by Mr W and Mr Y with an issued share capital of 5,000 shares held in equal proportions. In 2003 Mr W and Mr Y each transferred some shares to their respective wives, so as to result in Mrs W and Mrs Y holding their current shareholdings. In 2006 Mr W transferred 400 shares to Mr W Junior, who had a short while previously been appointed a director of WWL. Mr and Mrs Y were unhappy about Mr W Junior's increasing involvement in the running of WWL's business, but acquiesced in his appointment as a director for fear of offending Mr and Mrs W. Thereafter relations between Mr W Junior and Mr Y deteriorated rapidly, with one of the main areas of dispute being the sector of the market at which WWL should be aiming its goods. Mr and Mrs W have been inexorably drawn into taking sides with Mr W Junior against Mr and Mrs Y. The shareholders have recently agreed that the current situation is untenable and is having a harmful effect on WWL's business, and have agreed in principle that if it were legally and commercially feasible for WWL to purchase all of the shares of Mr and Mrs Y, that would be a mutually acceptable compromise.

It has now been agreed that this last-mentioned proposal is both legally and commercially feasible, provided that the proceeds of sale of the shares fall to be taxed not as income but as capital. WWL's auditors have put a value of £250,000 on the combined shareholdings of Mr and Mrs Y. It is proposed that WWL should purchase the entire shareholdings of Mr and Mrs Y for the sum of £250,000 to be divided between them in accordance with their shareholdings and to be paid by bankers' drafts. The entire £250,000 will be drawn from

WWL's reserves of distributable profits from earlier years. Under the proposal, Mr and Mrs Y will resign their directorships upon completion of the purchase of their shares.

The 'W' family hope that, with Mr and Mrs Y out of the company, WWL will regain the confidence of its suppliers and will be restored to profitability during the coming year. Mr and Mrs Y intend to use the proceeds of sale as capital for setting up an import/export business of their own.

We confirm as follows:

(1)   Mr and Mrs Y are resident and ordinarily resident in the UK.

(2)   The tax affairs of Mr and Mrs Y are dealt with by HM Inspector of Taxes _____ District under reference _____.

(3)   Mr Y has beneficially owned his 2,000 shares in WWL for more than 5 years. Mrs Y has beneficially owned her 500 shares ever since they were transferred to her in 2003 by Mr Y, who had previously owned them since 2001.

(4)   It is proposed that Mr and Mrs Y will sell their entire shareholdings simultaneously, with the result that, immediately after each purchase, the interests of both of Mr and Mrs Y will be 'substantially reduced' within the meaning of section 1037 of the CTA 2010.

(5)   After the purchases, neither of Mr and Mrs Y will be 'connected' with WWL within the meaning of section 1042(1) of the CTA 2010.

(6)   Neither of the purchases will form part of any scheme or arrangement falling within section 1042(2) of the CTA 2010.

(7)   None of the main purposes of the proposals is to enable Mr and Mrs Y to avoid tax or to participate in the profits of WWL without receiving a dividend.

We enclose copies of the accounts of WWL for its accounting period ending 31 December 2010.

We would be glad if the Board of Inland Revenue would confirm that they are satisfied that, in the event of the above-mentioned proposals being implemented:

(a)   no notice under section 748 of the CTA 2010 and/or section 701 of the ITA 2007 ought to be given in respect of them; and

(b)   section 1033 of the CTA 2010 will apply to them.

Yours faithfully,

Appendix J

SP2/82 – COMPANY'S PURCHASE OF OWN SHARES (CTA 2010, SS 1033–1048)

Editorial note: the statutory references in this note have been updated to reflect the rewrite of the provisions to the CTA 2010; the HMRC version of the Statement of Practice (most recently re-published 6 September 2010) still contains references to the ICTA 1988. References to 'Inland Revenue' and 'the Revenue' have been replaced with 'HMRC'.

Where a company makes a purchase of own shares which involves a payment in excess of the capital originally subscribed for the shares, the excess constitutes a distribution. However, such a payment is treated as not giving rise to a distribution if, among other conditions, the purchase is made wholly or mainly to benefit a trade carried on by the company, or by one of its 75% subsidiaries. This Statement indicates how this test is applied by HMRC.

The Annex to this Statement gives guidance on how companies should apply for a ruling on whether or not a purchase will be treated as a distribution.

Section 1033(1), (2) – The 'Trade Benefit Test'

1.   The Company's sole or main purpose in making the payment must be to benefit a trade carried on by it or by its 75% subsidiary. The condition is not satisfied where, for example, the transaction is designed to serve the personal or wider commercial interests of the vending shareholder (although usually he will benefit from it) or where the intended benefit for the company is to some non-trading activity which it also carries on.

2.   If there is a disagreement between the shareholders over the management of the company and that disagreement is having or is expected to have an adverse effect on the company's trade, then the purchase will be regarded as satisfying the trade benefit test provided the effect of the transaction is to remove the dissenting shareholder entirely. Similarly, if the purpose is to ensure that an unwilling shareholder who wishes to end his association with the company does not sell his shares to someone who might not be acceptable to the other shareholders, the purchase will normally be regarded as benefiting the company's trade.

Examples of unwilling shareholders are:

* an outside shareholder who has provided equity finance (whether or not with the expectation of redemption or sale to the company) and who now wishes to withdraw that finance;

* a controlling shareholder who is retiring as a director and wishes to make way for new management;

* personal representatives of a deceased shareholder, where they wish to realise the value of the shares;

* a legatee of a deceased shareholder, where he does not wish to hold shares in the company.

3.   If the company is not buying all the shares owned by the vendor, or if although the vendor is selling all his shares he is retaining some other connection with the company – for example, a directorship or an appointment as consultant – it would seem unlikely that the transaction could benefit the company's trade, so the trade benefit test will probably not be satisfied. However, there are exceptions; for example, where a company does not currently have the resources to buy out its retiring controlling shareholder completely but purchases as many of his shares as it can afford with the intention of buying the remainder where possible. In these circumstances, it may still be possible for the company to show that the main purpose is to benefit its trade. Also, the Board do not raise any objection if for sentimental reasons it is desired that a retiring director of a company should retain a small shareholding in it, not exceeding 5% of the issued share capital.

ANNEX TO SP2/82

Applications for advance clearance under s 1044 CTA 2010

Procedure

If clearance under s 1044 is desired the application should be sent to:

Clearances and Counter-Action Team
Anti-Avoidance Group
22 Kingsway
London
WC2B 6NR

Editorial note: address has been updated from that shown in the latest version of SP2/82

If clearance is also being sought under Section 701 ITA 2007 and/or Section 748 of CTA 2010 (regarding transactions in securities), a single application may be made under both provisions and should be directed to the address given above with an extra copy of the application and enclosures. Such an application should open by stating clearly the provisions under which it is made and should be expanded to include any additional information needed for the application under the other provision.

Form of application – General

Sections 1033–1048 contain conditions which must be satisfied before the tax treatment afforded by s 1033 can apply. A comprehensive application which has regard to each of these conditions will remove the need for lengthy fact finding enquiries and enable the Board to come to a decision on the application with the minimum of delay.

To assist companies in preparing clearance applications under Section 1044 and to facilitate their consideration by the Board, an outline of the basic information needed is given below. However, it is not an exhaustive list, and in giving the particulars of the relevant transactions required by Section 1045(1)(b) the applicant must fully and accurately disclose all facts and circumstances material for the decision of the Board (Section 1045(6)).

In what follows, references to purchase of shares include references to repayment or redemption of shares.

It will be helpful if applications follow the order set out below, each item being expanded as necessary and any further information being added at the end.

Application for clearance under Section 1044(2)

It should be stated at the outset whether the purchase of shares is regarded as falling within Section 1033 by virtue of Condition A or Condition B. If the purchasing company has previously made any application under Section 1044 it will be helpful if the Board's reference(s) can be quoted.

A.   Purchases within s 1033(2)

1.   *The Company*

    a.   The name of the company making the purchase;
    b.   its Tax District and reference;
    c.   confirmation that it is an unquoted company as defined in
        Section 1048(1);
    d.   its status, that is, 'trading company' or 'holding company of a trading group' within the Section 1048(1) definitions or some other type of company not within the definitions.

2.   *Groups*
Where the company is a member of a group (see below):

    a.   the names of the group companies together with their Tax Districts and references;

    b.   a statement or diagram showing the shareholding interests of each group company in other group companies.

A group for the purpose of this paragraph is the largest 51 per cent group to which the purchasing company belongs (Section 1047(1)), but the meaning of 'group' is extended, where appropriate, by Section 1047(2), (3).

3.   ***The payment***

    a.   Details of the shares to be purchased, the name of their present owner, the purchase price and the method of payment.

    b.   Details of any other transactions between the company and the vendor at or about the same time.

    c.   Confirmation that the company's Articles of Association allow it to purchase its own shares.

4.   ***Shareholders***

    a.   A list of the current shareholders in the purchasing company, and where appropriate, in each company in a group as in 2 above, together with particulars (amount, class, dividend rights etc) of their current holdings;

    b.   a statement of any relationships of the shareholders to each other;

    c.   where the shareholder is the son or daughter of another shareholder, an indication that he or she is over 18 or else details for their age.

5.   ***Prior transactions***

Particulars of any prior transactions or rearrangements to be carried out in preparation for the purchase.

6.   ***Purpose and benefits***

A statement of the reasons for the purchase, the trading benefits expected and any other benefits expected to accrue, whether or not to the purchasing company.

7.   ***Conditions in s 1033***

Confirmation, together with all relevant information, that the purchase etc does not form part of a scheme or arrangement the main purpose or one of the main purposes of which is to enable the owner of the shares to participate in the profits of the company without receiving a dividend, or the avoidance of tax. Confirmation that the vendor will receive no other payment from the company, or details of any such payment to be made.

8.   ***Conditions in ss 1034-1042***

a.   The present residence status of the vendor and any intended change (s 1034);

b.   the tax district, reference and National Insurance number of the vendor, or if not known his or her private address (s 1034);

c.   the period of beneficial ownership by the vendor of the shares to be purchased (s 1035);

d.   confirmation, if appropriate, that the vendor's interest will be 'substantially reduced' (s 1037(1));

e.   confirmation, if appropriate, that the combined interests as shareholders of the vendor and his 'associates' (see s 227) will be substantially reduced (s 1037(2));

f.   confirmation, if appropriate, that the vendor's interest as a shareholder in the group will be substantially reduced (s 1039(3));

g.   confirmation, if appropriate, that the combined interests as shareholders in the group of the vendor and his associates will be substantially reduced (s 1039(4));

h.   confirmation that the vendor will not, immediately after the purchase, be 'connected with' (see s 1042(1)(a)) the company making the purchase or with any company which is a member of the same group as that company (s 1042(1)(b));

i.   confirmation that the purchase is not part of a scheme or arrangement within s 1042(2).

9.   **Accounts and other financial information**
The application should be accompanied by:

a.   copies of the latest available financial statements for the purchasing company and for any group companies (see paragraph 2 above), and in the case of a group the financial statements for the group;

b.   a note of any material relevant changes since the balance sheet date or confirmation that there are none;

c.   details of any loan or current account which the vendor maintains with the company or with any group company.

B.   Purchases within s 1033(3)

1.   *Company*

a.   The name of the company making the purchase;

b.   its Tax District and reference;

c.   confirmation that it is an unquoted company as defined in Section 1048(1);

d.   its status, that is, 'trading company' or 'holding company of a trading group' within the Section 1048(1) definitions or some other type of company not within the definitions.

2.   *Groups*
Where the company is a member of a group (see A.2 above):

    a.   the names of the group companies together with their Tax Districts and references;

    b.   a statement or diagram showing the shareholding interests of each group company in other group companies.

3.   **The payment**

    a.   Details of the shares to be purchased, the name of the present owner, the purchase price and method of payment.

    b.   details of any other transactions between the company and the vendor at or about the same time;

    c.   confirmation that the company's Articles of Association allow it to purchase its own shares.

4.   **Inheritance Tax**

    a.   The name and date of death of the deceased;

    b.   the reference of the deceased at the Capital Taxes Office;

    c.   the amount of the outstanding tax and whether or not liability has been finally agreed;

    d.   the extent to which the purchase price is to be applied in satisfaction of the tax liability;

    e.   a full explanation of the circumstances in which there would be 'undue hardship' if the tax liability were to be discharged otherwise than through the purchase of own shares from this or another such company;

    f.   the Tax District and reference of the person to whom undue hardship would be caused or if not known the address of that person, and their National Insurance number.

5.   **Accounts and other financial information**
The application should be accompanied by –

    a.   copies of the latest available financial statements for the purchasing company and for any group companies (see paragraph A.2 above), and in the case of a group the financial statements for the group;

    b.   a note of any material relevant changes since the balance sheet date or confirmation that there are none.

C.   **Applications for clearance under s 1044(3)**

1.   **Company**

    a.   The name of the company making the purchase;

    b.   its tax district and reference.

2.   **The payment**

a. Details of the shares to be purchased, the vendor, the purchase price and the method of payment;
b. confirmation that the company's Articles of Association allow it to purchase its own shares.

3. ***Accounts and other financial information***

a. Copies of the latest available financial statements for the purchasing company;
b. a note of any material relevant changes since the balance sheet date or confirmation that there are none.
c. A statement of the reasons why it is believed that the proposed payment does not fall within the provisions of s 1033.

INDEX

References are to paragraph numbers.